Ready to Serve, Ready to Save

—

Strategies of Real-Life Search and Rescue Missions

By

Susan Bulanda

Doral Publishing, Inc.
Wilsonville, Oregon

PUBLISHED BY DORAL PUBLISHING
8560 SW SALISH LANE
WILSONVILLE, OREGON 97070
1-800-633-5385
HTTP://WWW.DORALPUB.COM

PRINTED IN THE UNITED STATES OF AMERICA

EDITED BY MARK ANDERSON
COVER DESIGN BY RANDY CONGER
INTERIOR LAYOUT BY MARK ANDERSON

LIBRARY OF CONGRESS CARD NUMBER: 99-60315

Front Cover: Terry Crooks and his dog, Jess, practice their rappelling at Kootenai Falls. (Photo by Lisa Lovegrove)
Back Cover: Terry Crooks and Jess await their helicopter at a CARDA training on Durrand Glacier. (Photo by Duncan Daniels)

Bulanda, Susan
   Ready to serve, ready to save : strategies of
 real-life search & rescue missions / Susan Bulanda ;
 edited by Mark Anderson. – 1st ed.
   p. cm.
   Includes bibliographical references.
   LCCN: 99-60315
   ISBN: 0-944875-63-7

   1. Rescues--United States. 2. Rescue work. 3.
Rescue dogs.   I. Title.

HV553.B85 1999   363.3481
                          QBI99-500286

Acknowledgments

Many people have contributed facts, insights, and material for this book. Without them, this book would not have been possible. To all of you I am deeply indebted. Your faith in me to produce a book of this magnitude has kept me going through the hours of hard work. Your willingness to trust me with your mission is something I deeply value. Also, I am grateful for the support I received from the search and rescue community overall, and to all of you who have waited for this book to be printed. I am especially grateful to Marcia Koenig and Andy Rebman for their support at the very beginning of this project. I also especially want to thank Diane Skuzinski for her help in proofreading this book. Her suggestions and insight were a genuine help to me.

Nevertheless, without a publisher, this book would not have happened at all. I am very lucky to have a wonderful publisher who has faith in my ability to put a book of this nature together. Both Dr. Alvin Grossman and Mark Anderson continue to be a delight to work with. Their support has helped me throughout this project.

—Susan Bulanda
Pottstown, Pennsylvania

Table of Contents

Foreword

Ready to Serve, Ready to Save: Strategies of Real-Life Search and Rescue Missions is an impressive collection of missions demonstrating the reality and ingenuity of search and rescue. From California to Maine, Alaska to Africa, lost persons, suicides, murders, drownings, bombings, and firestorms are examined by strategies, techniques, resources, and circumstances in order to use teams as effective clue generators. Each mission is professionally organized in a clear format making reading effortless and analogous.

However, the real essence of this book is in the honesty and humility of those reporting the searches. Since we learn from mistakes and difficulties, I found myself smiling at the accounts of surprise when a dog performs in spite of our doubting, questioning, and the nervousness that we all feel at times. So often in search and rescue the "glory hunter" boasts of the accomplishments of their multifaceted, multi-trained "robo-dog." But not here. The section on search tips illustrates honest descriptions of lessons learned by experience—the hard way. From false alerts and conflicting clues, to lack of equipment and search limitations, and last, to the "need to speak dog."

The fear of being wrong when standing behind your dog's alert is a real issue. As you will learn from these mission accounts, valid alerts on human scent involve all sorts of deciphering problems due to terrain, wind, temperature, and human debility. This experience is not only well covered in this book, but is a common thread throughout the searches. We are, after all, perfectionists and we wouldn't be in this field if we were not. It is obvious that our need to succeed is a positive attribute when reading this manuscript. That is why the negative search devastates us.

Search safety is also an issue well explored and evaluated in this work. From dealing with moose and bear to toxic waste, hazards vary throughout these missions. The need to identify safety issues during a search is paramount. Thank you all for giving practical data on dealing with search hazards. This information is valuable to all of us in search and rescue.

Another common thread throughout this book is the subject of death itself. Death, from suicide to murder to natural causes, is obviously a natural part of search and rescue. As written in this book, it is apparent that we in search and rescue are very much remembered for putting closure to an emotionally charged incident and I commend Alameda SAR for taking the risk and opportunity to be a part of a family's ceremony at a crash site. However, how we handle death comes from our training and preparation prior to being mission ready. As we read through these pages, one realizes the fragility of being and the dread of non-being. Therefore, preparation and desensitization are a necessity for every search and rescue team. This may not be easy, but it does help put death into perspective.

An uncommon thread of death, but a force of even greater impact is the response to terrorism. The Oklahoma City bombing and the U.S. embassy bombings in Nairobi, opened up a Pandora's box for search and rescue. Since the Oklahoma City bombing was America's first large act of terrorism on home ground involving massive death, it brought with it great pain, many lessons, and many unanswered questions. This mission was personal to the Federal Emergency Management Agency (FEMA) response teams, but devastating to the first responders. Terrorism at the U.S. embassies in Kenya and Tanzania set off flashbacks of Oklahoma. The same "why?" questions were asked, but the psychological involvement was different. What we have learned will be examined in this book and what we do not know is obvious.

One thing I have learned from working in the field of death and dying and search and rescue is that it is an honor and privilege to be a part of someone's end of life. Body recovery work is difficult and painful at times, but it is an opportunity to be a part of a special closure. This is a very personal experience. Always remember that it is not a personal failure to ask for help from comrades and professionals who are trained to handle difficulties in dealing with death and dying.

Thank you, Susan, for allowing me to evaluate and be a part of this valuable book. The information is a must for all of us in search and rescue and those thinking about going into search and rescue. It has been a special privilege to be a part of this educational and sensitive collection of missions.

—Marilyn Neudeck-Dicken, Ph.D.
Diplomat to the American Psychotherapy Association, the American Board of Medical Psychotherapy, and to the American Academy of Pain Management

Introduction

Unless you are involved in search and rescue, understanding the emotional nature of search and rescue is difficult. Even some search and rescue neophyte's have not experienced the emotional impact that search and rescue can have. As one contributor to this book remarked,

> Someone who has not worked with police or SAR dogs cannot understand the type of emotion this type of find brings to a dog handler. It is not just the end product of a day's work with other search resources and the temporary "team" formed for that day, but the end product of raising a dog, training it every day of its life, nursing it through sickness and health, and spending day after day with other SAR dog unit members training for search and rescue work.

This sentiment is not limited to dog handlers. It's true for all people in the search and rescue field. The joys and heartaches are real, they are deep, and they are lasting. Sometimes the emotional aftermath of missions can destroy families and, perhaps unexpectedly, the lives of the searcher. Sometimes those emotions can be the thread that keeps them together, but they are never neutral and they rarely go away. These thoughts have never seemed truer to me than when I was working on this book. I shared the emotion, the joys, and the anguish that each searcher experienced through their missions.

What has gone unsaid in this book is the struggle each searcher faces. There are struggles to overcome during training, both search-and-rescue-dog training and team-member training. The team as a group is a living, growing, and fluid unit. People fail and quit or people get hurt and are forced to quit and when that happens, the team suffers. A very real psychological struggle is that you can pass their training and never have a "find." In fact, it is possible to go through your whole search career and never have a find. Even so, you are still an important contributor to the search effort, and yet, somehow, it still doesn't feel as rewarding when you actually find a clue. The real mission is to solve the mystery, to find the clues, to "clear" the area. Searches that last for months and even years are ever present on the minds of the searchers. The unsolved ones forever haunt you with echoes of "why" and "where." You grieve for the families, you wonder if you could have done more. You ask, "Did I miss something?" Should I have looked somewhere else? You doubt yourself, and if you are a dog handler, you doubt your dog. Yet when you do solve a case, the feeling of both individual and unit pride and accomplishment is well deserved.

Search and rescue can be frustrating in other ways. Sometimes political agendas enter the picture and hinder a search effort; sometimes politics get things done. At times incompetent people are fielded and make your job more difficult, and sometimes incompetent people are in control of the mission.

Search and rescue is a volunteer activity that takes up much of your time. It eats up your vacation time from work, your sick days, and your family time. It robs you of a night's rest, a relative's birthday party, a holiday celebration, or your own special day. Still, to those of us who stick it out, it is rewarding.

The contributors of this book and I hope that you will get a glimpse of what search and rescue is really about. Not what is portrayed in movies, on television, or in fiction books, but what it is like in real life. I hope that as a searcher, you will learn from this book and solve that mystery, find that lost person alive and well.

Organization of this Book

This book is based on a two-part outline, which is given below. The first part of the outline is written with the incident commander (IC), or the search team leader, in mind. It gives the reader an overhead, team point of view. The second part of the outline is from the searcher's point of view to give the reader an idea of what it's like to do the searching. Sometimes the same person has written both parts because they worked both sides of the mission.

In some cases, some sections of the outline were not applicable and were therefore left out, but as much as possible, the contributors conformed to the outline. This way, all of the information is presented in the same order so that the reader can follow the pertinent data easily.

In the outline below, when appropriate, some of the logic behind key questions is explained to help the reader understand the nature of the questions in the outline. This will help the reader understand the contributor's answers as well as why the question was included in the outline. A copy of the actual outline that was sent to contributors can be found in the appendix.

OUTLINE

THE MISSION

Mission Type

Contributors were asked, *Is this search short or long, or does it illustrate inefficient search techniques or circumstances?*

There are many types of missions. Some last for less than an hour, some for weeks, and some remain unsolved. Therefore I have asked each contributor to state the mission type in a simple manner.

The Victim

Contributors were asked to provide the *gender, age, physical condition/health, habits (if any), equipment/clothing, date victim went missing, and any other relevant circumstances or information.*

The information about the victim is one of the most important aspects of the search. It is the part of the search that is on everyone's mind, the focus of the whole event. In order to find someone, you have to know what they look like. When a photo of the victim is not available, searchers have to rely on a physical description. Searchers not only need a physical description, but they need to know the habits of the victim as well, because their habits may dictate what choices they might have made.

Different types of people behave in different ways when they get lost. For example, a person who wants to commit suicide will behave differently from the lost hunter. All of the information about a person will give the search manager clues as to where and in what direction the person would likely go. This will bear heavily on which direction must be searched first. A good IC and/or overhead team, will be able to use this information to compare to the statistics on lost person behavior. A good, seasoned searcher should know about lost person behavior as well. This information may help the searcher decide how to search his sector.

Point Last Seen

The PLS is critical when looking for someone. This gives you a starting point. However, the PLS may not always be correct. Sometimes the information is sketchy because people just do not know where the person was before they failed to return home or wandered away.

Why did the incident take place?

For example, a hiker did not return, person fishing fell overboard, child wandered away, etc.

Where did the incident take place?
When did the incident take place?

Terrain Features

Terrain and other features about the area are critical. Since many searches are conducted at night, it is important to know if there are mine shafts, cliffs and other dangers in the area. If the area contains a toxic waste dump, it may be necessary for a hazardous material team to search that area and everyone else to stay out of that area. If your area includes some low hills or small mountains, you need to develop your search strategy in a manner that will conserve your energy so that you can search your sector properly. If you are using a dog to search the area, the terrain can help or hinder your efforts by channeling the wind and scent. You must know how to use the terrain to your favor. Also, unusual features in an area may attract the missing person.

Weather

Contributors were asked to give the weather conditions at the time the victim went missing, current and what was expected for the next eight hours, including: temperature, wind strength and direction, and precipitation.

Special Dangers

These could include mine shaft, weather changes, unexpected sharp ravines, heat, cold, swamp, etc.

Any Other Special Information

Sometimes information that the family or other searchers consider unimportant can give an extra clue. So you need to gather all of the information that you can about the missing person. Even what you consider not relevant to the mission could later turn out to be a big clue.

Search Personnel and Equipment

Contributors were asked to provide the resources they would have like to have as well as the resources they actually received. There is never a typical search and very few ideal searches. This is because the circumstances in each search are different. It is also because many search and rescue teams are volunteers and do not have unlimited resources. Even the paid professional search teams do not have unlimited resources in their unit. This is why many searches turn into joint missions with other units. In terms of trained man-power, for the most part, searchers, both paid and volunteer, are highly trained and experienced. However, there are always the few who should not be in the field for one reason or another. Sometimes units will allow off-the-street volunteers to participate in certain aspects of a search mission, but to my knowledge, this does not happen often. In some cases, volunteers from other disciplines will help in a search mission. For example, fire-fighters or the police may help with a land search by manning a grid line with trained land search leaders.

Searching is not easy, it is not an exact science. While the missing person only went in one direction, you often have to search in all directions. Search areas become exponentially large, quickly.

Search Strategy

There is no one correct method or strategy for searching. This book illustrates some of the many ways that experienced searchers perform their job. There are many factors that determine how a search is conducted. Some of these factors are the weather, terrain features, how long ago the person went missing, the resources that were available, the condition of the missing person, the age and sex of the missing person, the mental state of the missing person, and the circumstances that surround the person's disappearance (this can help determine if the search is a criminal incident or not). All of the information about the victim, the weather, and terrain will help to decide the urgency, boundaries, and segments of the search. This is usually done by the IC and the overhead team.

They will also decide the probability of area (POA). The POA helps the overhead team decide how likely the missing person is in any given segment. Next, you can find the Probability of Density. The PDEN is determined by dividing the POA by the size of the segment. PDEN = POA/Size. The higher the PDEN the more likely it is that the person will be in that segment. By using these methods to figure out the likelihood that the missing person is in a certain segment, you can focus your resources on that area. When you have more area than you can cover, you have to decide where to look first. This way you have a better chance of finding the missing person quickly.

Some of the methods that are used in searches are confinement. This is when you patrol the perimeter of the area (if it is not too big, and you have the manpower) with human patrols. The idea behind this is to keep the missing person from wandering outside of the area while searchers look for them. Another method is to set up lights or make noise such as turning on a siren at regular intervals. This can attract the missing person to base camp. This is similar to firing three shots to signal help. It is up to the search manager to decide what methods to use on a search mission.

Contributors were free to respond to this section however they needed to. They asked themselves pointed questions, such as, Did I use the resources I had to keep the search area from getting bigger or to try and find the victim? How did I determine the urgency of the search? the boundaries of the search? Did they segment the search area? And they also recounted how they determined the Probability of the Area.

Assign Resources

Based on the information they have been given about the missing person, their experience with the local terrain and what they knows about lost person behavior, the search manager will assign their available resources.

Suspension

The suspension of a mission can be one of the most gut-wrenching aspects of searching. Of course if the missing person is found, the mission is called off. If the missing person is deceased, experienced searchers will be relieved that the person was found. But if the person is still missing, and the search is unresolved, it can haunt the searchers for years and cause the family endless torment. For people who are not found, you reach a point where it becomes hopeless to keep looking. Either the missing person is not in the area or you have exhausted your manpower. I have been on a number of searches where the person left with another person and just was not to be found using traditional search methods. It would have been foolish to continue searching.

Results of the Mission

This can be a successful find or, in some cases, a victim is never found. These latter ones are the missions that can haunt searchers for years, sometimes never knowing the full story.

What are Your Feelings About the Mission?

Searchers were encouraged to share their feelings about the mission. Many times, in the media, only the effects on the victim and the family are considered, but little or nothing is said about the effects that a search has on the searchers. A particularly good example of this is the article by Dr. Marilyn Neudeck-Dicken who deals with the aftermath of the Oklahoma City bombing.

Additional Comments

Search Tips

Respondents were to offer any search tips that they could. Normally, in this section, the contributors offered search tips for the incident commander.

Biography

A brief biography. It would take a book in itself to give the contributors the full credit due them or to credit them with all of their searches and qualifications.

THE SEARCHER

DOG HANDLER TEAM

Ideally someone who used a dog team to search a sector for the reported search mission was to fill out this section. The sector did not have to be one in which a find was made. It should, however, represent some of the problems unique to the search.

Who are you?

The IC, the dog handler, field technician, etc.

The Callout

Respondents were asked, *Where were you when you received the callout? How long did it take you to reach the search site? What special arrangements did you have to make to respond to the search?*

Many searchers are volunteers. Few, if any, searches occur at a convenient time. You can be in the middle of dinner, out for the evening (but never away from your pager), or even on vacation. I have been on vacation a number of times with my dogs and I wound up on a search mission. Responding to missions means you may have to skip your child's birthday party, school function, or special event. You may have to go out at night, search for twelve or more hours and then go right to work. On a regular basis, a great deal of personal time is spent training, especially if you are a dog handler. Some people give up every weekend for unit training. To be on call means that you have to have all aspects of your life covered, such as babysitters on a moment's notice, and petsitters for the pets you leave behind.

Search Sector

Who decided the sector you were to search?

Sometimes you can decide where you want to search when you respond to a mission and many times you are told where you must search. If you are told where to search by a search manager, you may not agree with that decision, but you have to do your job anyway. The searcher may not know the whole story or why he was given that particular sector.

How large was your sector? How long did it take to complete?

This question was intended to give the reader an idea of the range of sector size, since different areas of the country have different terrain features and vegetation, the size of the sector can vary a lot. The weather also factors into the size of the sector.

How did you decide where to start?

Deciding where to start your sector can be critical. If you do not work your dog and the wind to the best advantage, it can take longer to search an area. If you do not take into account the terrain features, you can become too tired to finish your sector, you can take longer to search it, or your probability of detection (POD) will be lower than you would like it to be.

Problems Encountered

Contributors were asked, *What problems did you encounter? Did you expect the problems you encountered?* No one, of course, can predict the problems that one could encounter on a mission. These can range from sudden weather changes to wild animals.

Were you prepared for the conditions you encountered?

By knowing your geographical area, you can be prepared for most "surprises." This includes bringing the proper equipment, and clothing, staying in shape if your search area tends to be rugged, and being trained to handle the local conditions.

The Dog

Contributors were to *Describe how you and the dog worked. What did you notice and what did you do?*

This section is an explanation of how the dog worked. A dog is not a machine. They have good and bad days, just like people. The mystery of the search is "where is the scent?" The dog is the only indicator of how much, if any, scent is available. Scent is just one clue in the whole search effort. The way the dog acts when he finds scent are the signals that the dog gives to the handler, but often these signals are subtle. They are not the hard, excited "alert" signal that the dog gives when he has found a person. Reading these signals is an art that must be developed between the dog and handler. It takes practice and careful observation. Dogs cannot talk. If they could, then searching would be nearly 100% accurate. Nor do dogs have the reasoning skills to take into account what we humans are aware of, such as how terrain features can trap scent, or how wind can "bounce" or "skip" over the terrain. Therefore, it is truly a collaboration between dog and human to solve the mystery, each relying on the other's strengths.

One of the biggest problems in canine SAR is that handlers can miss a signal. Sometimes this happens because the dog is working out of sight of the handler. Without learning how to read your dog, it is almost impossible to trust your dog. Trusting your dog comes from working with him and seeing time after time that the dog is correct. Sometimes, you may think that your dog has given a false alert when he is really telling you something is there. And yes, sometimes dogs do give false alerts.

Probability of Detection

Contributors were asked, *What Probability of Detection did you calculate for the sector you searched? Why?* It is important for the searcher to be able to give the IC a POD. This tells the IC how thoroughly the area has been searched, based on what the searcher and his dog were able to do in that search. With this information the IC can decide if the area needs to be searched again or if it can be eliminated from the area that needs to be searched, which will allow him to make the best use of his resources. He can also decide what priority the area should have if it does need to be searched again.

How Successful were You?

Success does not mean that you found the victim. Success is decided by how effectively you searched your area. By the clues you found or by clearing the area. If the searcher feels that he has a high POD then he was successful in searching or clearing that sector.

What are Your Feelings About the Mission?

As above with the mission commander section, this is a personal response, not a professional one.

Search Tips

Respondents were to offer any search tips that they could. Normally, in this section, these dealt with tips for dog handling.

Biography

A brief biography.

Missing Person, Possible Murder
Wilderness Airscent

Jane and John Aspnes of P.A.W.S. Search and Rescue Dogs
Mission Location: Fairbanks area, Alaska
Dates of Mission: June 1, 1993, through October 11, 1994

Mission Type

This was a very long search because of lack of clues identifying which areas to search. We searched more than 12 different geographic areas in and around Fairbanks, Alaska.

The first week's area that we searched eventually stretched to a radius of approximately five miles. The initial search strategy was based upon the theory that this was a lost person either geographically confused or overtaken by a health problem. Following the clearing of the area surrounding the PLS (the subject's home), the initial search was closed down. It then evolved into a criminal investigation and eventually into a search for a deceased subject. As more clues became available through the 17 months we searched, new areas, some as far as 50 miles away from the PLS were cleared. In addition, the Alaska State Troopers (AST) searched several specific sites (mining claims) accessible only by small single-engine planes. Also, included was the burial site in Canada of the subject's wife.

The Victim

A male, 80 years old. The victim had a heart condition, a slight memory problem, bad leg, but was otherwise physically vigorous for an 80-year-old person. Victim had also

The hills around Fairbanks. The Aspnes search family (left to right): Maya, Chaco, Jane, and Inca.
(Photo by John Aspnes)

shown some vague signs of depression. The subject was independent and lived alone; he'd been a miner and real estate developer throughout most of his life. He had been wearing outdoor-type clothing when he went missing on May 30, 1993. His wife, with whom subject had a close relationship, had died in January 1992. The victim was a VIP and the leader of the Alaska Independence Party; he was a former candidate for governor of Alaska. He had verbal confrontations with many individuals and carried a small caliber handgun.

Point Last Seen
Why did incident take place?
The cause of disappearance was unknown. The case evolved into a suspected robbery.

Where did the incident take place?
The incident was assumed to have taken place at or near the subject's home.

When did the incident take place?
The incident took place May 30, 1993. Friends talked with the subject on that date. Friends discovered that he was missing two days later, on Tuesday morning, June 1, 1993.

Terrain Features
House lots on a south-facing hillside, each of which were one to five acres in size, interspersed by occasional undeveloped wooded areas and larger areas of thick undeveloped woods along the top of the ridge behind the subject's house, which descends into a valley of tundra[1]. Marshy, small shallow ponds and willow brush. Elevations in this search: PLS 950' above sea level; main road 500'; back valley 550'; ridge, over 1100'.

Weather
Mostly sunny, in the high 80s during the day, down to a low of 50°F in the evening; 24 hours of light (0–5 mph) wind, and occasional showers.

Special Dangers
Old military bunkers, mine shafts in some areas, moose, and short-tempered landowners. The moose are a problem because they are unpredictable and can kick with great force. They have been known to kill or injure dogs. In fact, they have been known to kill or injure almost all dogs in a sled dog team. This will happen when a musher surprises a moose on a trail and the dogs are in harness and cannot escape. Many consider moose to be more hazardous than bears. We have had numerous encounters with moose and grizzly bears. So far we have had no problems with either species. We hope that our luck continues! Female moose are a particular problem when they have small calves with them. Males are more aggressive during mating season, but we have not had firsthand experience with that. Bears can be a problem around camps or if they are surprised. Female

---

1 The official tundra is the treeless area between the northern limit of the taiga (northern) forests and the frozen arctic to the north. There is also a transition zone called wooded tundra. Fairbanks has some of these transition areas. The tundra is a cold desert, swampy with dwarf shrubs, moss and lichen.

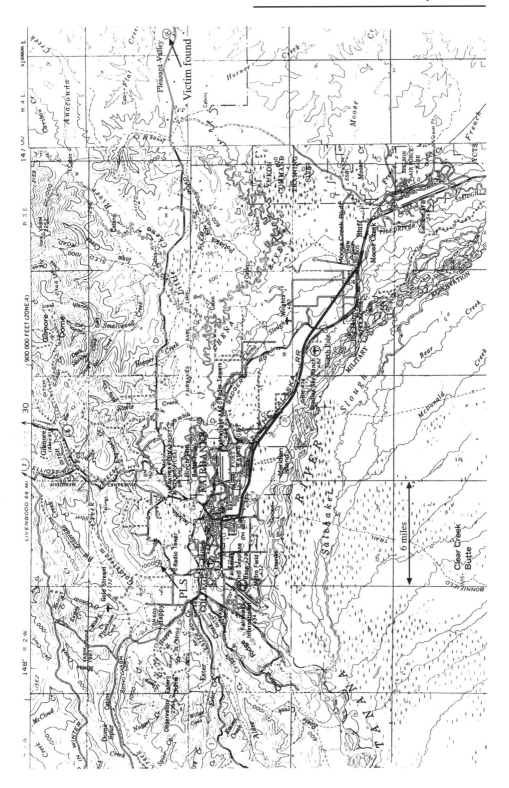

bears with cubs are probably the most problematic. Porcupines can be a problem for dogs. So far we have not had problems with porcupines either. Alaska has no poisonous snakes.

Any Other Special Information

Because of the duration (17 months) of this search, there was a wide range of variables such as weather and clues available.

Search Personnel and Equipment

The resources that we would like to have had were exactly what we had available, although it would have been nice to have trailing dogs that were adept at 24+ hour trailing. The resources that we received were PAWS search and rescue dogs (nine handlers and dogs), a team from Wilderness Search and Rescue (WSAR), Alaska State Trooper personnel and helicopter, more than 60 volunteers for grid searching, and volunteer horseback riders.

Search Strategy

The search began as a lost-person search working from the area of the subject's home as the PLS. A dog search of the home and close dog searches of the immediate area and hasty searches of the surrounding area with continual helicopter coverage was the initial approach. This evolved to grid searches of the area within a one mile radius of the PLS. Careful dog searches up to a five-mile radius and some confinement teams on the outer reaches of the search area were used. Other searchers interviewed all of the neighbors within a mile. Interviewers asked everyone within the large area to individually check their yards for anything obvious as well as any changes.

After several days, PAWS, WSAR, and the AST believed that there was a very low probability of the subject being located in the search area. The AST suspended the search, and PAWS and WSAR awaited further callouts. The AST chose all search areas based on clues that they were gradually gathering.

The following spring, we began clearing areas with a search focus on potential burial sites. Between May and October 1994, we carefully searched an additional nine locations for evidence and supposed burial sites. We searched all areas to a high POD. Search areas included mine shafts, caves, auto junkyards, steamboat interiors, burned houses, foundations, abandoned buildings, woods, thick brush, and marshy areas. Other than some vague interest in marshy areas, possibly due to naturally occurring methane rather than from a human source, and some heightened interest in junked cars, which may have resulted from the vehicles having been in accidents causing human injuries, we never had any strong alerts. (All decomposing material gives off methane gas and sometimes a dog will hit on the methane gas, and if a car was in an accident and blood is left in the vehicle, a dog will hit on it.) Since the subject was a VIP, there was considerable interest from the press. Because of this, we conducted most searches at unusual times, out of uniform, and sometimes under the guise of searchers being berry pickers.

Finally, in October 1994, after several autumn snowfalls, the AST called us out after dark to clear a wooded area 25 miles out of town. Right from the very beginning the dogs seemed more excited than usual even while waiting in the car. It happened that it was Maya's turn to go first. She ran about 250 feet into the woods, stopped at a location briefly, and then disappeared momentarily. She returned 180° opposite from where she had disappeared, apparently cutting a large circle. She continually returned to a depressed area containing a few small saplings, and wanted to dig and gave a bark alert. Suspicious that scent may have flowed into this low area, we had her check the higher areas, but she showed no interest and would go back to the low spot. Five other dogs showed a similar search pattern. The following day the body was found where the Maya had alerted. It was buried at a depth of 3.5 feet, wrapped in a blue plastic tarp, which someone had sealed with lots of duct tape. The snow depth was two to three inches, and the temperature was in the 20°F range.

Because of the burial depth and the cool Alaskan ground temperature, the body was in identifiable condition despite being in that location for 17 months.

Although we searched many areas to a high POD, we of course were very relieved to find out that we had not missed anything.

If we'd had reliable trailing dogs available at the time the search began, it is possible that the dogs may have confirmed that the subject had not left the driveway of his home on foot, the search might not have covered such a large area around the PLS, and it might have evolved to a criminal investigation sooner.

We believe that because of this search, our group has achieved, and maintains, a higher level of competence in trailing and cadaver search techniques.

Additional Comments

As a result of this and previous searches during the summer of 1993, Andrew Rebman and Marcia Koenig provided our team with a cadaver search seminar. This resulted in cadaver proficiency for 12 PAWS dogs. We used this training extensively for the remainder of the search.

Another result of this search was that in the summer of 1994, Andrew Rebman and Marcia Koenig provided a trailing course for PAWS. Although all PAWS certified dogs passed a basic trailing requirement, many of the various breeds of PAWS dogs are now proficient at 24-hour-old trails with some working trails up to the 72-hour level. It is now normal procedure at searches to run some trailing dogs from the PLS and at locations where evidence or visual sightings are reported by troopers or witnesses.

Search Tips

Train a group of dogs (they don't have to be bloodhounds) to a high level of trailing and use this expertise.

Have dogs cross-trained for cadaver searches.

THE SEARCHER
DOG HANDLER TEAM

Who are You?

I am a dog handler.

The Callout

We were at home when we received the callout. It was ten minutes to the search site.

The Search Sector

Who decided your sector?

Dog Operations leader, in coordination with WSAR Ops in coordination with the AST, decided my search sector.

How large was your sector? How long did it take to complete?

While the search was for a missing person, the sectors averaged a half-mile to one mile on a side for the early searching, and three to five miles on a side for containment. As the search continued, the search areas became one-eighth to a half-mile on a side. The smaller areas were assigned to look for evidence. Because of the heat, most people alternated working their dog with observing another handler work her/his dog so the dogs got plenty of down time.

How did you decide where to start your sector?

Wind direction, terrain, and access determined strategy for working the sectors.

Problems Encountered

Most problems were urban problems: loose dogs and curious people, because we worked so close to homes.

Were you prepared for the conditions you encountered?

Yes.

The Dog

The dog worked well. However, because she had a black coat, the heat affected her on hot days, particularly when in the direct sun.

Probability of Detection

By the end of the search, I expected a high POD because of the tight pattern and overlapping of searchers.

How Successful Were You?

In hindsight, the group was very successful, although at times it didn't feel that way. We eliminated many areas.

What are Your Feelings About the Mission?

Because of the ultimate success, the group gained tremendous credibility with the public. Because of clearing so many areas and ultimately finding the subject, we enhanced our credibility with the AST.

Waiting for callout! P.A.W.S. dogs (Photo by Richard Hansen)

Suicide
Wilderness Airscent

Mission Location: City of Fairbanks, Alaska
Dates of Mission: February 13, 1995, through February 14, 1995

Mission Type

This was a short search in cold winter conditions.

The Victim

"Phil" (name changed to protect his identity) was a male, 23 years old, who was in okay physical condition and mental health, except that he had a history of depression. He was a heavy consumer of alcohol. He was dressed in appropriate outdoor clothing and had a blanket when he went missing on February 11, 1995. On February 10, 1995, he was charged with D.W.I. and spent the night in jail. He'd had a previous suicide attempt.

Point Last Seen

Phil had been last seen at the apartment of a friend.

Why did the incident take place?
Suicide.

Where did the incident take place?
The incident took place in urban Fairbanks.

Terrain Features

Typical city blocks, housing areas, school and playground, and a city recreational area—soccer fields, city snow dumps, and woods.

Weather

Mostly clear, with temperatures from 0° to -20°F, the wind was light, 1–3 mph, with no precipitation.

Special Dangers

There was drug activity in the neighborhood and busy roads.

Search Personnel and Equipment

Although on the second day of the search, we did not have sufficient mantrackers, we had mantrackers, dog teams, a helicopter, snowmobiles, and four-wheelers.

Search Strategy

The callout was at 1800 on February 13, 1995. The search began at 1930 and was halted for the night at 2330. Hasty searches consisted of the neighborhoods surrounding the PLS and the city recreation area or a radius of approximately 0.5 to 0.7 mile. Conditions were dark and the air temperature was -10°F.

On the next day, February 14, 1995, operation leaders from PAWS and WSAR sent teams to recheck areas of heavy brush and woods, which were areas of low POD. They sent four-wheelers and snowmobiles to check trails and areas along a nearby river for containment. They assigned two dog teams to a new area of heavy woods (0.5 mile by 0.4 mile). The dog handlers could drive along two sides of the new area for a hasty visual search, looking for tracks in the snow. Two main trails were located plus one smaller trail and one tiny track into the woods. One dog team took one main trail and the other dog team took the other. We were fortunate to be able to work into the wind from the road access. Snowshoes were necessary and it took about 1.5 hours for the two teams to clear approximately 50% of the area with some overlap. Primary emphasis was on checking all tracks leading away from the main trails. POD was high because of searchers being able to visually determine if areas were not accessed or were still pristine (i.e., no tracks into the woods).

Following that section, the two teams went to the remaining area. One team started to check along the edge of a main road, which bordered the search area. The second team was to specifically check the one small track into the woods. When that handler came to the small track and was trying to decide if it was made by a moose or a human (snow depth was 18 to 24 inches), the dog took off into the woods. By the time the handler had crawled up over the snow berm at the edge of the woods, the dog had found the subject. Phil had committed suicide.

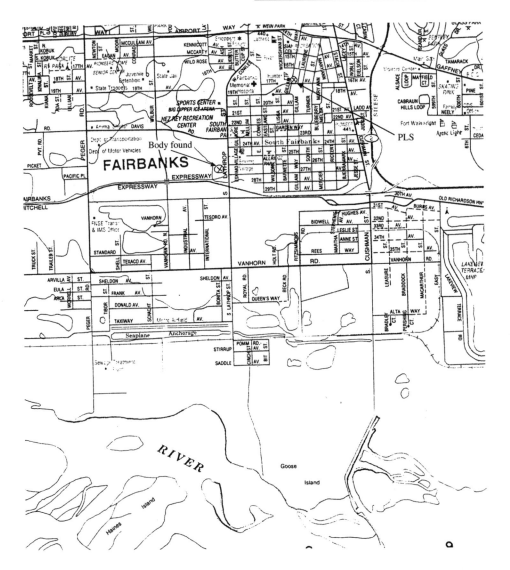

Search Tips

Snow can be very helpful in efficiently covering large areas. Check with the local weather service to correctly establish what weather conditions have happened between the time that the subject was last seen and the commencement of the search (any new snow, wind, blowing snow, and temperature). On this search there was confusion due to a rumor that new snow had fallen since the subject was last seen, which would have covered his tracks. In fact, there had been no snowfall during that interval.

If there is a good snow covering and no new snow, tracks into woods or pristine areas are obvious. Perimeter searches are valuable here and can give a high POD without having to minutely cover the entire area. Doing a partial (two sides) perimeter hasty search by automobile established strategy on this particular search.

THE SEARCHER
DOG HANDLER TEAM

Who are You?

Dog handlers.

The Callout

We were at home, and it was 45 minutes to the site.

Search Sector

Who decided your sector? What information did you need?

The dog Ops leader. We needed the boundaries and subject description.

How large was your sector? How long did it take to complete?

Our sector 0.4 mile by 0.4 mile first assignment, 0.5 mile by 0.4 mile second assignment using two handlers and two dogs.

How did you decide where to start your sector?

We used wind direction and access to decide our starting point.

Problems Encountered

Darkness, cold (-10°F), and deep snow, which was not unexpected.

Were you prepared for the conditions you encountered?

Yes.

The Dog

The dog ranged well, handled snow and cold well, and gave an alert when finding a blanket giving off human scent.

Probability of Detection

On the first night, we determined that we had an average POD. The darkness, though, kept one from having a good feel for POD in thick brush and rough area.

How Successful were You?

We felt that the coverage was very good considering the conditions and that effective searching by the entire team reduced the potential areas very quickly.

What are Your Feelings About the Mission?

We felt good about the mission having had the opportunity to apply extensive training in a successful way.

Drowning

Mission Location: Nenana, Alaska
Date of Mission: January 15, 1994

Mission Type

This was a short, one-day search for a drowned subject. The Nenana River was partially frozen at the time of the incident, but had totally frozen over at the time of the search. Ultimately, conditions were considered too dangerous and difficult to continue.

The Victim

The victim was a white female, 30 to 40 years old in good physical condition. She was riding a snowmobile at the time of the incident and was dressed for outdoor activities. She disappeared the evening of January 3, 1994.

Point Last Seen

Why did the incident take place?

The subject was on a snowmobile that went through thin ice or an open patch in the evening. A female companion was able to pull herself out of the water onto thick ice and was rescued.

Where did the incident take place?

The incident took place on the Tanana River across from the town of Nenana, Alaska. The subject became the object of considerable dragging for the following two weeks.

Any Other Special Information

Four dogs, three handlers, and one observer were brought to the site on January 15, 1994. The conditions were -20°F with wind

Water search—John Aspnes "Captain," Tsuugi, & Cathi Carr-Lundfelt. (Photo by Jane Aspnes)

about 25 mph gusting to 35 mph. The wind created clouds of dust and silt in the air.

Search Strategy

The area from the PLS to the highway bridge downstream (about 300 yards long by 100 yards wide) was divided into small search areas and gridded by different dog teams.

In an area just above the bridge abutments, one dog showed some interest. A second dog team was sent to the area and interest was confirmed by the second team.

A group of the original river searchers arrived and with an ice auger drilled a series of holes. All four dogs were then worked on these holes. The dogs consistently alerted on only the holes just upriver from the initial alert area.

Suspension

The recommendation was made to concentrate dragging in that area and upstream from the alert areas.

Results of the Mission

No body recovery was made but this search was an interesting problem resulting in good training for working in difficult conditions.

What are Your Feelings About the Mission?

We will always wonder about the alerts since there was no body recovery.

Search Tips

When working on ice that may be of questionable safety, be sure of the safety of searchers. Consider being roped. Always question sources of safety information. When searching on ice, assign small segments and use a tight grid pattern.

THE SEARCHER
DOG HANDLER TEAM

Who are You?

I am a dog handler and observer.

The Callout

I was at home at the time of the callout. Since there was no chance that a live person could be recovered, the search was arranged at everyone's convenience.

The Search Sector

Who decided your sector?

We had a small group so we decided on the sectors ourselves, always keeping half the

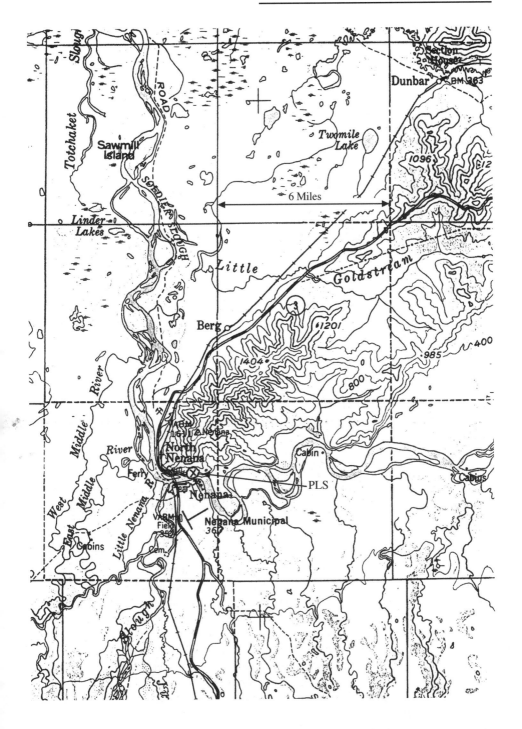

The area around the Nenana River where the victim was last seen. No body was ever recovered.

group on shore in case problems arose.

How large was your sector? How long did it take to complete?
We searched different sectors about 100 yards by 300 yards and 100 yards by 200 yards.

How did you decide where to start your sector?
We used landmarks on shore to divide sectors and worked into a heavy wind.

Problems Encountered

It was cold, windy, and dusty, with very slippery footing in places. We only expected the cold.

Were you prepared for the conditions you encountered?
Yes.

The Dog

The dog worked very well except in the combined extremely slippery and windy areas.

Probability of Detection

I determined a low POD. Searching for a body under ice was new to us, and we weren't certain what level of alert to expect.

How Successful were You?

We all felt good about our approach to the problem and the work the dogs did but were unsuccessful in locating the body.

What are Your Feelings About the Mission?

After the fact, we discovered that parts of the river we were asked to search had frozen only the day before. We regret the risk in which we placed our dogs and ourselves.

Biography

Jane and John Aspnes are advocates of the idea that "a family that searches together, stays together." Their family includes Maya, a Bouvier, and Inca, a Beauceron, both certified by PAWS Search and Rescue Dogs of Fairbanks, Alaska, as well as North American Search Dog Network (NASDN). Jane is a NASDN board member, evaluator, and instructor. Jane and John have been training Bouviers since 1966 and have shared the exploration of Alaska's back country with their canine companions. The most recent addition to their family is Chaco, a yellow lab that is also certified by PAWS. All three dogs have taken their handlers through the Find 'em Search School courses. Jane and John feel privileged that their canine searchers enable them to be members of P.A.W.S. where Jane is presently training officer and John is secretary. They are also members of Wilderness Search and Rescue of Fairbanks, Alaska.

Note on Permafrost

There are large areas of so-called permafrost in the arctic and subarctic. Fairbanks is in the subarctic zone. We have permafrost in low, swampy areas and often on the north side of ridges and hills. Permafrost is permanently frozen ground. There is a so-called "active" layer above the permafrost that thaws seasonally. This thawed layer may be a few inches thick in the high arctic and many feet thick in the sub-arctic. Building on permafrost is risky. If done, it is necessary to have pilings placed in the permafrost and then it is critical to keep it frozen. Thawed permafrost in silty soils can be a soupy mess that does not support structures. If the permafrost is in gravel, it may not be such a problem.

Permafrost does not affect our missions in the winter when the active layer is frozen. Areas of permafrost could affect our missions if we needed to search places that turned into swamps in the summer. There are sometimes craters that form when ice lenses in permafrost melt. These might present a hazard, but it has not been a problem so far.

Fairbanks temperatures range from a record low of about 66°F below zero and a record high of about 96°F above zero. The average over thirty years of data gives a normal annual low of about 23°F below zero and a normal annual high of about 73°F above zero. The average (mean) annual temperature in Fairbanks is about 25.7°F above zero.

From left to right: Maya (Bouvier), Jane Aspnes, John Aspnes, and Inca (Beauceron).

Missing Walker

Larry S. Bulanda
  Phoenixville Fire Department K-9 SAR Unit
  Mission Location: Ridley Creek State Park, Pennsylvania
  Mission Date: August 1990

Mission Type

This was a short search using a diverse range of resources.

The Victim

"Davis" was a white male, 58 years old, and was 5'8" tall, weighed 140 pounds, and was in good physical condition. Mental condition: diagnosed as mildly schizophrenic, non-violent. Davis was a resident of a supervised care facility located a few towns away from the PLS. There were no outstanding habits reported, except that Davis was a brisk walker. Davis was dressed appropriately for the season but did not carry any equipment or food. The victim went missing on Monday, August 27, 1990, approximately 1530. Two friends had brought Davis to Ridley Creek State Park for an outing. Their intention was to walk some marked trails and return the subject to his care facility. Davis had no family in the area.

Point Last Seen

The subject's friends identified the PLS as the intersection of two hiking trails in the park.

Why did the incident take place?

The incident occurred because of a moment of inattention when Davis became separated from his friends. The mental condition of the subject and his fast walking pace contributed to his disappearance.

Where did the incident take place?

The incident took place at Ridley Creek State Park in Delaware County, Pennsylvania. The park comprises more than 2600 acres and is bordered by residential and semi-rural areas. The park is popular with hikers, bikers, fishermen, and other outdoor enthusiasts. It contains miles of marked trails and many unmarked trails created by fishermen, deer herds, etc.

When did the incident take place?

The incident began Monday, August 27, and ended Wednesday, August 29.

Terrain Features

The park consists of rolling hills, some of which are steep. It is wooded and has many areas of thick brush that are difficult, if not impossible, to walk through. Some wide but shallow streams also run through the park.

Weather

The weather was mild for the season. Daytime temperatures ranged in the upper 70s with higher humidity. Nighttime temperatures were in the 60s. There was no precipitation during the period.

Special Dangers

At various spots along the stream, the banks were slippery and steep. Although the streams were not very deep, the chance for a drowning was present. The thick brush and stickers could also pose a danger to anyone trying to navigate it.

Search Personnel and Equipment

The head park ranger was the IC for the mission while I shared the command of the canine resources. The IC had called in the following resources during the mission: several local fire departments, park rangers, one police and one medical helicopter, a mantracker, and our canine unit consisting of six dog teams and support personnel.

As for the resources we would have liked to have, as in most other searches involving large areas, extra dog teams would have been welcomed. Regardless, our unit had been structured to act in a stand-alone mode or as part of a larger team. We provided our own dog teams, support personnel, maps, first aid, communications, and transportation. Our specific resource demands included park rangers to provide information on the park and access to areas and outbuildings. We also requested that the park be closed to the public for the duration of the search.

Search Strategy

The IC began the search late Monday afternoon when the subject was reported missing. Following interviews with the subject's friends, the IC deployed hasty teams to check high-probability areas that included trails, outbuildings, pavilions, and other public areas. The fire department vehicles were deployed as containment and as attraction devices with their PA systems used to call the subject. The air search included two helicopters but they were quickly determined to be ineffective due to the thick canopy over most of the park. The search continued throughout Monday night and late that evening, the IC contacted our canine unit to deploy the following morning.

Assign Resources

Our unit mobilized and arrived on the scene early Tuesday morning. Following our briefing by the IC, we set up base near the PLS, distributed maps and subject profiles to our teams and began to deploy. Our strategy was to revisit all of the trails and outbuildings that had been previously searched hastily by park rangers. We felt that with the favorable weather and the subject's good health, he probably was on the move somewhere within the park. Since many trails formed long loops, it was felt that Davis could have become easily disoriented if he moved during the night. Initially we started a tracking dog from the PLS to try to track the subject. An airscenting team was held in reserve to work, if need be, at the end of the track should the tracking dog lose the track. Other dog teams were deployed to cover trails, buildings and public areas.

The tracking dog worked to a point where a footprint was found. A mantracker on the scene was sent to the site and determined that the print could have been from the subject. The print was not legible enough for a 100% ID but the probability was high. The tracking dog continued but began to work inconsistently. As other teams came in from their assignments, they were re-deployed on trails and in areas around and beyond the footprint location. Our teams continued to work throughout the day and showed some interest along trails and in some areas. After plotting the team's results on a map, I concluded that we were closing in on the subject but were always "a few steps" behind him.

Suspension

At approximately 1800, Tuesday August 28, the IC called a status meeting with both the canine and fire department personnel. Based on what had been accomplished, the IC felt that there was a strong possibility that Davis had left the park. He chose to terminate the search at that time but planned to keep the park rangers on alert during their daily routines. By this time the subject's photo and description had been broadcast on all the local television stations and an alert had been sent to the local and state police. The local police departments were apparently satisfied with the search effort and chose not to continue a full-scale mission outside the park.

Results of the Mission

On the following day, Wednesday 29 August, Davis found his way out of the park and proceeded down a secondary highway. Tired, hungry, and disheveled, the subject went into a local tavern where the bartender quickly recognized him from news broadcasts. The authorities were notified and the subject was treated and returned to the care facility. During his travails, the subject suffered two broken toes, broke his glasses, and lost a shoe but was otherwise in good shape.

After Davis had recovered, I contacted his friends and requested a meeting with the subject so we could determine if our search strategy and our assumptions had been correct. They agreed to the meeting and we all returned to the park to reconstruct the events surrounding the search. We questioned the subject regarding his actions during the search. His answers seemed fairly reliable given his mental condition but some of his statements and thinking were obviously flawed. He showed us some of the trails he walked during the search and we were all surprised at how quickly this individual could walk. Keeping up with him was difficult and he was obviously a searcher's worst nightmare—a moving target, and a fast one at that. Although we did not retrace his entire voyage, he covered enough ground to show us that we were indeed on the right course during the mission.

In hindsight, the perfect strategy would been to have deployed teams well ahead of our forward teams and have them work toward the forward teams in a pincer-type movement. This tactic would have required more resources than we had available to us so it could not have been done properly even if we had the wisdom to carry it out.

I felt that the most interesting part of our reunion was the response Davis gave to our questions. We asked if he had heard the PA systems calling him, and he said yes but he had not answered because he wanted to conserve his energy. We asked if he had seen other people in the park during his time there. He said he had seen some bicyclists on a trail but he did not talk to them or follow them because they were traveling in a direction opposite to his direction of travel. This sounded ludicrous at first but made sense when you consider that he knew he was lost: Where he was coming from was clearly not where he wanted to go or be and that is where the cyclists were going. He said that he had spent some time on his hands and knees searching for his glasses that he had dropped and broke. During the two evenings out, he slept in the brush. We were not able to establish exactly when he broke his toes or how much that had hindered his progress. Hunger and injury had to slow his progress significantly toward the latter part of the search. Our session with him became less fruitful as he seemed less willing to talk so we decided to part ways with the valuable lessons we had learned.

What are Your Feelings About the Mission?

Like most search missions, this one had its burden of frustration. Too few resources to cover too large an area. It was unique in that it gave us an opportunity to question the subject and determine what had happened during the search. Many searches in our area are for suicides, drownings, runaways, and the like. These afford almost no chance to question the subject to determine actions and motives. One major regret for us, and I am sure for the IC, was not continuing the search into Wednesday. Knowing when you have done enough and then terminating the search is the most difficult part of any search mission.

Search Tips

Consulting with local mental healthcare professionals to learn more about the general characteristics of common types of mental patients would be useful for any search teams. The Alzheimer patient should also be included in this study. To be effective at searching for this type of individual, the team must understand how this subject may react to being lost.

Although contacting the news media can pay off, it can also create more work. In most of the cases that I have been involved with, missing person reports put out over TV, newspapers, or radio has generally resulted in a flurry of false sightings spread over a wide geographic area. Checking the validity of these potential clues is time consuming. However, in this case the TV coverage was a key tool in finding the subject.

The decision to terminate a search usually has life or death consequences. It should be done by consensus involving as many of the management team as possible. Although not always possible, the decision should not be made under situations of frustration or fatigue.

If your subject is on the move or can move, don't forget to revisit previously searched areas. There is a natural tendency to want to break new ground rather than cover old real estate.

Close the park or keep it open? Closing the park to all traffic helped us do our job more efficiently; however, having the benefit of dozens of other "searchers" (hikers and joggers) in the park would also have been an advantage.

Biography

Larry Bulanda's involvement with emergency services began in 1970 when he joined a local rescue squad. The first search he participated in was with that unit and it was his baptism by fire. His team found the body of a nine-year-old drowning victim in the Hackensack River in New Jersey. Since then he has been involved with three SAR units, two of which he helped to create and run. Larry has obtained his Managing the Search Operation certification, his Federal Incident Command Certification, and his state Water Rescue Certification. To date, Larry has been on more than 200 missions during his career. He enjoys both the management and ground-pounding aspects of missions. When Larry is in the field, he is teamed with his Border Collie partner, Jib. His previous and first search dog, Ness, was also a Border Collie and to his knowledge was the first Border Collie to do SAR work in the United States.

Larry Bulanda and his Border Collie, Jib.

Missing Person
Suburban Search Scent Specific

Susan Bulanda
  Phoenixville Fire Department K-9 SAR Unit
  Mission Location: Upper Merion, Pennsylvania
  Mission Date: October 3, 1992

Mission Type

This was a short search. It illustrates how confusion and lack of communication can hinder a search effort. It also illustrates teamwork between a dog and handler.

The Victim

"Andy" (name changed to protect his family) was a 36-year-old male in good health, with no known habits. Although the victim had taken hunting gear, pants, and coat, with him, no one was exactly sure what he was wearing when he disappeared on October 2, 1992. Andy had gone to an area of woods to set up a deer stand for bow hunting and did not return.

The incident took place next to an active train freight yard in a suburban area of Pennsylvania, and the callout came at 1930. The terrain was flat and wooded; the Conrail freight yard was dusty and open. The weather was fair, clear, with temperatures ranging in the 50s–60s. After we reported to the site, we learned that there was a toxic waste dump in the area. Along with the man's vehicle, the police found a bloody shirt in the parking lot, and the wife of the victim verified that the shirt belonged to the victim.

Search Personnel and Equipment

We had all of the resources we needed. In fact, for this mission, it would've helped the search effort if we'd had fewer resources. There were too many people and things going on for the size of the area that we had to search. Although we did not request nor receive the assistance from them, thirty-six units responded within a 24-hour period. These units included four canine SAR units, nine EMS units, and 23 fire companies.

Search Strategy

When our unit arrived on the scene, I assessed the situation. The police department that was in charge of the investigation had specifically called us to try to find a track. Their police dog was not able to find a track around the vehicle.

I asked one of our unit members to interview the officers involved to decide what had been done and found. After the interview, I examined the area where the man had parked his vehicle.

The man had disappeared 24 hours ago. The wooded area where Andy disappeared was about five hundred feet wide and two to three miles long and was situated on the other side of an active train freight yard and between residential neighborhoods. His vehicle was found in the freight yard. The wife and another family member had looked through the car for a note; only family members had entered the vehicle. The bloody shirt had been found about 200 feet from the vehicle. Before we arrived, Andy's wife identified the shirt as his. A police officer had picked up the shirt and put it in a brown paper bag and then returned it to same spot where it was found.

Because this was a scent-specific problem, I did not set sectors or boundaries. I planned to obtain a scent for my dog and let him try to follow a track.

Assign Resources

This mission had a very specific purpose and our unit was not going to do an area search. Therefore, I assigned two field technicians to follow me while I ran the track.

Suspension

Once we ran our track we suspended our part of the mission.

Results of the Mission

We found the track, reported the results to the police officer in charge and left.

THE SEARCHER
DOG HANDLER TEAM

Who are You?

As well as being the dog handler, I was in charge of the mission. This happened because at that time my dog was the only scent-specific dog available. My dog was a Beauceron named "Scout."

The Callout

I was just finishing dinner with a number of our unit members when I received the call-out. We had a guest instructor from the Department of Environmental Resources who was certifying our unit members for the Managing the Search Operation (MSO) course. We were fortunate to have this person with us to go on the mission. He could provide a "fresh" set of eyes and critique the mission the next day in class.

I did not have to make any special arrangements for this mission, since we had enough unit members handy to cover the mission. Because we were out to dinner, I already had a babysitter for my five-year-old son. The search site was local and it only took about a half an hour to reach the search site.

The Search Sector

Who decided your sector?

Since I was in charge of our unit's operation, I decided where and how I was going to search.

How large was your sector? How long did it take to complete?

I had no idea at the beginning of the mission where Scout would lead me, or even if he would lead me at all. As it turned out, it only took about thirty minutes to run the trail.

How did you decide where to start your sector?

After reviewing all of the information about the case, I discussed it with the DER K-9 SAR manager and my husband, who is also an Incident Commander. I decided to start Scout at the car rather than at the shirt. We were all in agreement that if Scout led me to where the shirt had been found, he was on the right track.

Problems Encountered

The police department who was investigating the incident called us to the mission. It was not until we arrived that I learned that there were approximately five other fire companies and one other search unit on the scene.

The police had roped the car off with yellow tape before we arrived. At least twelve people were milling around the vehicle. Fire trucks were running in the parking lot and a train was creeping through the freight yard. Approximately fifty to one hundred people had walked through the parking lot within the twenty-four-hour period since the man went missing. There were groups of people standing around throughout the area.

It also appeared that three separate search functions were going on at the same time. The police were conducting their search, the fire department was conducting theirs, and another search and rescue unit was conducting theirs. The police were not involved with the other searches. I am still not clear just how this mission got so out of hand. This made it impossible for us to find out exactly what the other units had done. We did not know what areas the other units had searched and what they had found, if anything.

Were you prepared to face the conditions you encountered?

All of our unit members (including the dogs) were experienced in the proper procedures and methods that we needed to get the job done.

The Dog

First I questioned the police officer who had tried to find a track and the officers who were investigating the incident. Next, I collected a scent pad from the vehicle. Two family members had been through the vehicle and had sat in the front seat. A jacket was lying in a heap in the hatchback part of the vehicle. I questioned the police officer who was present while the family went through the car and he assured me that they had not handled the jacket. So I took a sterile gauze pad and placed it deep in the folds of the jacket to collect scent for the dog. After I had created the scent pad for Scout, I stored it and scented him on the jacket.

Scout took off like a shot and went directly to the shirt in the parking lot. From there he led me across the railroad tracks. At that point I heard yelling and turned to look back. My two field technicians were calling and waving to me to come back. Thinking that they had found the missing man, I called Scout off the track and went back. A Conrail freight yard official was upset because I had gone across the tracks without his permission. When I went back to him, he started to reprimand me for crossing the tracks in front of a train that was creeping along the tracks. The train was moving so slowly that I could not tell that it was moving. Of course I had to cross the tracks in front of the train to get back to the man and then cross them yet again to continue my mission. Once I re-crossed the tracks, I took Scout back to the point where we had stopped the track. I gave him his "find" command and he picked up the track again. He tracked at a brisk pace into the woods along a trail. We came to two different intersections in the trail. Both times he circled the intersection and then led me down one of the paths. Along the last leg of the trail, he stopped for a brief second to show to me that scent had left the trail. I had my field technician mark the spot with surveyors' tape as we continued along. A little farther down the trail, Scout turned and headed along a stream. Because of the toxic waste in the area, I didn't allow him to go near the water because he would've taken a drink. After following the stream for about 500 yards, Scout came to a sudden stop. Up to now, Scout had been moving at a quick pace for the entire length of the track. Scout stood there for what seem like a long time, but in reality was just a few minutes. Then he made an acute angle turn into the woods, not following any visible path. When we again returned to the path, it was exactly at the spot that they marked with tape. It was the same spot where Scout signaled on the way in and my field technician had marked with tape. Scout continued to lead me out of the woods back to the parking lot where the scent ended.

Based on the indications that Scout gave, it appeared that the man had gone into the woods. He walked along the path, along the creek and went back to the parking lot where he left by another vehicle.

After I gave my report, the police took the shirt and the vehicle so that a forensic team could examine them. The shirt had blood on it, but it seemed suspicious. There were no rips or holes in the shirt. Also, the blood on the shirt had the same pattern on the front and the back. Apparently someone had poured blood, or a similar substance on the folded shirt.

Once Scout was done with his track, the police and our unit left the search site. The rest of the units stayed to search the area, but didn't find a single clue or the man.

Probability of Detection

I was very confident in the track that Scout ran. I felt that the man was not in the area and gave Scout a POD of 95%.

How Successful were You?

Later investigation by the police department verified that Scout had been 100% successful and correct in what he indicated. It turned out that Andy had left the area. Officials suspected that he may have flown to London, staging his own disappearance.

What are Your Feelings About the Mission?

As far as Scout was concerned, I thought that he worked very well. I have always felt awed when he comes through in difficult circumstances. As far as the mission itself, I was pleased with the way the police and our unit worked efficiently. We got done what we had to get done and wrapped it up. I was not happy with the way the rest of the mission grew and got out of hand. The lack of coordination and confusion made it difficult to work. When I was ready to run the track with Scout, I had to ask at least a dozen people to move. As it turned out, some were standing right on the track.

The DER IC stopped at another command post, which was being run by one of the SAR units and asked to see their log and paperwork. We wanted to gather information to help us with our job. No paperwork or log existed. This person had no idea who was in the field, what units they were associated with, where they were sent, or what they were doing. No one checked the area for dangers, and therefore they were sending dogs and people into the toxic waste area. When I see people involved in SAR who do not know, or will not follow, a safe standard of operation, it upsets me.

I was pleased with the way our unit performed, however, and how well we worked with the police department. I was also very pleased with how accurate Scout was. Yet I was upset about the way the rest of the mission was handled. The rest of the searchers continued for another 18–24 hours

Search Tips

Always follow the correct procedures for conducting a mission. If you are called out on a mission where the procedures are not safe, your unit should decide if they will participate in the mission or not. Not following the procedures, or getting involved in a mission without order, can cost the lives of the searchers and the victim. For example, one time our unit responded (in the middle of the night) to a mission. When we arrived on scene, everyone had gone home. The person in charge did not contact us to let us know that they suspended the mission. Nor did they leave anyone at base to account for all of the people en route or in the field. They just went home.

Learn to trust your dog. This cannot be said enough. The only way to learn to trust your dog is to train in as many different conditions as possible. If you are working a dog in scent-specific work, push the circumstances to the limit. Don't be afraid to work beyond what you think your dog can do; this way you will learn what your dog can and cannot do. However, only do this after you train your dog and he is proven. The same goes for airscenting dogs.

Take a course in managing the search operation. Searchers who do not want to be a part of the overhead team should have the course as well. This will help everyone on a mission work together. It will also help the searcher understand what the overhead team needs and why they do what they do.

A search unit should work as a team. Each member should trust all of the members in the unit. This doesn't mean that you have to like each person or dog, but you must be able to trust them. To do an efficient job in the field, a unit has to be able to work independently as well as in harmony with other units.

Be sure to keep an objective outlook regarding your dog. If your dog is getting old, having a bad day, or not feeling well, pull him from the mission. Trust your unit members to spot these circumstances when you do not.

Biography

Susan Bulanda has been a dog trainer since 1961. Professionally, she has been a practicing ethologist (dog and cat behaviorist) since the 1970s. Susan holds a bachelor's degree in psychology and a master's degree in education, in addition to course work in the behavioral sciences and mathematics. Her involvement with canine SAR spans more than fifteen years. During that time she has been the head trainer for two units. Susan is currently with the Phoenixville Fire Department K-9 SAR Unit, and formally with Coventry Canine SAR Unit. She is certified by the state of Pennsylvania in Managing the Search Operation, holds her federal Incident Command Certification, and the Pennsylvania Phase One Water Rescue certification. Susan and her husband, Larry, were honored to receive the George Washington Medal of Honor from the Freedom Foundation for their work in search and rescue.

Missing Child

Patti and Dan Burnett
Summit County Rescue Group
Mission Location: Kenosha Pass, Colorado
Mission Date: October 1987

Mission Type

This search was short primarily because we used several different search techniques simultaneously. They had a police dog, my search dog, ground searchers, ATVs, etc. The search lasted about four hours. I was only involved the last two hours of the operation.

The Victim

It was Saturday, October 3, 1987. The victim, Michael, was a toddler camping with his family. Michael was about two-and-a-half years old and was in excellent health. His mother reported that he would not walk more than one-quarter mile before he got tired. He toddled around like a typical toddler and was not in the habit of wandering far. At that point he would lie down and sleep. Michael wasn't potty trained. All that he had with him was the diaper he was wearing.

Point Last Seen

Why did the incident take place?

Michael was playing on a sand dune with his brothers and sisters. The older kids were on bikes. Their mother instructed them to watch Michael but the kids got distracted and lost track of him around noon. The parents called the sheriff's office immediately via 911. In Colorado, most search and rescue groups are under the authority of the county sheriff's office.

Where did the incident take place?

Kenosha Pass, Park County, South of Denver, Colorado, between Bailey and Fairplay off Route 285.

Terrain Features

The terrain was hilly and went through marshy fields where cattle were grazing. The rest of the area was dry, pine forest.

Weather

At the beginning of this search, it was warm (approximately 60°F), but the temperature dropped rapidly. In October, once the sun goes down, the temperature often drops to below freezing. The wind was approximately 5 mph, ideal for working a trail. It was also dry, with no precipitation.

Special Dangers

There were a few bulls in the herd of cattle. My dog, Hasty, did not lose sight of his mission despite all the smells and sights. We were fairly close to the highway in one portion of my search. Mission command had the added concern that Michael could be picked up by a passing motorist.

Search Personnel and Equipment

I do not recall having very good maps and we desperately needed more radios. We should've brought some from our own county. The trail was only about four hours old, so because Hasty was working a fresh trail, I got separated from the rest of my search team. I learned that keeping the team together is always important, even if it means making the dog wait and then restarting him.

For a scent article, I was given the little boy's soiled long underwear that he had slept in the previous night.

Search Strategy

I was able to keep the search from getting bigger by establishing the direction of travel. There was a high urgency. The boy was literally wearing only a diaper, which was probably wet by now. His mom was sure that he was exhausted by this time, which by now was nap time. As the sun dropped in the west below the mountaintops, the temperature was plummeting exponentially. When I arrived there was still a fresh track. We worked the PLS—the sand dunes where the children were playing. Hasty had to discriminate Michael's scent from all the scents of his siblings, the other searchers, and the police dog. We worked a fine-grid search, zigzagging back and forth through the area for about ten minutes before Hasty picked up the little boy's scent. After that, all we did was follow Hasty on the trail for at least two hours, traveling mostly north the entire time. The tactics that we used were confinement, segmentation, attraction, and detection.

Assign Resources

We used a variety of resources on this search. There was a police dog, my search dog, 30 ground searchers, four-wheel drive trucks, ATVs, horses, helicopters, and mantrackers.

Results of the Mission

After trailing the boy for about 4.5 miles, an ATV came up alongside us. I told them to continue heading north ahead of me and they would probably find him soon. I felt that we were close because Hasty kept going faster while trailing him. They immediately came across the boy (within five minutes and less than a quarter mile). Hasty was correct. And the mission was called off after the successful find.

THE SEARCHER

DOG HANDLER TEAM

Who are You?

I am Patti Burnett and I was the second dog handler to arrive on this mission. The first dog team was a white German Shepherd canine handled by a sheriff's officer, who was not familiar with friendly searches. My dog, Hasty, mostly works airscent but also works some trailing. The first dog had not established a trail.

Kevin Kelble unloading Hasty from a Flight for Life helicopter at Copper Mountain.

The Callout

I think I was home at the time of the callout. We were first paged at 1400 and put on standby. They called us back at 1515 and asked us to respond. From the callout, it took approximately 45 minutes to reach mission base. We probably should have been dispatched earlier considering how much urgency that this mission had.

The Search Sector

The IC did not have much experience with SAR dogs and consequently asked me where I thought we should deploy the dog. Since the trail was still less than four hours old, I asked to work the PLS to establish a trail and direction of travel. All the boy's siblings confirmed the PLS.

How large was your sector? How long did it take to complete it?

The trail we worked was about 4.5 miles long and it took us about two hours to work it, from 1600–1800.

Problems Encountered

If there were any apprehensions, they would have been with the other dog and the bulls. I was uncomfortable about being separated from the rest of my search team. I learned from my mistake. In the ten years I have worked SAR dogs since then, I have not allowed myself to be separated from the rest of my search team.

Were you prepared for the conditions you encountered?

I was a new SAR dog handler at the time. A novice handler is never completely prepared for everything that can happen on a search. Preparedness comes with experience.

The Dog

Hasty and I worked well together. One thing that I have enjoyed about Hasty has been his all-business manner of searching. Anyone who knows golden retrievers knows that they love to play. Witnessing the transformation in Hasty when I started him was remarkable. Although he was not quite two years old at the time of this search, very little distracted him when he was searching.

Probability of Detection

Our POD was about 80% for the trail. This is higher than it would've been if we were airscenting.

How Successful were You?

We successfully brought the mission to completion. We did not find any clues until we found the little boy.

What are Your Feelings About the Mission?

Overall I was pleased with the outcome of the mission. The boy was cold, tired, and hungry, but otherwise doing very well. When we found him, he was not even crying. I wish that my team had stuck together better. However, being a less experienced dog handler, I placed a higher priority on working and watching my dog than keeping the team together. Separating from my team handicapped me, since they had the only radio we were assigned. Park County only had a skeletal SAR team at this time and I was glad that we could help them with some resources.

Search Tips

Always keep a search team together. Take the time to ensure that no one gets separated from the rest of the team.

When traveling to a search in another area, get appropriate maps ahead of time because other SAR teams may be under funded and unequipped. Good maps are a good investment.

The dog handler should always be aware of their dog's position in relation to themselves. As we were working the PLS, the police dog's only interest was aggression toward my dog. When a dog is not working, handlers must put it in a place where it is not a nuisance to SAR operations.

Always have enough radios, even if it means buying your own Mountain Rescue Association radio or programmable radio.

Trust a dog handler when he or she gives the direction of travel. It can save a lot of time.

Expect a child to travel farther than you would think. Michael was more than 4.5 miles from the PLS.

Avalanche

Mission Type

This avalanche was one of many that occurred in the Colorado Rockies during the winter of 1991–1992.

The Victim

Takashi Fujii was an approximately 27-year-old male from Osaka, Japan. He was a high school ski coach and gymnastics instructor and was in excellent health. Fujii was also a technical executive with the Bolle sunglasses/goggles company, and a very strong skier. At the time of this incident, he was staying with friends in Dillon, Colorado. Fujii was an excellent, highly experienced skier. He had the normal gear for back-country skiing. His rescue beacon was rendered inoperable when it was ripped from his body[1]. Fujii was not found during the beacon or the Recco[2] search. During the hasty search, there is always a beacon search, a scuff search for clues on the surface, a coarse probing of the most likely points of deposition, and a dog search if a dog is available. He disappeared on March 29, 1992.

Any Other Special Information

We were given Fujii's sweatpants for a scent article, but we did not use them. Typically, avalanche dog handlers do not use scent articles. For one thing, scent articles are not normally available quickly enough for avalanche searching, and time is always a crucial factor. Also, the avalanche dog is trained to alert only on the scent that is coming from underneath the snow and disregard scents on the surface.

Point Last Seen

Why did the incident take place?

At 1530 Sunday, March 29, Fujii was skiing an extremely rugged back-country area with a group of about ten snowcat skiers. Snowcat skiers are people who pay for a guide to take them up the mountain and ski down in the area that the guide directs them. They are transported up the mountain in a cab on the back of a snowcat, which usually hold about 10–12 people. Snowcats carry the skiers to the top of a steep chute and pick them up again at the bottom once they have skied. These are people who are bored with ski-area skiing and want an added challenge on ungroomed, steeper terrain. They ski terrain much the same as that skied by people who are doing helicopter skiing.

The snowcat and helicopter guide services are flourishing in Colorado because a certain element of the skiing public thrives on this form of "extreme skiing." Customers usually purchase a trip that either goes out for a day or half a day. All of the patrons are briefed on safe back-country skiing procedures since the areas they are skiing are not at populated ski areas. The terrain is usually steep, not compacted by skiers, and full of unmarked obstacles. The snowcat operators purchase permits that allow them to use the Forest Service land for such enterprises.

They had already been skiing the Montezuma area for about six hours. They were careful to make their turns one at a time, as instructed by their guide. This diminishes the odds that multiple skiers would get caught should a slide occur. Fujii did not follow the guide's

---

[1] A rescue beacon is an electronic device that allows rescuers to home in on buried avalanche victims. Every back-country skier and snow safety worker should wear a beacon inside their jacket anytime they are in avalanche terrain. All people initially have their beacons in the transmit mode. If someone should get buried, everyone else goes to the receive mode, and tries to pick up the transmitting signal that is being emitted from the beacon of the person buried. You can usually pick up the signal within 100 feet. The best way to search is to grid and triangulate.

[2] Reccos are little Band-Aid type of diodes that people put in their ski parkas or on their ski boots. They are not that popular in the U.S. I believe they were developed in Canada. To find someone buried with a Recco you need a Recco receiver, which is a larger (about the size of a medium size backpack), more expensive piece of equipment. The Recco receiver sends out a signal to the diode and then picks up the signal of the diode and returns it to the receiving instrument.

instructions and skied beyond the "safe" zone. Safety is all relative in the back country. There are no guarantees. However, tour guides study the areas where they take guests. They know which areas are more prone to sliding depending on the time of the year, recent wind directions, recent snow depths, etc. When he triggered the slide, he was the only one caught. The other members of his skiing party watched as Fujii was carried through the debris and had a vague idea of his location at the time he disappeared in the snow out of sight.

Where did the incident take place?

The slide occurred in the Equity Chute, which is near Saints John, an old mining town southeast of Keystone and south of the town of Montezuma.

Terrain Features

The area we searched was all steep avalanche debris. In those places where the debris was deep, it was well consolidated. As we got closer to the flanks and the tail of the debris we post-holed, because of the effects the warm temperature had on the snow. In the early mornings in the spring, the snow is well consolidated because it is still frozen granular. However, as the day wears on, warm temperatures cause water to percolate through the snow pack, and the frozen granular become unconsolidated corn snow, like slush. Post-holing is when you walk through snow and it does not support your weight, and you end up sinking through up to your hips and waist. The travel was difficult on this search. The elevation was above 11,000'.

Weather

Spring days in the Colorado Rockies are warm and sunny, and this day was no exception. The winds were steady and light, 0–5 mph, which were ideal for an avalanche search. The wind direction was downslope Sunday night and upslope Monday morning. During this weekend, more than 100 avalanches were reported in Colorado, many triggered by skiers. About 26 inches of heavy, wet snow fell since Saturday—the day before the search—on top of older snow layers covered with an ice lens, creating dangerous avalanche conditions. The ice lens is created after a particularly warm day when the surface of the snow is saturated with water. Over night the lower temperatures cause the surface to freeze. The Colorado Avalanche Information Center had rated the hazard for the Montezuma area as high. On March 29 there was also a rockslide in Boulder Canyon indicating the high level of precipitation and runoff.

Special Dangers

The largest danger for the rescuers occurred Sunday night when we searched in an area that continued to have an avalanche hazard. With the approach of darkness, the danger increased. In the dark there is no way to find out whether a pillow of snow is being deposited in the starting zone of a slope over the search area. Also, the avalanche guard is ineffective because he has no way of telling if an avalanche is descending upon the searchers. The avalanche guard is a rescuer who stands in a strategic location from where he can see if there are any new avalanches that might descend upon the rescuers so that he can alert them to the danger. He is in a location where he will not be hit by the avalanche himself. Keep in mind, that it is rare that rescuers will go in if there is any remaining danger; however, you cannot always be 100% sure.

Search Personnel and Equipment

The only resource that I wished we'd had was the ability to cut through red tape Sunday afternoon to get the necessary explosives to mitigate the hazard. By not bombing the remaining hazard that was hanging over the areas we searched, we were in a great deal of danger ourselves. I doubt I would take the risk again if I were put in a similar situation. Putting the rescuers in danger doesn't make any sense.

The Summit County Rescue Group coordinated the mission, under the auspices of the sheriff's office. Alpine and Grand County SAR teams assisted along with ski patrollers from Arapahoe Basin, Keystone,

Andrea Reller with Skadee and Pager during Rapid Deployment Training.

and Copper Mountain. Approximately 40 rescuers were involved. We had five different search dog teams that worked Sunday night. The three teams from Copper Mountain were John Reller and "Skadee," Todd Goertzen and "Cache," and myself and "Hasty." The team from Keystone was Tom Resignolo and "Donner." and from Arapahoe Basin the team was Peter Heckman and "Alex." We were shuttled to the slide area via snowmobiles and snowcats.

Search Strategy

The size of the search is well defined for most avalanches. The victim's not going anywhere. Though we arrived at the site only an hour after the slide occurred, we had to wait until 1900 to enter the debris. The reason for the delay was that mission coordinators were attempting to have control work[3] performed. This could have been a fatal error. It had been 3.5 hours from the time of the incident before we began searching, and yet we still held out a glimmer of hope that he would be found alive.

Since there was still a possibility of hangfire[4], a minimum number of searchers ven-

---

[3] Control work is when snow safety technicians (usually ski patrollers) go into an area to mitigate the danger, using ski cutting techniques, bombing, removing cornices, etc. Unfortunately, the control work could not be performed that first night because of politics; i.e., forest service land, permits, explosives, etc.

[4] Hangfire is any remaining danger after an avalanche occurs. Often a number of avalanche slopes funnel into one drainage or gully. If only one slide has occurred, it may be that others will go out as a result of losing their support from below.

tured out on the slide. An avalanche guard was stationed higher up the slide path to alert us if another slide were triggered. Rescuers included a few beacon searchers, coarse probers[5], all the dog units, and a navigator/prober for each. All five teams worked at the same time. As I worked, I received an alert from Hasty fairly close to where we entered the debris area. I had my navigator probe the area and he was not able to get a strike. A "strike" is that awful feeling a prober experiences when he hits a buried body. (Note: The debris was 15–20 feet deep in places, this means that there were times when the 12–15 foot probe poles could not hit ground.) About an hour later, Skadee got a stronger, more specific alert in the same place. Unfortunately, again we got no strikes. By 2030, it was very dark, and the site commander called it a night.

Monday morning at 0700, the fireworks began. A helicopter transported snow safety technicians from Colorado Heli-Ski to reduce the remaining avalanche hazard by throwing hand charges from the helicopter. These are usually two-pound primers with an igniter fuse. The shot placements effectively started a slide that covered a large portion of the area we had been walking on the previous evening. This was extremely sobering for me. We had three search dogs Monday: Hasty, Donner, and Alex. We took a different strategy this time and decided to work each dog separately for 15 minutes. With the different wind directions (downslope Sunday night and upslope Monday morning) Hasty alerted about 40 feet above his and Skadee's alerts from the previous night. He also did an article alert where Fujii's ski pole was buried. An article alert is much more subtle—and in some ways, more incredible—than a live or dead body alert, since a metal ski pole buried under the snow gives off very little human scent. At 1030 the Site Commander sent a probe line directly through Hasty's and Skadee's alerts and got a strike exactly between the two. This was a perfect example of where wind changes worked in our favor. Fujii was buried under ten feet of snow, another factor that affected the distance of the alerts from the body. In most avalanches, the mostly likely places of body deposition are at the toe of the slide, below ledges (terrain variations), above trees and other obstacles, and on the outside of turns.

Suspension

It is difficult to say whether the mission should have been called off on the first night any sooner or later than it was. The consensus was that the possibility of a live recovery was worth the risk. However, the one constant in an avalanche rescue is that the safety of the rescuers should always be paramount (Dan Burnett).

Results of the Mission

Success. We found him, finally, on the second morning.

What are Your Feelings About the Mission?

The mission was a tremendous success in interagency cooperation and coordination. The tragedy of a vibrant life lost and the use of resources in an avoidable accident are memories that many rescuers will carry for a long time (Dan Burnett).

---

[5] Coarse probers probe with a pole in those areas that are the most likely places of deposition in an avalanche.

Additional Comments

Fujii was the fourth person to die in Colorado avalanches in a little more than a month.

Search Tips (from Dan Burnett)

There are many potential dangers to avalanche rescuers and the possibility of accidents should not be underestimated. Among them are:

1. Accidents (helicopter or car) can occur while en route to the avalanche. Usually the weather during and after avalanches is bad, snowy, windy, etc., and helicopters are a dangerous way to travel. I have lost several good friends in helicopter accidents. My second dog, Sandy, was born the day my friend, Sandy (a flight-for-life nurse) was killed in a helicopter performing a SAR mission.

2. Entering unstable terrain to effect a search.

3. Exposure. Usually to unequipped or poorly motivated rescuers.

If the mission leaders feel that the remaining avalanche hazard is too great, then it probably is and the risk should not be taken.

Putting forth the effort to establish relationships between agencies before missions always pays off.

Have a checkpoint for people going into the field to ensure proper equipment and attitude for the mission. At the first sign of an

Sandy at the top of Copper Mountain.

ego problem, the IC should pull potentially dangerous rescuers. On this mission, on Sunday night, I chose to work with Kevin, a navigator whom I had worked with often and who was a paramedic. However, another person was creating problems because he wanted to go into the field. He felt he was more qualified since he had been on more avalanche missions. I knew, though, that he had a tendency to create division rather than unity in team situations. Kevin was someone who'd helped me train Hasty, so he was familiar with Hasty's alerts and also had a higher level of paramedic training than the other person. I told the other person that we had already predetermined that Kevin would be my navigator and this was not the time to be making changes. There is always stress at staging areas anyway. If there are rescuers who have a hidden agenda and do not have the welfare of the victims as their top priority, then anxiety is going to be increased. Fortunately, this is more the exception than the rule. Most rescuers (who are all volunteers) have a focused perspective that nothing else will be allowed to get in the way of their objective of finding and helping the victims.

Waiting to start the search until all of the necessary precautions are taken is the smart thing to do. This shows a lot of expertise and maturity, though it is not always a popular move.

Biography

Dan Burnett has been active with the Summit County Rescue Group since 1980. He has been a mission coordinator since 1985 and a past group leader. Dan has been involved in approximately 30 avalanche missions and another 200 general SAR missions. Dan is a real estate broker with Columbine Management and Real Estate in Dillon, Colorado. He is married to Patti and they have two children, Bethany, who is eight years old, and Rachel, who is seven years old.

THE SEARCHER
DOG HANDLER TEAM

Who are You?

I am Patti Burnett and I was one of the avalanche dog handlers on this mission.

The Callout

One member of Fujii's skiing party must have skied out and called 911, while the remaining skiers probed the area. There may have also been someone in the town of Montezuma who witnessed the slide and reported it. I was patrolling at Copper Mountain when the call came in at 1600. I carry a mission coordinator pager at work so that I hear the first call for avalanches. Sometimes when we get avalanche calls, it is not clear whether someone is truly buried. There was no question this time. The reporting party had witnessed the slide, which buried his friend. After receiving permission to respond, I got Hasty down the mountain using a snowmobile and then drove the 25 minutes to Montezuma. I arrived at the trailhead at 1630.

The Search Sector

Who decided your sector?

The dog handlers agreed that we would split the area and search different areas. At various times we changed sectors so that dogs could confirm the alerts of other dogs.

How large was your sector? How long did it take to complete it?

The size of the entire avalanche was approximately 40 yards by 400 yards—a steep, narrow chute.

How did you decide where to start your sector?

The first night we divided the area and individual dog units took different sectors.

Problems Encountered

The first night it got very dark. I do not recommend working an avalanche in the dark, if just for the hazard reason. Even with headlamps, searching avalanches at night is a harrowing experience.

Were you prepared to face the conditions you encountered?

I did not expect to enter the debris with an avalanche hazard remaining. This had never happened to me before and has not happened since.

The Dog

The first night we searched for 90 minutes before the mission was called off until morning. The following morning it took us about 90 minutes to get another alert on Fujii and get a strike with a probe pole.

Probability of Detection

With so many dogs and searchers on the slide, the POD was high, about 75–80%.

How Successful were You?

Hasty had considerable experience doing avalanche searches, and both he and Skadee alerted on Fujii, and Hasty alerted on one of his ski poles.

What are Your Feelings About the Mission?

I was happy to see so many dogs from different ski areas work so well together. Though it was a sad outcome, it is always rewarding to bring an avalanche search to conclusion.

Search Tips

In an avalanche search, the dog alerts are strongly affected by the wind direction and speed. In this search, Sunday night's downslope winds caused the alerts to be 20 feet below the body. Monday morning's upslope winds caused the alert to be 20 feet above the body.

With a deep burial, expect the dog alerts to be farther away from the body than for shallow burials.

I use different commands for live and dead searches. This is a strategy I learned from Dick Epley. I command my dog to "Search" when he is looking for a live person. I command him to "Slow Search" when he is looking for an article or a dead body. I begin every avalanche mission with the "Search" command. If this produces no results, I switch over to the "Slow Search" command. I have found that this technique gives the dog the motivation to alert enthusiastically, even on dead bodies. Before I began to employ this strategy, Hasty's alerts on dead bodies were more difficult to discern.

Make a point of training with as many distractions as possible. Have more than one dog work at a time with multiple burials; bury people very close to each other or almost on top of each other; have people sitting over the buried subject; have probers yelling for the dog to "check here, check here"; and have people digging in areas other than where the subjects are located.

Never ever forget to take all the necessary safety precautions: radios, the triangulation of burial sites, rescue beacons, safe caves[6] buried in advance, etc.

I recommend that avalanche dogs be neutered or spayed. With the close working con-

---

[6] Safe caves are snow caves that are buried under the snow. They are made by digging a hole straight down in the snow about six feet deep. Then a cave is built into the side of the hole. The cave has a small entryway, about four feet wide and about two feet high. The cave itself has a floor that's about two to four inches above the level of the entrance hole bottom. It is roughly six feet long, three feet wide, and about two and a half feet high with a domed roof to increase the stability. It is large enough for a person to roll over in and has approximately three hours worth of air (I would guess). If an avalanche starts, you can run to the nearest safe cave.

ditions required in an avalanche search, there is no room for a territorial dog. I had Sandy neutered at six months and he has a wonderful temperament for a working dog. He will work with any dog and never have a problem.

Biography

Patti Burnett has been a member of the Summit County Rescue Group since 1980. She has been a past mission coordinator. Since 1986 she has worked two SAR dogs (both golden retrievers) with Summit County Rescue Group—her local SAR group—SARDOC (Search and Rescue Dogs of Colorado), and the Copper Mountain Ski Patrol. She was instrumental in writing the original standards for SARDOC and has been a past director-at-large, secretary, and area director for SARDOC. She regularly holds Avalanche Dog Schools at Copper Mountain. She is supervisor of the ski patrol at Copper. Her retired dog, Hasty, was operational in avalanche, wilderness, and water from 1987–1998. Her four-year-old dog, Sandy, is operational in wilderness. Her husband, Dan, is a mission coordinator with SCRG. They have two children: Bethany is eight and Rachel is seven years old.

Patti Burnett and Sandy

Suicide: Wilderness Scent Specific

Dave Cook
Durham Search and Rescue
Mission Location: Durham, North Carolina
Mission Date: June 18, 1987

Mission Type

This is a short search generally illustrating efficient search techniques.

The Victim

"Ron" was a 49-year-old male. He was an Insulin-dependent diabetic; his last dose of insulin was at 0200 on June 18, which was 10.5 hours before he was reported missing. Ron was depressed about his deteriorating health, he'd lost a toe from diabetes, and his parents reported that he would not survive long without two insulin doses daily. Also, the subject was considered suicidal. Ron lived with his parents. He frequently walked in the area around his home with a tendency to stay on travel routes. He also often walked around the golf course near his home. The victim was wearing blue slacks, a blue T-shirt, a white sweatshirt, and blue slip-on shoes with Velcro closures. He disappeared on June 18, 1997.

Point Last Seen

The night of June 17, 1997, the victim had his second seizure in a week due to low blood sugar levels. He was treated at Baptist Hospital in Winston-Salem and released at 0300 on June 18. He told his parents and his doctor that he was not going to take his insulin any more. That morning he wrote and mailed notes to his doctors canceling all of his appointments. About 0900 he told his mother again that he had decided that he was not going to take his insulin. At about 1000, his mother went to check on him and could not find him. The victim had locked a door behind him and left his house without his insulin, glucometer, money, keys, or fanny pack.

The victim was last seen at his home. The area around his home is primarily residential with single-family homes, a golf course winding through a large subdivision, and interspersed with blocks of undeveloped woodlands. This is typical North Carolina Piedmont, hilly with several small steams and ponds. Temperatures were warm and conditions dry.

Any Other Special Information

Rural Hall is a small town adjacent to Winston-Salem in the mostly urban Forsyth County. The Forsyth County Sheriff's Department (FCSD) admits that they have not had training or experience in SAR. However, they interacted very well with the out-of-county resources that were called in.

Search Personnel and Equipment

We would have liked to have additional trained search crews to clear the lower priority segments, an effective uniform radio system, and more fresh command personnel.

However, we did receive a great deal of resources, which included the following:

- FCSD, consisting of 65 searchers that included command, confinement, and investigation units, along with radios
- FCSD Bloodhound
- Special Operations Response Team (SORT), a Winston-Salem-based emergency medical response team of eight persons with radios
- Stokes County Mountain Rescue, which included command, hasty and search crews, radios, one bloodhound, and 23 persons
- North Carolina National Guard Helicopter
- American Red Cross that provided food and supplies
- Durham Search and Rescue; command, search crews, two dogs, radios, five persons
- Guilford Search and Rescue; command and search crew, two persons
- NC Search and Rescue Dog Association; two dog teams, radios

Search Strategy

The victim was first noticed to be missing by his parents. They drove around their neighborhood looking for him for two hours before reporting the disappearance to the FCSD at 1243. FCSD took this report seriously. Extra shifts were called into check hospitals, nearby communities, the home, the nearby golf course, and to patrol area roads. At 1632, having found nothing, FCSD turned to the only local resource with SAR experience, the Special Operations Response Team. SORT had supported SAR events with medical teams and had some introductory SAR training. A command post was set up at the Rural Hall Fire Department, about three miles from the scene. SORT was prepared with USGS topographical maps of the area and put searchers in the field. Knowing their limitations, SORT convinced FCSD to call the nearest trained SAR resource that they were familiar with. They called Stokes County Mountain Rescue.

Stokes County Mountain Rescue (SCMR), which is primarily a technical rescue team, had gone through "Fundamentals of Search and Rescue" training in February and two members had taken "Managing the Lost Person Incident" in April. Although they had experience on a few short searches, this was their first major search. SCMR arrived about 1800, and their chief was assigned as the Incident Commander. Their assistant chief was named Operations Chief. A SORT officer provided documentation and logistics. The IC interviewed the parents and filled out a Lost Person Questionnaire, which yielded a lot of valuable information. SCMR sent out multiple hasty teams and a bloodhound team until about 0300 on June 19.

With limited experience SCMR did a number of things right. They searched travel routes both natural and manmade around the PLS. They also searched in and around the home. Initial missions were well mapped and documented, and they kept good records of events. FCSD maintained road patrol confinement. Between 0015 and 0210, a helicopter with FLIR (Forward Looking Infrared) was deployed over the search area but located nothing. Hasty teams and the Bloodhounds had the same results. The IC maintained the investigation continuously throughout the incident by canvassing the neighborhood and

Search Area with
Sectors

interviewing the local residents.

Even though they did a number of things right, SCMR made a couple of mistakes that originated out of the fire-service experience of many of the members. The mistakes were as follows: While the IC was working with other command staff at the command post, the Ops Chief was set up in a separate staging vehicle in the search area. The end result of having the Ops Chief separated from the IC was essentially that two command posts were in operation. As a result of this, the OPS Chief sent returning teams out on subsequent missions. While these missions were valid assignments, they were not documented or communicated adequately with the IC command post. Fortunately this did not negatively impact the search outcome.

Possibly the most important accomplishment of the IC was convincing the sheriff—who was unfamiliar with SAR and worried about using resources he knew nothing about—to call in outside SAR agencies.

Assign Resources

The search urgency was high because of the subject's medical condition and suicidal statements. Investigation determined that his intent was to hide somewhere and allow himself to die.

Road patrol confinement was maintained throughout the search. Additionally they alerted the surrounding neighborhoods to watch for the subject. Unless the victim had hitched a ride, we were reasonably confident that he had not left the area. Accepting a ride was considered a serious possibility; the parents confirmed this likelihood. However, the consequences of suspending the search based on that probability were too serious to ignore. The IC suspended investigation prior to my arrival but resumed it aggressively at daylight.

When Durham arrived, they brought the most experienced and trained dogs so far on the scene. Those were sent to re-search the PLS and the immediate surrounding area. Experience has shown us that this is sound strategy when untrained and inexperienced resources have done previous searches. The rest of the Durham searchers were sent to hasty search a drainage and creek going northwest from the PLS that had not been searched by SCMR earlier.

With the hasty searches in the field, we turned our attention to setting up the search management and planning the third operational period strategy. We defined the search area using a combination of statistical information on despondent people, our previous experience with despondent people in poor health, and the profile of the subject's walking habits. This resulted in a search area roughly four miles north to south and 2.5 miles east to west, about ten square miles. A factor in determining the areas to be searched was identifying undeveloped areas in the ten square miles where the victim was known to walk and could hide. This would prove to be a proper assessment. The search area was split into eleven segments using roads, creeks, drainage, and power lines as boundaries. Using the CASIE III computer program, a consensus of the probability level (POA) of the segments was done by the Ops Chief, Durham SAR Chief, and myself. We determined that segment six, which was north of the point last seen (PLS) and in the center of the search area, had the highest POA. A factor in evaluating POA was that segment eight, which contained the PLS, had been the most intensely searched thus reducing the likelihood that the subject was in sector eight. Segment six, on the other hand, had significant undeveloped areas, ponds, and portions of a golf course where the victim normally walked.

The strategy of the third operational period strategy was directed by our objectives, which were to, one, locate the victim by 1800 hours due to decreasing survivability, two, search the segment areas that had a high probability based on the subject profile, and three, continue confinement and investigation.

Eight missions for dog teams and search crews were drawn up and prioritized. A helicopter mission was prepared. As the third Ops strategy was started, missions were issued in priority order with consideration for crew capability. Because the search resources arrived throughout the morning of June 19, coupled with new information due to the ongoing investigation and debriefings, we were able to re-evaluate our priorities. This flexibility proved valuable. The missions were based on two common themes that are used in SAR that is associated with despondent people. The victims are usually found hidden, either a short distance off of a travel route, or they are at a specific destination that has significance or allure for them. Attraction devices were never considered since we knew that the victim's intentions were to hide.

Suspension

A North Carolina Search and Rescue Dog Association (NCSARDA) dog team was assigned to work the drainage ditches in segment five. A Durham/SCMR combination search crew was sent to search a ridge and farm road in segment five. A Durham/Guilford search crew was sent to search eastern segment six. A SCMR search crew was sent to search around several ponds and lakes around the boundaries of eastern segment five and northwestern segment six. A NCSARDA dog team was sent to search segment nine paying particular attention to three lakes in that segment. The original Durham dog team deployed during the second Ops strategy continued to search areas north of the PLS. These areas had higher POAs because they contained wooded areas where the victim could hide, attractions such as ponds, creeks, hills, roads, and the golf course where the victim was known to walk. Some of the other segments were densely populated. However, the sheriff's department thoroughly covered this area and asked the residents to watch for the victim. Because of this we believed that it was likely that if the victim were in that area the residents would have let us know.

Early in the third operations stage, we noticed that a large hill in segment six had not been searched. Teams had worked or were working all around its base and east of it. A Durham dog had shown mild interest at the base of the hill during the night, about 500 meters southwest of the summit. The USGS map showed that this hilltop was wooded and adjacent to the golf course. However, intelligence from debriefing crews and scene surveys by management revealed that since the last revision of the map, much of the area depicted as wooded in the search area had houses built on them. To get accurate information about the current condition of the hilltop, the sheriff's department secured large aerial photographs of the search area. These photographs showed that the hill was still wooded. It was located about 1,350 meters due north of the PLS. Because of its high probability location and suitability as a destination for a person who is despondent, that hill became a priority.

At this point there were six crews in the field and two available at the command post. At 0855, SCMR crew eight was sent to area search the hill. While they were en route to their drop-off point, the IC, with assistance from the sheriff's department, was continuing the investigation. At 0850 the IC located a resident of Eagle Crest Drive who had seen the victim at 1100 the previous day, one half-hour after he was noticed missing. Eagle Crest is about 800 meters due north of the PLS. It is a short residential street dead-ending in woods on the side of the hill where we had sent the SCMR crew. According to the resident, he had seen the victim walking north on Eagle Crest toward the hill. The resident gave an accurate description of the subject. Now that we had a new PLS we radioed SCMR Crew eight to go to Eagle Crest.

At 0910 SCMR Crew eight reported that they found a single set of footprints going north through the brush at the dead end of Eagle Crest. The tracks matched the size and shape that the victim would have. The IC, who was on the scene, ordered the crew to stand by. He then requested that a dog team take over. The original Durham Dog Team was still working in the vicinity and was directed to Eagle Crest and arrived at 0930. The dog picked up a scent and headed north toward the hill's summit. At 0950 he located a pile of human fecal material, later confirmed to be the subject's. Continuing north at 1000 he located the subject's socks and shoes. Crossing the summit and continuing north, the dog team found the victim at 1035 in the woods not far from the golf course, about 1,450 meters north of the PLS.

Results of Mission

Remarkably, the victim was in good condition even after a day and a half without insulin, possibly due to not eating during that time. According to the searchers on the scene, he was angry that he'd been found. An EMS team was deployed to the scene and after they checked him out, he was transported to Baptist Hospital at 1125. All search teams in the field were notified of the find and were out of the field by 1145. There was some confusion regarding the picking up of crews. This part of the demobilization should have been planned better.

The Forsyth County sheriff was so impressed with his first SAR event that he took all of the outside personnel that was available to lunch.

What are Your Feelings About the Mission?

This search went like it should. What went very well was the cooperation between the responding agencies, which were both local and outside aid. Resources were deployed correctly and deficiencies quickly rectified. It was a testament of the effectiveness of the confederation of North Carolina's specialized SAR resources that have developed in recent years.

When the clues started rolling in, I recall telling the lead sheriff's department representative in the command post something that I have often heard and believe: Once we have a direction of travel, we have the victim. They can run, but they can't hide. The investigation gave us the clues and made the clues meaningful. The clues led us to the victim.

Search Tips

Assume from the start that every search will be long and plan on multiple operational periods. It is better to demobilize a search than be unprepared when the victim is not found quickly and need to call in additional sources.

When debriefing teams, have them indicate on a map exactly which areas they searched. This improves documentation of the search coverage beyond the debriefing report, which is often hastily done and not always clear.

When teams are debriefed, make sure any references to locations are backed up with grid coordinates, especially landmarks that are not shown on the map.

Responding quickly saves lives and relieves suffering. Be ready to go, which means 24 hour packs are ready, incident command boxes are packed, and uniforms are washed as soon as a mission is over.

Do not assume that someone is dead just because their intent was to commit suicide. Between October 1995 and June 1997, Durham SAR has been involved in finding four victims who hid and attempted suicide. All four victims were unsuccessful in committing suicide. All four were in bad condition but survived, even though they were found between 12 and 24 hours after their suicide attempt.

Biography

Dave Cook has been involved in search and rescue for 12 years as a Carolina State Park Ranger. Currently he is the Superintendent of the Eno River State Park. Since 1993 Dave has volunteered with Durham Search and Rescue as a field searcher, in search management, and serving as a training officer. He is a NASAR FUNSAR Instructor and SAR Tech II & III Evaluator. He is on the North Carolina Search and Rescue Advisory Council Board of Directors.

THE SEARCHER
DOG HANDLER TEAM

David Hancock
Durham Search and Rescue/North Carolina SAR Dog Association, Inc.

Who are You?

David Hancock, Chief of Durham SAR, President of the Central Unit of the North Carolina SAR Dog Association, Inc. (NCSARDA).

The Callout

I was at home when I received the call from Dave Cook. He had taught a fundamentals of SAR course to the Stokes County Mountain Rescue Team for NASAR and they had his home phone number. My office, the Durham/Durham County Emergency Management Agency, is responsible for the callout of Durham SAR and the Central Unit of NCSAR Dog Association. Our callout is done via an alphanumeric pager system. I also contacted the Western Unit of NCSARDA and they began a callout of their personnel. I was contacted at 2358 on June 18. We arrived on scene at 0230 on the 19.

The Search Sector
Who decided your sector?

A conversation took place between Dave Cook, who was the Plans Section Chief, and myself to decide where to begin the search with the canine. On previous searches, we had to work large areas because we were told that the immediate area around the PLS had been searched, only to later find the missing subject nearby. Therefore we elected to begin close to the residence of the subject and let the dog take it from there.

Prior to beginning our search, we received a briefing sheet with details about the subject that had been gleaned from the investigation. We also talked to the family and secured a valid scent article, a hat belonging to the subject. Using sterile techniques (i.e., sterile latex gloves) we cut a baseball cap belonging to the subject into four pieces and secured these in unused Zip-Lock plastic bags labeled with the subject's name, date acquired, and my initials.

How large was your sector? How long did it take to complete?

Although this may sound strange, however, it is my belief that the dog determines the sector. We let the dog decide the direction that he wants to go. The only thing that we do as far as a sector goes, for the canine, is that we will begin in a specific sector and that's all we guarantee. If the dog shows interest and wants to work in an adjacent sector, we let the dog go there. If the dog does not show a specific direction and interest, we will then work an assigned sector. This would be in sector eight as identified on the enclosed map.

How did you decide where to start your sector?

We scented the search dog, Gus, on the scent article in the backyard of the subject's home. He worked behind the house, along a small brook (about two feet wide, one foot deep), and worked around the home. Gus did not show any particular interest in any one area initially so we began an area search of the golf course sector.

Problems Encountered

There were no major problems encountered on the initial search mission. Once that mission was completed, I sat in my vehicle to provide communications relay between two teams from our western unit. I was frustrated that I was doing communication relays instead of being given another assignment, but our job was beneficial because a clue was found that ended up leading us to the victim.

These types of problems (not being given a new assignment) can normally be expected in any large search with numerous resources involved. The Plans and Operations Sections become overwhelmed trying to keep up with the status of all the different units. The other problem encountered was that the golf course was open for business shortly after daylight. This meant that there were golfers everywhere, including the areas that needed to be searched. This is where our scent discrimination training paid dividends. The area where the subject was found was between two holes on the golf course. We entered our sector on the putting-green area, which was across from the tee-off area, and an active golf cart path ran between the two areas.

Were you prepared for the conditions you encountered?

The sector that I worked was very open, due to it being a golf course. Because of the vast terrain differences from the mountains to the coast of North Carolina, we are always prepared for whatever conditions we may encounter in the field. Some of the other dog teams were working cut-overs and briar patches. These make searching very slow with low PODs.

The Dog

I walked a zigzag pattern on the golf course, paying special attention to a creek that ran along one side of the course. Gus ranged well and worked effectively. I re-scented him several times during the search. I normally do this just to assure myself that he is working the correct scent. I do this especially when I see that his ranging has decreased. Near daylight Gus did show interest at the base of a small hill between two holes on the golf course. I searched the hill and found no clues there. As I was walking back to our vehicle,

I encountered Denver Holder, the president of our western unit. I asked him to come look at Gus' behavior at the base of the hill and we both agreed that he was "winding" the subject. We again searched the hill. (This area turned out to be about 500 meters from where Gus located the subject.)

After searching the hill with no success, I returned to the command post and gave my debriefing report to the command staff. As I stated above, I was not given another assignment immediately and noticed that two members of our western unit were having difficulty with radio communications to the CP, so I parked my truck in a cul-de-sac to act as a communications relay for them.

While I was sitting in my truck, I was called and asked to search an area with Gus where it was suspected that the subject had gone into the woods at the dead-end street. Three members from the Stokes County Mountain Rescue were standing at the end of the dead-end road near a footprint, believed to belong to the victim. I gave Gus the scent and he immediately ran off, out of sight into the woods. The SCMR team began to track the subject.

I knew by Gus' speed and intensity as he took off into the woods that he was on a strong scent. He wears a bell and I followed the sound of it into the woods for about 50 meters when I saw Gus standing and smelling something on the ground. Gus was sniffing a pile of fecal material that appeared to be human waste. I called the find into the command post and they asked me to flag the waste. Due to the urban area that we were working in, I was only carrying water with me, so I had to return to my vehicle for flagging tape. I then scented Gus again and he ran about fifteen meters to my right and stopped again with the same posture as before. On the ground were a pair of tennis shoes, with a Velcro closure, and a pair of socks. When I called this in, the IC asked that I bag the articles and flag the location. Again I had to return to my vehicle for the bag and tape.

About this time, the western unit canine team finished their search and called me on the radio with a request to be picked up. They were not sure what road they were on and tried to describe the residence that they were standing near. While I was talking on the radio, Gus was throwing his head up, airscenting with keen interest.

I could tell by Gus' body language that he had a strong scent. I became anxious and handed the radio to one of the SCMR team members and turned our unit radio off so that I could concentrate. From a point between the shoes and the fecal matter, I began to work a spiral pattern. On the second spiral, Gus ran away from me toward an area that was overgrown with knee-high ferns. Gus initially ran past the victim, and I saw the victim just as Gus was turning around. The victim was lying beneath a tree. I called the victim's name and he responded by telling me that he had been lying there hoping that he wouldn't be found. He offered to sign whatever was necessary to absolve me from responsibility so that he could lie there and die. I called for the deputies and secured the victim.

Probability of Detection

For the first sector that I worked, I calculated a POD of 20%. For the area where the victim was found, the POD would have been about 40%.

How Successful Were You?

I feel that we were successful not only because the victim was found, but because our training methods utilized scent discrimination. This allowed us to focus the dog on the victim and not find everyone on the golf course. The dog had a specific scent that he was to look for, and that was the only scent he focused on and found. If he had not been trained in this method, we would have had to find all the golfers in the area as well as the two deputies before we found the victim. It is very possible that if the dog had led us to the area where the golfers were located, we might not have stayed in the area where the subject was found.

What are Your Feelings About the Mission?

I was elated because this was Gus' first live find and I feel that the victim would have died if we didn't find him. All of our training paid off. I'd always have believed that I'd be so proud because we (Gus and I) made the find and saved a life. What happened was just the opposite. I was humbled because I realized that we were just a tool. If it hadn't been for the work of all of the other people on the search, we wouldn't have been successful. If it hadn't been for the deputy's ongoing investigation and canvassing the neighborhood, they wouldn't have found the neighbor who pointed us in the direction where the victim was found. I realized on that search that we, as a dog/handler team, don't "walk on water," everyone is important. A search is a team effort by everyone involved in the search.

Search Tips

Train realistically and often. We train every other Tuesday night and every Saturday.

Learn to read your dog. There is no such thing as the bomb-proof alert. It may be the small behavior change and the subtle things that the dog does that make you successful.

Train using scent discrimination and scent articles. If it had not been for this method of training, we would have "found" everyone on the golf course, not just the missing person, since there was no way that we would've been able to shut down the golf course. It's unrealistic to think that every time that you go on a search, the area that you are working can be cleared of all non-search personnel.

Understand that as a dog handler, you are part of a team. So many times we as dog handlers are looked at as the "experts," but we're only another tool to be used in the search effort. We need to quit acting like "prima donnas" and need to realize that our role is no more important than any other is. If all the things that are theorized about dogs and handlers were true, there would only have to be two or three dogs in each state because we would find everybody. It just doesn't work that way.

Train with other teams so that each one knows the capabilities and limitations of the other. When there is a search, you know what to expect from the other team.

Biography

David Hancock began his emergency service career in 1983 in Baton Rouge, Louisiana, with Central Volunteer Fire Department. He was a volunteer firefighter and became a nationally registered Emergency Medical Technician. He left his job as a machinist and went to work with Regional Ambulance Service. In 1985 he went to work for the East Baton Rouge Parish Sheriff's Department where he attained the rank of corporal as supervisor of the jail medical department. In 1988 he moved to Durham, North Carolina and is currently an Emergency Management Coordinator with Durham and Durham County Emergency Management Agency as well as the Chief of Durham SAR.

David is also the president of the Central Unit of the NCSAR Dog Association, Inc. His partner is Gus, a four-year-old Doberman Pinscher, certified by his unit in scent discriminating airscenting, and land and water cadaver searches. The two of them have worked on searches in North Carolina, Tennessee, and Virginia.

Dave Hancock and his partner. Gus.

Missing Hiker: Mountain Scent Specific

Julie L.S. Cotton and Dave Bigelow
   Larimer County Search and Rescue
   Mission Location: Rocky Mountain National Park
   Mission Date: August 10 and 11, 1995

Mission Type

This search is a long search utilizing extensive resources of various types. It illustrates that while the dog team may not be directly responsible for finding the subject, it can contribute information that leads to finding the subject by other resources.

The Victim

The subject of this search was a 16-year-old female in good health. "Sara" was described as athletic, adventurous, active, and levelheaded. She was not considered a risk taker and had no history of drug or alcohol abuse. Sara had a positive attitude toward her first overnight solo hike. She had learned about the hike at summer camp and planned to do it on her own while vacationing with her parents in the Rocky Mountains.

Sara was from Tennessee. She had attended the summer programs at Cheley Camp near Estes Park, Colorado for several years. Sara had extensive experience hiking in the Colorado Rockies because the program, designed for children ages nine through seventeen, included hiking in and around Rocky Mountain National Park. A particular hike in Rocky Mountain National Park, "The Mummy Kill," had been mentioned at camp as one of the "cool" hikes to do. The Mummy Kill entails hiking to the top of six mountain peaks in the Mummy Range. The hike begins at Chapin Pass (11,140' elevation) and continues to Mount Chapin (12,454'). From there it goes to Mount Chiquita (13,069'), Ypsilon Mountain (13,514'), Fairchild Mountain (13,502'), Hagues Peak (13,560') and finishes at Mummy Mountain (13,425'). The hike extends about 14 miles and is mostly above the timberline. In addition, over half the hike is off-trail. It is a hike than can be completed in a very long day. Most people begin the hike in the middle of the night[1].

At the time of this incident in August 1995, Sara had just finished another summer program at Cheley Camp. After joining her parents, she mapped a route to attempt "The Mummy Kill" on her own. Sara was well prepared for her first overnight solo hike. She had with her a wool sweater, long-sleeved shirt, rain gear, and she was wearing leather hiking boots. She was carrying a day pack that was well equipped. It included a compass, topographic map of the area, emergency blanket, wool hat, first-aid kit, whistle, matches, food, and water. Additionally, through her participation in the summer programs, Sara had

---

[1] Because the initial part of this hike is not bad, it can be done at night. It is across a worn trail until you get close to Mount Chapin. At Mount Chapin you must cross a ridge, which also can be done at night. It is just time consuming to move across the rocks. The closer you get to Ypsilon, the worse it gets, but by then it is daylight if you started your hike at 0300. Many hikers choose to start the hike at night so that they will not be on the ridges during the time of day when thunderstorms are likely.

learned what to do if she ever became lost.

Point Last Seen

Sara's parents dropped her off at the Chapin Pass trailhead at 0330 Wednesday, August 9, 1995. After ascending the six peaks, she was to complete the hike by descending the Lawn Lake trail to join her parents at their back-country campsite in the Roaring River drainage. Her parents expected her at the campsite around 1800 Wednesday evening, several hours before dark. When she was overdue, her parents hiked up the Lawn Lake trail expecting to meet her. Since it was possible the hike took longer than anticipated, Sara's parents waited, and slept, on the trail throughout Wednesday night. They hiked out to the Lawn Lake trail Thursday morning to report Sara missing.

The hike Sara set out to do was challenging but not impossible. From the beginning of the hike to the Lawn Lake trail, about a mile south of Mummy Mountain, the "trail" is above timberline across the tundra. The mountain slopes consist primarily of loose talus,[2] which either shifts slightly or slides down the mountainside with each step. Where there is not loose talus, the rocks are large and passage requires jumping from one boulder to another. Good balance is required to stay upright and not twist an ankle. In some places fairly gentle slopes form the mountain ridges. In others, the steep slopes come together sharply forming a narrow blade of a ridge. There is no protection from foul weather, or the intense sun, while hiking the ridge line from mountaintop to mountaintop. For the portion of the hike between Mount Chapin and Ypsilon Mountain, a distance of approximately 3.5 miles, the closest protection is 2,000 feet below the ridge. This is where stubby and wind-twisted pine trees mix with the rock and tundra. Beyond the first three mountains, protection from the elements is scarce for another five miles until reaching the Lawn Lake trail. The ridge line between the final three mountains is rugged and does not allow for a fast descent if needed[3].

Wednesday afternoon, a particularly strong thunderstorm had passed through the Mummy Range area where Sara had been hiking. Aside from that strong storm, the weather before and during the search was fairly typical for midsummer. Thursday, the day was clear and temperatures were in the upper 70s—a hot day in the mountains. Thursday evening there was a light wind primarily out of the northwest, but down-slope winds predominated at nightfall. Near the Saddle, the proximity of the numerous mountain peaks created a whirlpool effect so that the wind swirled and switched directions continuously. Late Thursday night another storm system moved into the area. While it brought some precipitation, the storm consisted primarily of abundant thunder and lightning. With the incoming storm, the stable down-slope winds became shifting and unpredictable. Friday morning, the westerly winds were forty-plus miles per hour, which made it difficult to move across the boulder-strewn mountain slope without being blown off balance. The skies were overcast and the temperature was in the low 40s.

---

[2] Talus is formed by the rock debris. The debris is not stable and will move underfoot. It will fall down the slope but usually not too far. Talus is formed by large boulders that break down to form smaller rocks. Talus will range in size from gravel to rocks the size of a car. Typically talus does not refer to the rocks that are the size of a car, so it would be gravel size to those just smaller than a car.

[3] When a person hikes in the mountains, it is necessary to descend quickly if a thunderstorm approaches. This is necessary to avoid lightning strikes. In this particular area, a fast descent was not possible. This meant that Sara could have been a lightning casualty due to the storm that came through the area while she was missing.

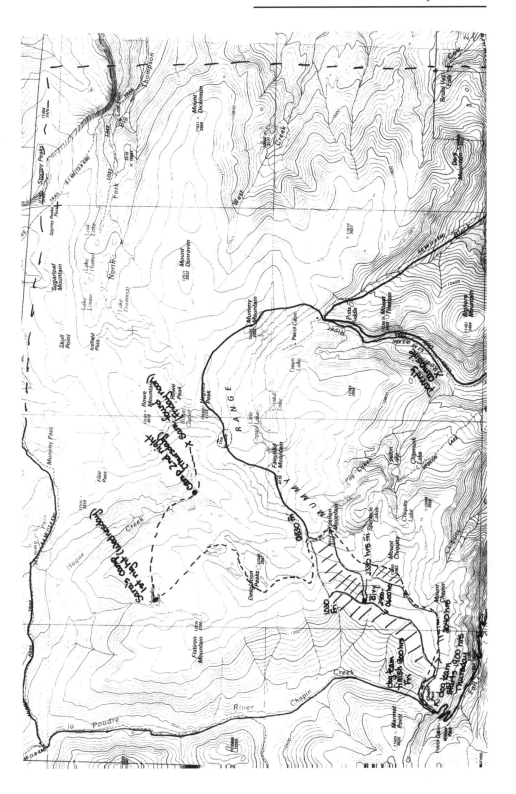

During her solo hike, Sara was exposed to several hazards typically associated with alpine mountaineering in Colorado. In the Colorado Rockies thunderstorms are nearly a daily occurrence; they form suddenly and lightning strikes without warning. It was possible that Sara was on an exposed ridge when the strong storm passed through the area Wednesday afternoon. Besides lightning, the storm would have created another safety hazard, rain-slicked rocks. Slick rocks are a hazard not only because safe footing becomes uncertain, but also because the rain loosens the rocks from their tenuous hold to the earth, sending them tumbling down the mountainside. The wind is a hazard because it can be so strong that it is difficult to remain upright. This was the case Friday morning when Sara was still missing. Although it was midsummer, there were still many dangerous snow fields on the steep mountain slopes that had to be avoided. Serious injury can occur if a person slips and falls several hundred feet down a snow field.

Besides weather and terrain, a serious danger in the mountains is altitude sickness. Although Sara had spent a couple of weeks near Estes Park, her hike was over 5,000 ft. higher in elevation than her camp was located. This made altitude sickness a good possibility. The symptoms include general malaise[4] followed by nausea and a headache. As the sickness progresses, judgment is clouded and apathy and dizziness increase. In severe cases of altitude sickness, a person may develop a high-altitude pulmonary edema or cerebral edema[5]. As a solo hiker Sara would be in additional danger since she had no one to assist her if she should succumb to altitude sickness. Moving to a lower elevation usually relieves the symptoms of altitude sickness. However, since a person may not recognize they are experiencing altitude sickness, they may continue to move to a higher altitude, which could worsen their condition.

Search Personnel and Equipment

Many different resources were requested for this search. Foot teams, airscenting, and trailing dog teams, and a helicopter was requested once Sara was reported missing.

A total of seventy-five people and five dogs were used in the search effort. Two foot teams made up of park rangers were fielded immediately early Thursday afternoon when Sara was reported missing. Two airscenting dog teams from Larimer County Search and Rescue and a helicopter was also utilized Thursday afternoon and evening. Friday, two additional airscenting dog teams and a trailing dog team were fielded along with six foot teams and one helicopter. There was the possibility that a television news helicopter would also be available.

Search Strategy

Overdue hikers and climbers are common due to inclement weather and underestimating the time to complete a hike. The report of a person who is overdue on the morning following a particularly long hike possesses no special urgency, especially if the hiker is as prepared as Sara was. However, since Sara had not returned by early afternoon Thursday, the situation was upgraded to urgent.

---

[4] Malaise is when you generally do not feel well. Sort of like the beginning of the flu. You suffer from a lack of energy and enthusiasm.

[5] Pulmonary edema is when fluid builds up in the lungs and cerebral edema is fluid in the brain. Both cause death quickly.

The search area was very large and remote, covering over 50 miles in rugged terrain. We used two initial foot teams along trails on two sides of the search area for containment. Other than that, there was no containment in effect in the remote northern section of the search area. Management at the check-in site at Corral Park, northwest of the primary search area, was notified about the missing subject in case Sara exited via the Mummy Pass trail.

The extended first operational period, from 1300 Thursday afternoon until 0600 Friday morning, was primarily a hasty search to get teams in along Sara's intended path of travel. Hopefully they would find clues to further direct the search effort. Segments and boundaries were determined for the second operational period, which began Friday morning at 0600 hours. The high priority segments were based on clues obtained by the hasty teams, the history of overdue hikers in the area, and hazards encountered along the route. The descent off Ypsilon Mountain to Fairchild Mountain was identified as a likely place where Sara could have lost the route, as it is a particularly tricky descent. It was the highest priority area for Friday.

The Cache la Poudre/Chapin Creek drainage formed the western boundary. The Fall River Road was the southern boundary. The Black Canyon trail formed the eastern boundary, and the northern boundary went up toward the Mummy Pass trail. Most of the exit routes off Ypsilon Mountain, Fairchild Mountain, and Hagues Peak put hikers and climbers in the Ypsilon Lake and Lawn Lake drainage—the segmentation was extensive in this area.

On Thursday, the two hasty foot teams were used for confinement, clue detection, and attraction. Rocky Mountain National Park authorities called for dog resources mid-afternoon due to the size of the search area. The dog teams, and a helicopter, were used for clue detection and attraction. Friday, foot teams were used to search segments thoroughly rather than move quickly as hasty teams. The dog teams were also used to thoroughly search segments Friday.

Assign Resources

One ranger patrol foot team was assigned to follow Sara's intended path and check the register atop each summit to see if Sara had signed in. Another ranger patrol foot team was flown into the Lawn Lake ranger station to do attraction and man the station throughout Thursday evening in case Sara showed up.

The first airscenting dog team to arrive, Dog Team One, consisted of a handler and two rangers. They were flown to the Saddle to try to narrow the search area into one of four quadrants: two quadrants to the west of the saddle, one quadrant below Fairchild Mountain, and one quadrant below Mummy Mountain. The direction of the search effort would be determined by the information that Dog Team One obtained. The trailing dog was unavailable, so the second airscenting dog team, Dog Team Two, was assigned to follow Sara's intended route using any up-slope winds to cover a wide area. Dog Team Two consisted of a handler, two additional Larimer County Search and Rescue Team members, and a ranger.

The last resource available for the search Thursday afternoon was a private helicopter contracted by the National Park Service. The helicopter flew the intended route and searched around the mountain peaks. After these resources were fielded, management began planning for Friday. Resources requested for the next operational period were one trailing and two airscenting dog teams, foot team resources from Larimer County Search and Rescue, and additional helicopter time.

Information Obtained from Resources

Dog Team One was flown from mission base to the Saddle around 1700 Thursday. The airscenting dog teams in Larimer County are trained to scent discriminate and the dog, a black Labrador Retriever with two years of mission experience, was given Sara's scent. Immediately the dog indicated that there was a large amount of Sara's scent near the Saddle. The dog began to run back and forth with her head in the air; however, the switching winds made it difficult to determine from which direction the scent was originating. The dog team made grids across the Saddle, around the base of Hagues Peak, and circled Mummy Mountain. Based on the dog's behavior, the handler and search management thought that it could be possible Sara's scent was coming up out of the Hague Creek drainage; however, the handler thought it might also have just seemed that way because of the swirling winds. It also seemed unlikely to management that Sara was in that drainage since it meant that the dog had an alert from what was thought to be too far away. Additionally, since there was no response to attraction efforts made by Dog Team One, it was decided that, if responsive, Sara was not likely to be close below the Saddle on the north side. As a result, the Hague Creek drainage was considered only a slight possibility for Sara's location. However, the alert distance and the unsuccessful attraction methods combined with strong interest toward Mummy Mountain suggested that Sara was most likely in the Lawn Lake drainage. Dog Team One concluded its search for the evening around 2200 and stayed in the patrol cabin at Lawn Lake.

Dog Team Two started their search assignment at the Chapin Pass trailed at 1900 Thursday evening. The dog, an Australian Cattle dog with five years of mission experience, was given Sara's scent and the team started up the trail. At the trail junction for Chapin Creek and Mount Chapin, the dog started on the trail toward the mountain. As the team moved along the barely visible trail, the dog acted as if she was trailing. The dog's behavior showed the team that Sara most likely had been through the area, although they were unable to obtain any definite signs. Because of communication problems resulting from the terrain and distance, this information could not be easily relayed to the mission base. As the dog team progressed toward Mount Chapin, the winds switched to blowing down slope after having been predominantly up slope. An incoming storm later in the evening created strong, unreliable winds accompanied by thunder and lightning. The dog team was forced to retreat from the ridge line around 2330 due to lightning. The team bivouacked that night on the scree slope and resumed searching early Friday morning[6].

Most of the teams were not in the actual search area until a few before dark Thursday. Therefore the only clues obtained by Thursday night were those from the dog teams. They were the alerts in the Saddle area from Dog One and the continuing progress of Dog Two along Sara's intended path. Using this information, the additional resources Friday were assigned as follows: One airscenting dog team was to be flown to the Saddle to see if they could confirm the alerts from Dog One. Another airscenting dog team hiked into the Fay Lakes/Ypsilon Lake area to rule out the possibility Sara had descended off the east side of

---

[6] The scree (talus) slope was dangerous because it did not give us any protection from the elements, such as lightning. The rocks were not large enough to sleep on and were sharp, pointed, and jagged.

Ypsilon Mountain. A trailing dog team worked the intended route, a trail that was now over 48 hours old. Four foot teams had assignments as well. One foot team was sent to the Spectacle Lakes area to scan the slopes under Ypsilon Mountain in case Sara had fallen or attempted a descent. Two foot teams were sent to look on the Lawn Lake side of Fairchild Mountain in the Crystal Lake drainage. Another foot team was flown to the Saddle to further check the area around the Saddle and Mummy Mountain. They were sent there because Dog One had shown so much interest in that area. Unfortunately the teams to be flown in had to wait until midmorning when the raging winds had subsided and the helicopter could fly.

An airscenting dog team and a foot team were finally flown to the Saddle around 1000 Friday morning. The foot team worked its way around to the north-running ridge west of the Saddle. After about an hour, they heard three whistles in response to them blowing their whistle. The initial thought was "What kind of bird is that?" After a few cycles of this pattern they realized they were most likely in contact with Sara though they never could get voice contact with her. It sounded like she was directly below them at the bottom of the northern slope of the Saddle. They worked their way over truck-sized boulders as they descended. At times they had to remove their packs and pass them to another teammate to maneuver across the terrain. The helicopter flew over the area north of the Saddle while the foot team slowly worked their way toward Sara. The helicopter crew spotted Sara near a clearing in the Hague Creek drainage and could land and pick her up around 1200 hours. She was flown to mission base where she was reunited with her family.

Sara said she became disoriented after she was forced off the mountain ridge by the thunderstorm Wednesday afternoon. The storm passed through while she was preparing to cross the narrow ridge from Ypsilon Mountain to Fairchild Mountain. She opted to move westward around Desolation Peak rather than cross the narrow ridge between the other two peaks. The storm's intensity forced her to continue a descent off the mountain range, eventually leaving her in the Hague Creek drainage. She was unclear as to her location once the storm passed, so she decided to stay in one place Wednesday night. She figured out that she needed to move back to the south Thursday and tried to attract the attention of the helicopter crew Thursday afternoon to no avail. Friday morning she was able to get into a clearing and caught the attention of the helicopter crew after getting contact with the foot team via whistles.

Desolation Peaks and the Hague Creek drainage where Sara was ultimately located. This view is from Mummy Pass looking southwest. (Photo by Bill Cotton)

What are Your Feelings About the Mission?

These feelings about the mission are from Dave Bigelow who was acting as Situation Unit Leader for this incident.

As the Situation Unit Leader, I felt good about this mission for several reasons. First, the subject was found in good condition and all personnel involved in the mission returned safely to incident base. The mission was successful, in part, because the investigation by the National Park Service staff was excellent. The investigation, the subject behavior profile, the search urgency, and the determination of required resources all made the search a success. However, the search could not have gone as well as it did if the requested resources had not been available. During the hasty search, teams did generate useful clues, though they were sometimes conflicting. Lastly, the incident affirmed how easily resources from different agencies can work together using the Incident Command System.

Search Tips (from Dave Bigelow)

Dog teams make great clue generators. Clues can include the absence of detectable scent of a subject in an area so that a dog team may clear an area. search managers can then use information from the dog teams to triangulate to a high probability area. They can do this by evaluating dog alerts, interest, and corresponding meteorology, such as wind direction and the heating or cooling of the terrain. This type of hasty assignment, using dog teams as clue generators, is as important, and possesses the same urgency, as other SAR field assignments.

Airscenting dogs trained as scent discriminators have a huge advantage in public areas such as National Parks and Forests. A search segment does not have to be cleared of humans before a dog can work, and search managers don't waste valuable time and dog resources "finding" non-search-related subjects.

Re-deployment. Dog handlers and search managers must have an understanding that once in the field, dog handlers may need to adjust their tactics to achieve the search objectives in a given search segment. This may include re-deployment to an opposite side of a search segment or the temporary abandonment of the area because of unfavorable climate conditions during the assigned operational period.

Debriefing is very important. Handlers and search managers should spend extra time debriefing to elicit an in-depth discussion regarding the scenting behavior of the search dog during the mission. This post-mission discussion of dog behavior, as it relates to the eventual subject location, is the single most important training tool for search managers who are attempting to correctly utilize dog resources during future missions. You learn from your successes just as you learn from your mistakes.

You and your dogs are a team. While dogs are not always conscious of scent being trapped in valleys or other environmental factors that affect scent, sometimes you need to trust your dogs. Airscenting dogs that discriminate human scent may have valid alerts on subjects as much as a mile away or more. In the case of Sara, we'd considered the Hague Creek area to be low probability, because the humans thought it was too far away for the dog to detect, when it turned out the dog was right on. Handlers and search managers must consider this possibility when interpreting clues generated by the dog teams.

Biography

Dave Bigelow has been a volunteer member of Larimer County Search and Rescue in

Fort Collins, Colorado since 1979. He has been a search manager in his SAR team since 1992. His team routinely, and successfully, utilizes search-dog resources as a part of their search operations. The LCSAR team has a stable group of approximately six dogs that are available for most search and rescue operations. Their team is one of the SAR teams in the State of Colorado to support the organization Search and Rescue Dogs of Colorado (SARDOC). Dave is also a NASAR, MRA, and Colorado Search and Rescue Board member and has held a subcommittee chair in ASTM F32 (Search Operations and Management) since 1991. When he is not doing SAR related work, he is a full-time solar radiation researcher at Colorado State University.

THE SEARCHER

DOG HANDLER TEAM

Who Are You?

I was one of the two initial dog handlers who responded to the search Thursday afternoon. Since my trailing dog was still in training, I responded with my experienced airscenting dog, Tassie, an Australian Cattle Dog.

The Callout

My pager started emitting a series of tones around 1400 Thursday afternoon while I was at work in a research laboratory at Colorado State University. Based on the tones, I knew that the information I was receiving on my pager was search-related and urgent. While my employer allowed me some flexibility, my mission response could not be at the expense of

Tassie searches for a missing hiker on the Continental Divide in Rocky Mountain National Park, Colorado, in August 1998. Tassie is operational in airscent, avalanche, water, and evidence search.

any ongoing experiments. I had just started an experimental protocol that would take about two hours to complete. Following completion of that stage of the experiment, I had to start an overnight procedure. After that, I would not need to do anything further until the next morning, so I determined that I could respond to the mission later. I arranged with my coworkers to place my experiments in cold storage Friday morning after the overnight protocol was completed. I left my workplace around 1630.

I had to load my gear and dog into the car and then drive up the Big Thompson Canyon to Rocky Mountain National Park during high tourist season. I didn't arrive at the incident command post for briefing until 1800. Fortunately, for this mission, I did not need to take extra time making arrangements to have my younger dog cared for, since I was the only one in the household responding to this mission. My team and I did not reach the actual search site until 1900.

The Search Sector

Who decided your sector?

When I arrived at the incident command post, search management had two primary search objectives. The first was to get a dog team to the middle of Sara's proposed route, and the other was to have a dog team follow along her intended path of travel. The first dog and handler, who were available immediately when the pager toned, had been flown in by helicopter to the Saddle. They had been searching for a few hours before I arrived. I was briefed about the circumstances surrounding the search and given the objectives for my search area. While following Sara's planned route, I was to use the wind to see if the dog would show that Sara might be on the west or east side of the mountain range. Management hoped that I could use up-slope winds to determine if Sara had fallen down or descended the treacherous east face of her intended route.

Before I could leave the incident command post, I needed to obtain a scent article so my dog knew to search exclusively for Sara. I was given Sara's suitcase to select something suitable for my needs. The contents had not been touched by anyone else. Because the clothes had not been worn during Sara's vacation, my best scent article was one of her clog shoes. I had no desire to carry something that heavy and large with me while searching. Therefore I placed a sterile gauze pad inside a shoe to absorb Sara's scent while I briefed my team members about our assignment. Afterward, I collected and stored the gauze pad in a plastic bag to use as the scent article.

Two Larimer County Search and Rescue Team members and a park ranger, none of whom had worked extensively with a dog team before, accompanied me on the search assignment. One of them was tasked with keeping track of our route on the map. One of the search team members had to mark the locations and directions of any alerts or interest from the dog and write down the time we were at different landmarks. The rest of the team did attraction and looked for any visual clues. One team member monitored the radio traffic and communicated with the incident command post when needed. It was beneficial having the park ranger with us since he was familiar with the area.

How large was your sector? How long did it take to complete?

Because of the nature of my search assignment, the size of my search sector was vague. I was to follow Sara's planned route and use the wind to the dog's best advantage to cover the mountain slopes. The primary objective of search management was to try to cover the east face of the mountain ridge. The distance between the trailhead and Ypsilon Mountain entailed a hike of more than 3.5 miles across some tough terrain. This was only the first part of our assignment. We had three more mountain peaks to cover to follow the entire planned route. The wind pattern and terrain helped me to determine how much area the dog could actually cover. By the time we ascended to the ridge line, it became obvious that we would not cover any of the east face below the ridge line. The winds were down sloping rather than up sloping. I adjusted my search objective for Thursday evening and concentrated my efforts along the western slope of the ridge. The slope consisted of loose rocks that impeded our pace. It also got dark after 2100. We tried to work along the ridge line Thursday evening at an elevation of about 12,800', but a thunderstorm late Thursday night forced us to descend nearly 1,000 feet. We were between Mount Chiquita and Ypsilon Mountain. We had expended a lot of energy to reach the higher elevation, but the descent, at 2330, was necessary to lessen the possibility of being struck by lightning. Though we moved to a lower elevation, we were still on a very rocky slope that offered no real protection from the storm. We stopped for the night to get some rest. A few hours later, the rain stopped, the storm had passed.

Friday morning at 0600, after spending the night sleeping on rocks, we again ascended toward the ridge line. As we tried to move up and across the rocks, a 40+ mph westerly wind with strong gusts, hampered our movement. When we reached the ridge between Ypsilon and Fairchild Mountains at 0800 hours, we decided that the wind made it too dangerous to cross the ridge. I again adjusted my search sector. Though I could no longer cover Sara's intended route, I could search a sector from the ridge line down to the west toward Chapin Creek and work back to the Chapin Pass trailhead. We returned to the trailhead at 1300 Friday afternoon after having been in the field for 18 hours.

How did you decide where to start your sector?

Since our assignment was to follow Sara's intended route, we started our assignment at the Chapin Pass trailhead.

Problems Encountered

The problems that we encountered were expected due to the nature of searching in a mountainous and remote wilderness. The first problem became apparent almost immediately. I had a difficult time moving quickly along the trail. I had come from an elevation of 5,000' in Fort Collins and in less than three hours was at 12,000'. My body had a hard time adjusting to the fast altitude change. I was slow, sluggish, and had to make frequent rest stops. This was because I had not done much hiking at high altitudes that summer. My other team members were not having as hard a time as I was that night, so I set the slow pace. Typically I have problems with altitudes. However, the severity varies from incident to incident depending on the time of day and how much sleep and water I had before the mission.

Two additional problems our dog team encountered were weather-related and typical for the time of year and environment. The first problem happened late Thursday night when a thunderstorm moved overhead. All four of us were up on an exposed ridge and were the highest objects in the terrain. We were totally exposed to the lightning unless we descended below 2,000'. We opted to drop about 1,000 feet to reduce our exposure to lightning, yet maintain some of the elevation we had worked so hard to gain.

Friday morning we had to contend with the second weather-related problem, the wind. Maintaining our balance across the boulder fields with wind gusts was difficult. Because of the wind, we did not feel safe walking along the ridge line. Therefore, we could not get close enough to the ridge to see the east face of the mountaintops along our route. Further along the route, the wind prevented us from attempting to cross from Ypsilon Mountain to Fairchild Mountain. We were not surprised by the problems with the wind. I have participated in several missions in Rocky Mountain National Park where the winds were brutal above timberline. It can literally pound a person into the ground and force them to crawl across the terrain on hands and knees.

The last problem I experienced on this search assignment was rather unexpected. The problem was convincing my teammates to work to the dog's advantage. When the wind was up sloping, it made sense to my other team members to work along the ridge line, since that was presumably where Sara had walked. However, once the wind shifted to down slope, I could not convince them that we would cover more area with the dog by staying at a lower elevation. By doing so we could use the wind to cover the area above us. Not being familiar with working with a dog team, they felt their primary responsibility was to follow Sara's intended route, even if it hampered the dog's search efficiency. This meant that I did not search my area very effectively Thursday night.

Were you prepared for the conditions you encountered?

The Larimer County Search and Rescue Team is rarely requested to assist Rocky Mountain National Park on "easy" missions. Whenever I respond to Rocky Mountain National Park, I need to be well prepared for a search marathon, mentally, physically, and equipment-wise. This mission was no exception. I knew that since we did not start until 1900 Thursday and that we were doing a remote sector, I would be spending the night outdoors. I carried my bivy bag[7] and a sleeping pad in case we took a break to sleep. Since it was summer, I did not carry a sleeping bag, but I did carry several layers of warm clothes to wear inside my bivy bag if it became chilly above the timberline. I always have rain gear and some cold weather clothes in my pack, so I was prepared for the weather. I was prepared to minimize potential ankle injuries related to moving across the boulder and scree fields by wearing full leather boots. As far as preparations for my dog, Tassie could stay warm and dry during the storm since she was small enough to join me inside my bivy bag. Unfortunately, the rocks were abrasive on the pads of her feet. Her feet were tender when we completed the search. Booties, however, may have impaired the dexterity she needed to move from rock to rock.

The Dog

While Tassie is an airscenting dog, her initial six-month training entailed following the scent trail deposited on the ground during a person's passage through an area. Because of that training, she will indicate the presence of a scent trail under certain conditions. Shortly after the hiking trail begins at Fall River Road, it splits and continues either north along Chapin Creek or east toward Mount Chapin. At that junction, Tassie went east without hesitation. She did not appear to trail continuously, but she worked with her nose to the ground along various segments of our route. We felt she was indicating the presence of Sara's scent and passage. We noted it on the map.

When the storm moved into our area, we were forced to descend for safety reasons. The slope consisted of loose scree—lots of shattered boulder pieces that gave poor footing and made an even poorer sleeping surface. Eventually we found one boulder large enough for me to curl up on. We found another boulder about 100 feet away that was large enough for the other three team members to sleep on. During the storm, I crawled down inside the

---

[7] A bivy bag is a nylon or Gortex bag that you crawl into for protection from the weather. Since it is not a sleeping bag, it offers no warmth or padding. It only protects you from the rain. You can put a sleeping bag in it to keep dry and block the wind.

bivy bag and brought Tassie in with me so she could also stay warm and dry. Being a small dog at forty pounds has its advantages! Since we could hear rocks crashing down the mountain slope as the rain loosened them, we wore our rescue helmets throughout the night, and I kept my search pack against my back.

After spending a restless night on the rocks, we began to regain the elevation we had lost the night before while between Mount Chiquita and Ypsilon Mountain. But our movement was greatly hampered by the strong wind. With each step, my body would sway about until I had both feet firmly planted again. Slowly we moved toward the ridge. As we got closer, Tassie's behavior again appeared to indicate she was trailing. We continued north toward Ypsilon Mountain, being careful to stay off the ridge itself because the wind was so strong. Two of the team members hiked to the top of Ypsilon Mountain while another member and I and Tassie, stayed just below the peak. We wanted to reduce the team's exposure to the hazardous conditions. Because of the weather conditions Friday morning, we were all wearing winter-type clothing.

When we reached the ridge joining Ypsilon and Fairchild Mountains, we discussed possible routes across the ridge and potential hazards. As a team, we decided the risks were too great to cross over to Fairchild Mountain and that it would be best to redirect our search efforts. We no longer searched along the intended path of travel but chose to clear the sector between Chapin Creek and the ridge line, making up the route. As we moved west to the saddle between Ypsilon Mountain and Desolation Peaks, Tassie again began to act like she was trailing. I did not know what to make of it since, if it was Sara's trail, it was at least thirty-six hours old. I figured the wind had probably blown any residual scent from Sara's passage elsewhere so there should no longer be scent for Tassie to follow. Therefore, I did not feel it was possible she could be following Sara's trail.

As we moved westward off Ypsilon Mountain, we descended from 13,000' to about 11,600'. During the hike down the drainage, which was just northwest of Ypsilon Mountain, we had to cross running water from melting snow, little ponds that were formed from the running water, and wet moss. We then began to contour back to the south and toward Chapin Pass at 1030 hours. Rather than walking across rocks and boulders, we were now crossing the headwaters of numerous drainages. We walked through an open marsh and some willows. With the strong westerly wind that morning, I felt confident that our hasty search cleared from just below the peaks to possibly the 11,600-foot contour line. I came to this conclusion because Tassie only indicated she had scent along a trail and not in the air to the west. With our grid southward at 11,600', I hoped to cover the area down to the tree line, a distance about 400 feet below our intended contour/grid. When we were halfway back to Chapin Pass, around noon, we heard that Sara had been found and that she was in good condition. While proceeding to the trailhead just below Chapin Pass, I had one of my team members place Sara's scent article along the trail so Tassie could find it as she passed by. I did this for two reasons: first, it would reaffirm to me that Tassie was indeed still looking for, and aware of, Sara's scent. Secondly, after finding the article, she would get her reward, a Frisbee, for doing a job well done and working hard for over 18 hours. However, it did not work as planned. I had a support person place the article along the path. Just as we started to work Tassie, we noticed a bird swoop down and fly away with something in its feet. As we worked the path, we could not find the article. By the time we reached the support person, Tassie still had not given an alert. The support person took us back to the spot where he had placed the scent pad and then we realized that the bird had taken the gauze pad! To give Tassie a "find" we placed a scent article from one of the team members along the trail. I gave Tassie a new scent to find and she found the article and was happy. Normally I wouldn't switch scents on a dog like this, but under the circumstance's Tassie needed a find. Tassie can alert on an article that is 100 feet or so away. Under the right conditions she can alert on it even further.

Probability of Detection

The probability of detection was low for my assigned task. Both Thursday evening and Friday morning I had 0% coverage of the east faces of Mounts Chapin and Chiquita and Ypsilon Mountain. The wind was not conducive for coverage based on my location on the west side of the ridge. For the area between my grid Thursday evening along the 12,200–12,600 contour up toward the ridge, my probability of detection was around 20%, again because the wind was not reliable and constant. I felt the POD was not much better than 20% for the scree fields I covered Friday morning. I felt that way due to the size of some crevices she could have fallen into if she had been injured. However, the probability of detection was much higher for the sector between the 12,600-foot contour and tree line. Because the terrain was fairly open and even, and I felt the wind speed was high enough to cover much of the area, I assigned the probability of detection to be about 60%.

How Successful were You?

Although we could not follow Sara's planned route beyond Ypsilon Mountain, we were successful in completing our search assignment. As we later learned, the dog correctly indicated that Sara had passed through the area. And although I did not believe Tassie could still be trailing Friday morning, she was also correct in indicating that Sara had changed her direction and had not crossed over to Fairchild Mountain. Sara confirmed this when she described how she became lost. Our probability of detection was low for the scree slope, but we did feel we had cleared the lower part of the mountain with the dog. As we walked back to the trail before Sara was located, the team discussed how we would summarize our coverage of the area. We concluded we could confirm Sara's passage, but that our area was not a high probability area for finding her. We completed our assignment to the best of our ability and adjusted our assignment as needed so that we could still give valuable information to the mission management despite the weather challenges we faced.

What are Your Feelings About the Mission?

I felt good about this well-executed mission. In fact, this is one of my favorite missions because it so obviously demonstrates the overall team effort required to find the subject. I feel the team aspect is something that oftentimes gets overlooked because typically only one field team finds the subject. However, it takes the efforts from all of the other field teams to eliminate likely areas for the lost subject, or to provide clues that direct a team into the lost subject.

The team effort is clearly illustrated in this search. First, information from the first dog team and previous search experience in that area were required to keep resources concentrated in the upper region of the Lawn Lake drainage. While it was difficult to determine the correct side of the Saddle to search, it was deemed important to keep teams searching in that area because the dog had so much interest. Secondly, it was a foot team that established contact with Sara, but they were unable to actually get to her. She ended up being much further away from them than they had thought; however, they did determine she was down in the Hague Creek drainage, rather than in the Lawn Lake drainage. With this information, the helicopter crew expanded its flight path. It took the crew's efforts, and Sara's attempts to get their attention, to finally get a visual on her. And it was the helicopter crew that picked her up and returned her safely to her family.

Search Tips

I feel a dog handler should be a search and rescue person who happens to have a dog as a specialized search tool. The handler should be familiar with all aspects of search and rescue so that they can understand where they, as a specialized resource, fit into the bigger search picture. By not limiting oneself to just focusing on dog handling skills, the handler becomes a very valuable resource. A trained search and rescue person can take the information obtained from working with the dog and combine it with information obtained either at briefing, or gathered in the field. With this information the searcher can formulate a better understanding of what the subject may have done or where they might be.

As stated previously, trained dogs can, and should be, used as clue generators. Dog teams can indicate passage of the subject, but they can also clear an area or lower the probability of an area by having no interest or alerts in the area at all. Therefore, it can be significant that a trained dog does not find the subject in its search sector. They can also have alerts in a particular direction that helps to narrow down the search area. The training and experience of the dog/handler team, however, are going to determine how useful and reliable the dog team is as a clue generator.

It is very beneficial to pair the handler with other field team resources who are also experienced working with search dogs. Those team members are the handler's second set of eyes and ears. They might see an alert the handler missed because the handler may have been looking elsewhere instead of at the dog. In addition, if the person understands how search dogs work, they can provide another educated opinion to help develop and adjust the search strategy in the field. This will help the dog team be more efficient and effective. Handlers-in-training are excellent resources to fill this vital support role.

Using handlers-in-training as dog support actually has a twofold purpose. While they are a great benefit to the dog handler on a mission, it also provides invaluable experience for the handler-in-training. As a support person, the handler-in-training will learn the stresses of real missions. They will have the opportunity to observe how experienced handlers decide how to search their assigned segment. They will also have the opportunity to see how the dog's behavior during the search fits with the subject's eventual location. Also, by observing several different dogs that exhibit different working behaviors, the handler-in-training can develop a better understanding of what their own dog's behavior might mean. It is also important to work with the dogs often enough so that an unusual behavior during a search is noticed. I have found that when my dog does something unusual during a search, it is significant and I need to pay attention. By accompanying handlers on missions, a handler-in-training will learn these tricks and is better prepared to work their own dog.

Trust your dog, trust your dog, trust your dog. On this mission, both dogs indicated correctly. But both of the handlers, and management, felt the indications were possibly not valid as the alerts were coming from too far away, or the scent trail was too old. Since this mission, we have had experiences with our dogs where they worked scent coming from the subject when the subject was over a mile away. This is very dependent on terrain and most commonly occurs in a drainage. We learned a valuable lesson about trailing on this mission. Some scent had been blown away but much of it was still deposited in the rock crevices and not accessible to the wind. The rain helped to rejuvenate the scent.

Search work needs to be fun for both the handler and the dog. Actual missions can be stressful for all involved, so it is important to make training fun, and to reward the dog following missions. Part of the stress can be reduced if the dog and handler have a good relationship outside of search work.

Biography

Julie Cotton has been with Larimer County Search and Rescue out of Fort Collins, Colorado, since 1986. She is active both as a search leader and as a technical rescue member. She has been training dogs with Search and Rescue Dogs of Colorado (SARDOC) since 1989. In 1990, Julie and her Australian Cattle dog, Tassie, became an operational airscent team. They have participated in over one hundred searches in Larimer County, across Colorado, Nebraska, Wyoming, and South Dakota since then. Together they have several finds and assists in both wilderness and water searches. In 1996, Julie became operational as a trailing, avalanche, and water handler with her younger dog, Zephyr. Her primary interest is water searching. She has been an officer of SARDOC since 1991, and has served as the statewide SAR Dog Coordinator for two years, and more recently as president. She has participated in national conferences to instruct classes in scent discrimination for airscenting dogs.

Above: Julie Cotton and her trailing dog, Zephyr. Zephyr is also certified in avalanche, water, and evidence search disciplines. (Photo by Allen Weaver)

Left: Julie Cotton and Zephyr practice searching in avalanche debris on Rabbit Ears Pass, Colorado, in February 1988. (Photo by Bill Cotton)

Walk Away Child: Residential Scent Specific

Lt. Daryl Anderson
Lincoln County Sheriff's Office and David Thompson SAR
Location of Mission: Libby, Montana
Date of Mission: March 27, 1995

Mission Type

This was a short search.

The Victim

An active four year old girl in normal health. "Jill" had shoulder-length brown hair and was wearing a shirt and pink pants when she went missing on March 27, 1995.

Point Last Seen

Jill was playing in her own yard and wandered off. See map for location.

Terrain Features

Although the location was a housing area with many outbuildings, it was on the edge of town and on the edge of a large flat field surrounded with underbrush and a creek.

Weather

It was 50°F, wind 5 mph from the west, partly cloudy, with no precipitation.

Special Dangers

The creek that ran by the house was in the early stages of flooding and contained large root wads. There was an old, broken down footbridge by the house. The railroad tracks ran by the place. The Kootenai River was not far away.

Any Other Special Information

Nine years ago, in 1986, a child had been abducted and murdered along this same creek.

Search Personnel and Equipment

Our wish list for this mission would have included trained personnel, a helicopter, radio equipment for each team, orange vests for volunteers, and pagers.

Trained personnel responded from the following associations: David Thompson SAR, Libby Volunteer Ambulance, Libby Volunteer Fire Department, and Lincoln County Sheriff's Office. I also received numerous citizens who had heard the call on their scanners and minimal radio equipment.

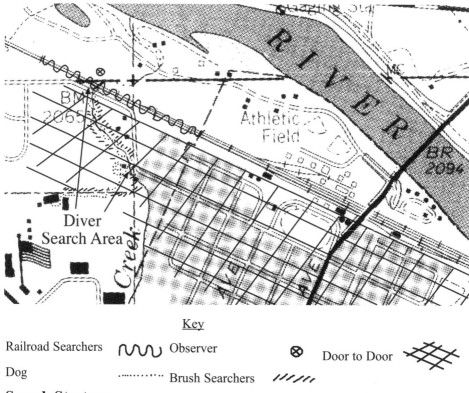

Key

Railroad Searchers 〰〰〰 Observer   ⊗   Door to Door ⧣⧣⧣

Dog ⋯⋯⋯ Brush Searchers ⫫⫫⫫

Search Strategy

The resources that I received were used both to keep the search area from getting larger and to try to find the victim. There were observers placed at the bridges and roads to contain the search area. The remainder of the available manpower was deployed in finding the victim.

Search Urgency

Since Jill was a four-year-old child and the creek ran past her yard, the urgency was high. If the child had fallen into the creek, it would be considered a cold-water drowning incident, therefore the "Golden Hour" theory was employed. Sixteen years previously, a two-year-old child had been revived from a cold-water drowning that occurred in this creek.

Boundaries of the Search: Initially the search area was defined by the creek, the railroad tracks, the field, and the ballpark. These boundaries were decided by the PLS and the time that had elapsed since the child had disappeared. These boundaries would be expanded as areas were cleared.

Segment the Search Area

The terrain was a determining factor in segmenting the search area. The area from the footbridge to the railroad near the creek was one sector. The houses and outbuildings with their respective areas were another sector. The brush piles and fence line was a sector, the field another sector. The last major sector was the area that covered the outlying homes from the driveway toward the town.

Probability of Area

The PLS and the nature of the segments or sectors, determined the probability attached to each section. We were trying to work within the "Golden Hour."

Prioritize Segments

The creek had to be given the highest priority because it was so close to the victim's PLS and the temperature of the water was ice cold due to the snow run off. If Jill was in the creek, we only had minutes to recover and revive her. There was no other area as nearly life threatening as the creek area. Secondly, since the railroad tracks were close to Jill's house and presented an immediate danger, the railroad was contacted to stop all trains in the area. Equal weight was given to the brush piles, outbuildings, the field, and other homes in the area. The possibility of a stranger abducting Jill was not ruled out. However, until it was determined that Jill was not in the area, that consideration would not be acted on.

Search Strategy

The tactics were straightforward. The resources that were available would be deployed to cover the sectors of the search area as quickly and thoroughly as possible. Observers would be assigned to help confine the search area. New segments would be outlined as old segments were cleared. Searchers were instructed to use their "singsong" voices to call for Jill. They were also told to search every hiding place carefully because of the small size and age of the victim.

Assign Resources

As they arrived, the resources were assigned to the high priority areas. Foot searchers were assigned to the banks of the creek, the root wads, and brush piles along side the creek. Observers were placed at the railroad bridge. The search dog and handler were assigned to make a hasty search of the creek and banks. A diver in an exposure suit, mask, and snorkel was deployed to the creek to search from the footbridge to the railroad bridge. With that area covered, searchers were deployed to check the railroad tracks. Others were assigned to search the fence line and brush piles. Ground searchers were deployed to the house and its outbuildings. The neighborhood was divided between the searchers and a hasty search was done in those areas. When the dog and handler concluded their hasty search of the creek, they obtained a scent article and tracked the victim. In total, approximately 90 people responded to this call.

Suspension

The report was called in at 1435. If necessary the search would have continued throughout the night. Searchers would have been relieved and areas redefined. The media would have been contacted and flyers would have been distributed. The areas would have been covered again at daylight. This search would have continued for the next 72 hours. Then our thoughts would have turned more toward stranger abduction and our options would have been reevaluated.

Results of Mission

Jill was located in a nearby apartment complex within ten minutes by the search dog and handler after the track was begun.

What are Your Feelings About the Mission?

Personally, I feel that this was a quality search. The volunteers and citizens were superb. Everyone did his part and performed the job that they had trained for. The response time was quick. I was pleased with our performance.

Search Tips

Always have the proper equipment and know how to use it.

Adequate radio communication is essential.

When you are assigned an area, work your section thoroughly. Cover it carefully and completely the first time. Lives depend on it.

Trust the dog.

Biography

Lt. Daryl Anderson is a veteran police officer with 29 years on the force. In 1969, he and several other law enforcement workers recognized the need for an organized search and rescue unit in the remote region of Western Montana. Together they founded David Thompson Search and Rescue. Since that time he has been highly involved in the organization, serving as president and holding other board positions. In 1982, Lt. Anderson was appointed as the sheriff's office coordinator for DTSAR. His years of dedicated service have helped to strengthen the organization and build its fine reputation.

THE SEARCHER

DOG HANDLER TEAM

Terry Crooks
David Thompson SAR
Western Montana Search Dogs

Who are You?

Terry Crooks, search and rescue dog handler.

The Callout

When the callout occurred, I was at home. My gear stays ready so there were no special arrangements that had to be made. The dog and gear were loaded. We arrived on the scene in approximately fifteen minutes.

The Search Sector

Two sectors were searched, Sector A and Sector B. In Sector A, because of the PLS, I realized that the dog could be of most use in the creek sector. The IC agreed.

In Sector B while the creek was being cleared, a dog-aware reserve officer arrived. We decided that the next option with the dog was to track from the PLS with a scent article. Returning to the residence, the reserve officer properly collected the scent article that was needed to run the track.

How large was your sector? How long did it take to complete?

Sector A was 200 yards of flooded creek. It took about fifteen minutes to complete.

In sector B, the track was around 300 yards of field and fence line. It took approximately ten minutes to complete.

How did you decide where to start?

For Sector A, the PLS was in the yard about halfway between the house and the foot bridge. We worked downstream from the bridge toward the river because this was the most critical place. A Cold water drowning has to be handled quickly.

In Sector B, the track was begun at the PLS.

Problems Encountered

While working the creek in Sector A, we encountered several brush piles along the shore where people were searching with difficulty. Although the brush piles were places where the dog could have searched more effectively than people, no scent article had been obtained. I was concerned that the dog would not discriminate between the searchers and the victim. The problems associated with the track were contamination and numerous other searchers. These problems had been anticipated and trained for. The other problem that I encountered that I had not prepared for was the scent trail ending at a closed door.

Were you prepared for the conditions you encountered?

Yes, the proper gear was used and our blaze orange vests clarified our purpose and made us easily identified by others.

The Dog

The dog was given the command to "Search" at the footbridge. We worked our way downstream in the water. The dog searched all the deep holes from the bridge to the road bridge. Next the dog searched beyond the road bridge to the railroad bridge. The dog gave no alerts, indications, or showed any interest along the way. No clues were detected.

Jill's pajamas were collected as the scent article. The dog was scented and given the command "track" at the PLS. The dog circled the garage several times and came back to me and heeled, which was uncharacteristic for her. The article was given again and the command "track" was repeated. The dog made a wider circle and entered a burned field. She caught the scent at the fence line and moved out ahead of us. She returned as if to say, "speed it up" and raced off again. At the end of the fence she veered left into a low-income housing area. The dog approached a door and paused for a moment. I stated that these buildings needed to be searched. The dog circled the building in an unexcited manner, as if the track had ended.

Probability of Detection

POD for the water search was 90%. The diver and searchers remained in the area to continue the efforts.

POD for the track was 100%. Jill was located in the apartment house. Several older children had gone to an apartment to play. Jill had followed along. The lady that lived there assumed that Jill was the younger sister of one of the other children. The woman did not know that an extensive search was under way for the child.

How Successful were You?

Sector A, the water sector, was effectively searched. We cleared that area and felt confident that the victim was elsewhere. Jill was located in the apartment housing in Sector B. This sector was searched with complete success.

What are Your Feelings About the Mission?

I am satisfied with the dog's work and our performance as a team. The dog was focused and did the job that we had trained her to do. The IC respected our judgments and used our talents well.

Search Tips

If you are a dog handler, be consistent, creative, and challenging in your training.

Be prepared to save yourself. Always have the proper clothing, training and gear for the mission. Carry food and water for yourself and your dog. Purchase a GPS system, which can pinpoint your location within a meter, and learn how to use it.

When tracking, it is best to train and work your dog on lead. This is safer for the dog and more effective.

Be realistic in explaining your dog's capabilities to the IC in each search situation.

Always issue a radio to the dog handler team and provide another search-trained person to accompany the team.

Biography

Terry Crooks comes from Libby, Montana, and has been a member of Western Montana Search Dogs for six years and David Thompson SAR for fifteen years. He has served as the president of DTSAR and currently is a mountain unit leader. His dog training includes water, avalanche, cadaver, wilderness, tracking, and trailing. Terry and his dog, Jess, have been credited with several tracking and evidence finds as well as one avalanche recovery.

Hospital Walk Away
Wilderness Airscent

Hatch and Judy Graham
Virginia Search and Rescue Dog Association
Mission Location: Roanoke County, Virginia
Date of Mission: June 10, 1978

The call came on Saturday evening, June 10, 1978. A 61-year-old patient was missing from Catawba State Hospital in Roanoke County. Virginia SAR dog handlers quickly loaded dogs and gear to convoy across the state.

Arriving at Salem just before midnight, they were met by the Roanoke County Director of Emergency Services who escorted them across the first folds of the Blue Ridge to Catawba. After a quick briefing about the situation and plans for the next day, he suggested they get a couple of hours sleep before the search resumed at 0700.

Those handlers didn't sleep much. Their new unit's reputation—and a woman's life—depended on what they did in the morning. And for all the training they'd been through, and all the testing, this would be different. This was the real world.

It had been almost a year since Marilyn Greene of Adirondack Rescue Dog Association had come down from New York State to give an introductory seminar on forming a SAR dog unit. Since then, dogs and handlers had been training intensively. Marilyn had come back eight months later, in April, to check on the unit's progress. As a result of that week-long evaluation, four dog-handler teams were declared ready for searches.

They'd worked hard to get there. Handlers trained their dogs almost daily, and got together as a unit every weekend—rain or shine, 90% humidity or ice storm. One time, they had to detour through an extra county because a bridge to the training site was underwater; when one handler didn't show up that drenching day, the others were worried that he must be sick or have car trouble. Excuses were rare. Everyone had one thing in mind—get trained and ready to go.

They didn't all make it. In January ten teams had been in training, three months later, one team dropped out. The April evaluation washed out another team, and one handler retired her dog and started a new one.

That was in April. Since then, there had been a few callouts, and long drives through the night, only to be turned around by radio en route when the missing person was found. Handlers wondered if they'd ever really get to a search. And, in the back of their minds, they wondered how they'd do if they ever did get there.

Now, Sunday morning, June 11, they were finally there. Since mid-afternoon Friday June 9, a patient—described as hostile and possibly combative, and weighing 250 pounds—had been missing. A compulsive flower-picker, she was last seen gathering flowers near the entrance to the hospital.

The search for her began as soon as she was discovered missing and continued through that first night. The next day aircraft scanned all the open areas around the hospital, and searchers on foot combed the places where the missing woman picked flowers every day. The only clues they found were some crepe-sole tracks headed east toward the main highway; no one could tell if the tracks were valid.

Surrounded by rolling green lawns and with the backdrop of 3,000-foot North Mountain behind it, Catawba State Hospital is picturesque. Handlers soon learned it was anything but easy searching.

Early Sunday morning, dogs and handlers began hasty searches along roads, trails, and firebreaks. Almost immediately the dogs began giving alerts but couldn't follow through. Handlers blamed the shifting and variable winds and broken terrain, since their assignments took them around and over knolls and into dense green hollows.

By afternoon Virginia Search and Rescue Dog Association's operation leader had divided the primary search area into sectors, assigning one to each dog team. The dogs continued to alert, particularly in the hollows. Still, they couldn't follow the scent to its source.

The next day, Monday, the teams worked farther east along the base of the mountain expanding the search area. At the same time they continued to recheck alert areas, using different dogs at different times of the day. The alerts were scattered over a wide area in hollows to the east of the hospital, with isolated alerts on the slope above—and north of— the institution.

The handlers were worried. In training, their dogs usually located the "victims" in short order; if they were having trouble pursuing an alert, the handlers knew how to work them around until they could solve the problem. But nothing the handlers did seemed to solve this problem.

As they'd learned in training, they reported every alert along with the wind direction at the time and any other pertinent information. The alerts were all logged on the base map. Between shifts, handlers studied that map, trying to discover a pattern.

Monday afternoon a severe thunderstorm hit that part of the Blue Ridge. As the storm cell passed over, dogs in widely scattered locations suddenly began alerting strongly. After the storm passed, as other teams tried to recheck the alerts, the dogs showed no interest.

By Monday night the handlers knew they were running out of time. The missing woman, if she was in the area, had been out for more than three days. While the weather had been generally warm, it had rained twice. Following the thunderstorm Monday afternoon, the temperatures Monday night dropped into the 50s. An earlier start was planned for Tuesday morning.

Before daylight dogs and handlers were re-searching the hollows east of the hospital, where the dogs had given so many alerts over the past two days. With the slopes still in shadow and air moving down, one dog alerted and began a long, hard run straight up the mountain. He lost the scent in a deep ravine.

Handlers regrouped on the side of the slope, higher than they'd searched before. They lined up and headed west, working parallel sweeps across the face of the mountain. At about 1030 one of the dogs turned and worked a short distance downhill; her handler followed and found the missing woman, face down on the ground.

She didn't move. Radioing for help, the handler examined her—and discovered she was breathing faintly.

Other handlers hurried to the spot. Hospital staff, with members of the county fire and sheriffs' departments, climbed the steep hill to evacuate the unconscious woman. She had fallen headfirst downhill and came to rest against a sapling with her right arm pinned under her. She weighed about 250 pounds and was unable to right herself. We could see where she had struggled with her left hand to get a grip on something to no avail. She was clutching a handful of leaves. Probably a combination of hypothermia, dehydration, and exhaustion caused her unconsciousness sometime during the three and a half days she was stuck there. With hospital care, she recovered fully, physically. (She was in the hospital care facility originally for dementia. We don't think the experience had any effect on her mental condition, good or bad.)

In retrospect, handlers had a lot of questions. Overweight as she was, how had the missing woman managed to climb so high on the mountain? Why had the dogs consistently altered in the hollows, when she wasn't there? And how did her scent get everywhere the dogs found it? Why couldn't they follow it to its source? What was happening during the thunderstorm? When the dogs finally found the missing woman, why was she so unexpectedly alive? And, most important, how might they have found her sooner?

As the handlers started to come up with some answers, they realized that the search at Catawba was some of the best training they'd ever had.

Technical Notes on Wind Conditions and Airscenting Problems

From June 10–13 the Virginia SAR Dog Association was involved in a search for a 61-year-old patient who wandered away from a state geriatric hospital near Roanoke, Virginia. The weather conditions, terrain, and vegetation created some difficult circumstances and situations that caused unusual airscenting problems and are worthy of some speculation and analysis.

No accurate weather records exist for the immediate area during the time of the search except for general observations of the eight dog handlers and support personnel involved. The author has been trained in micro-meteorology as it applies to forest fire behavior in mountainous terrain and has studied airscenting behavior of dogs for about four-and-a-half years. (See Syrotuck, Scent and the Scenting Dog). The hypotheses and conclusions are my own; they may or may not be correct, but the assumptions seem to be borne out by the facts recorded on the search and it is hoped, will be of help to others in similar situations.

The successful outcome gives us the advantage of knowing that the victim's location was on a steep, south-facing hillside. Though it was wooded, the victim and surroundings were exposed to sunlight for much of the day. The slope, calculated at 22.5° (50%), at latitude 37.5° N, approximates 75% of the insulation received on flat ground at the Equator, or the same as on the level in Guatemala at 15° N latitude.

The temperature—estimated from weather reports at about 80° (in the shade) on June 11 and 12—would be much higher in the sun on the south-facing slope. The victim was wearing white. This helped her survive but also reflected back the heat, causing thermal air currents to rise up from her body. It is assumed that the victim fell sometime after dark on Friday June 9, approximately 2200, and remained in the nearly the same position until she was discovered.

On a major mountain mass, the typical nocturnal wind pattern is downslope and down-canyon. Airscents emanating on Friday night and Saturday morning would be to the south into the hospital area.

During the day, airscents would be immediately borne aloft, influenced by the white surface of her clothes, the south slope, and the diurnal upslope drafts. Any scent cone developed during the night would soon be burnt off by the south-slope exposure. Thus there was little or no pooling of scent around the victim during the day. Most airscent would tend to be found upslope.

A very slight westerly breeze was noted sporadically on June 11 and 12 and is assumed to have been present on June 10; much of the time, cigarette smoke was rising vertically but occasionally would drift west, north, or south, with a little more orientation toward the east.

Any airscent moving to the east (or west) during the day would, at nightfall, be carried down the slopes and especially down the deeper ravines that dissected North Mountain. To the east, low hollows between the mountain and the foothills to the south acted as a natural trap to the down-flowing air. These hollows also, being shaded by the hills to the south, maintained cooler temperatures and retained the scent longer. The hollows would also, in the morning, tend to receive any airscents in the ravines pushed east by the prevailing westerly breeze.

In summary, on June 11 and 12, there was very little airscent on the ground near the victim. Much of it was rising up, being dissipated by erratic winds, coming to ground in different locations—mostly well up in the mountain above the statistically probable search areas that were receiving attention. The low hollows to the east and the shaded ravines, on the other hand, retained airscent brought in the night before.

On the afternoon of June 12, a major weather change occurred. A heavy thunderstorm passed over the area with strong downdraft radiating out from the storm cell and a cool air mass moved in from the northwest with strong breezes and more rain during the night.

During and after the storm, three dogs—two working adjacent sectors—gave strong alerts, but were unable to follow the alerts. On the morning of June 13, three dogs followed up on the two adjacent alerts of the night before. There was a steady west wind at 0600. The first dog gave a strong alert and started into the wind and uphill but was intercepted by a skunk. After some delay, a second dog was started in, upwind of the skunk incident. He gave a positive alert and moved northwest uphill at a sustained rapid rate. After about an eighth of a mile, he descended into a very deep ravine and obviously lost the scent. With the strong breeze (5–7 mph), it was obvious the airscent was flowing aloft from across the canyon without dropping into the ravine.

The three dogs regrouped on the west side of the ravine at about 1000. By this time, the strong westerly was slacking and the south slope was heating up. Spread out 500 feet apart, the trio moved toward the west. At 1039 the lower dog on the hill gave a weak alert and, following it, the handler spotted the victim. The second dog up the hill was also alerting but did not seem able to sustain a run to the victim as we have come to expect.

Again, it appeared that the location of the victim and the weather would not permit the development of a scent cone on the ground. The airscent, being initially borne aloft, was picked up as it later descended at considerable distance from the victim by all of the dogs at one time or another. Fortunately, all handlers informed base camp by radio of the location of all of their alerts and noted them on their maps. The developing pattern over the two-and-a-half days eventually led to the victim.

Our experience had generally been one of a single dog alerting and following through to the victim. All five dogs failed to do this on more than five occasions. We believe a careful study of weather conditions, terrain, and the careful noting of each alert are valuable SAR dog techniques. In this case, following up on previous alerts certainly paid off. After 84 hours, the victim was found alive and survived the ordeal.

Murder
Cadaver Search

Vi Hummel Carr
  Mission Location: North-Central Texas
  Mission Dates: February 11, 1996 to November 13, 1996

In keeping with the context of this book, no other search teams and individuals, other than Sheriff Carey Pettus and Chief Deputy Gary Barnett, are mentioned by name. The account of this case is printed with the full permission of the Young County Sheriff's Department.

Mission Type

This is a long search with some baffling circumstances. It was a multi-jurisdictional search and included law enforcement agencies from: Young County, Palo Pinto County, Stephens County, Erath County, and Eastland County. It also included: The Texas Rangers, Texas Parks and Wildlife Department, Brazos River Authority, Criminal Intelligence Service from the Texas Department of Public Safety, and the Texas Department of Public Safety dive team.

The search spanned ten months, during which there were more than 122 miles of roadside searches, including the search of rivers, creeks, ravines, buildings, vehicles, and hundreds of acres in five counties. In all, more than 140 profile areas were searched. Since I worked predominantly with the Young County Sheriff's Department and my callouts were from Sheriff Pettus, I wrote about this search from that perspective.

The Victim

A 27-year-old male who was a "quiet cowboy who loved animals." He was 6'4", 300 pounds, in good physical condition. "Hank" worked as a long-haul truck driver. He was reported missing January 20, 1996.

The Suspect

The primary suspect, was a 41-year-old female, who was in good physical condition. She was 5'6" and weighed 135 pounds. She was the five-year live-in girlfriend to the victim. She did ranch and yard work.

Point Last Seen

On January 16, 1996, when, uncharacteristically, Hank did not show up for work and could not be located, his employer notified the man's parents. On January 20, 1996, the parents filed a missing person report with the Young County Sheriff's Department.

That evening the Young County Sheriff's Department interviewed the Hank's live-in girlfriend. A Texas Ranger interviewed her again the next morning. A missing person report was circulated to other agencies. On January 21, 1996, in Palo Pinto, a bordering county, a curious landowner followed a set of tire tracks into a wooded, rural area near a popular lake. There he found the naked torso of a dismembered male (missing the head, hands, legs, and the buttocks). It was lying on a folded black trash bag amid a small amount of hay.

At this point Sheriff Pettus believed that the torso was that of the missing subject. But until DNA testing was completed this could not be verified. It took six weeks for the torso to be positively identified as the missing subject's. Hank was now a homicide victim.

The search now entailed not only looking for the missing body parts, but also for the victim's clothing, an unknown type of murder weapon, a dismembering tool, the crime scene (it was apparent that the victim was not dismembered at the location where the torso was found), the vehicle that had transported the body, black trash bags, and the rope that caused an abrasion across the chest of the victim.

The police tape blocks off the area where the torso was located, behind the trees.

Terrain Features

The area where the torso was found was flat with dead grass exceeding twelve inches in height, prickly pear cactus and scattered mesquite. However, the terrain in all of the search areas varied. Some areas were flat with low grass, hard-packed clay, and rocks. Others were steep bluffs or rolling hills. Then there were the rugged and heavily wooded areas and some with scattered or dense brush and high grass and weeds. The types of soil varied also. Some were a clay-type of soil referred to as "gumbo," because when it is wet, it becomes very sticky. In other places the earth was soft and still others had sandy loam. There was also soil called "caliche," which is sand or clay impregnated with crystalline salts, and can become harder than concrete.

When the rains came, the dry, hard-packed areas absorbed only a very small amount of water, causing severe run-off and sometimes flash flooding. Rivers, creeks, and culverts overflowed. Debris washed up and became tangled in strainers or embedded in thick underbrush. Because of this, the size of some search areas was expanded to include distances further down the streams. Almost every imaginable type of area was part of this search. We searched houses, cattle barns, fields, woods, trash pits, a variety of waterways, ravines, hilltops, roadsides, and many culverts.

This was typical of the terrain around the creeks and culverts.

Weather

At the time the family reported the victim missing, the temperatures had been in the 50s during the day and dropped into the 30s at night. Only .8 inches of snow fell in January. During the months of the search, which was not an everyday occurrence, the daytime temperatures ranged from the high 30s, through the 70s and into the 90s. The humidity factors varied from very dry to humid. The high humidity factors increased the heat index dramatically.

Special Dangers

During the spring and summer months of this search there were two extremely prevalent dangers. Poisonous snakes—including rattlesnakes, copperheads, and water moccasins—were one, fire ants were the other. Fire ants are extremely aggressive and will cling to your body and clothing, making them difficult to brush off. They range in size from 1/16" to 1/4" in length. Fire Ants have killed small animals and even newborn calves that got too close to their mounds. A single fire ant sting can cause shortness of breath, dizziness, or anaphylactic shock. Each person's level of sensitivity determines the severity of the reaction. However, in all cases there is local pain, swelling, itching, or pus-filled wounds that persist for several days or weeks. We also had to watch out for scorpions, Black Widows and other spiders, poison ivy, poison oak, and poison sumac.

Chiggers were not a danger but they were an annoyance. There wasn't any way to avoid chiggers, since they are almost invisible to the naked eye. The severe and prolonged itching caused by these blood-sucking mites told of their presence—after the fact. Body checks for ticks were another necessity for our dogs and us after each search.

Some other hazards to both dog and handler were barbed-wire fences, especially tangled masses of old, half-buried barbed-wire. Cactus, and painful grass burrs called "goat heads" posed another problem. Often throughout the day, the sharp grass burrs had to be pulled out from between the dog's pads. This sometimes left the handlers with bleeding pricked fingers despite protective gloves. The mesquite thorns, some as long as three inches, were also a hazard. In spite of the many things we had to be wary of to avoid becoming victims ourselves, they did not prohibit us or our dogs from doing our job.

Any Other Special Information

In an effort to provide a complete picture, to obtain additional information, and to confirm some aspects of this written account of the search, I met with Sheriff Pettus. I wanted a count of the number of search teams that participated, particularly on the two massive search days. I also wanted to review how the other teams worked their sectors and to see what problems they encountered. Sheriff Pettus stated that he did not receive search reports from any of the other volunteer search organizations.

The sheriff will not venture to estimate the number of teams that responded and any problems that occurred will go unmentioned. He can only say that there were "multiple teams" during the massive search operations. At this point in time, those reports are no longer necessary.

Search Personnel and Equipment and Search Strategy

Determining the POAs changed throughout this search, as did the boundaries. The search urgency factor, which also changed, ranged from moderate to very high over the first six months. After that our searches were usually done only on weekends.

The first search team was called out when the torso was found. An investigator with the Criminal Intelligence Services from the Department of Public Safety contacted a K-9 cadaver team he knew of from another part of the state. The team searched the area where the torso had been dumped but I was told that they did not find anything. Shortly after that, the Department of Public Safety dive team checked the lake for the remaining missing body parts. They also found nothing.

The first massive search was on February 11, 1996, in Young County. It was a cold and windy day. DNA tests for confirmation that the torso belonged to the missing man were not yet completed. However, the authorities had strong feelings regarding this case. Information from an informant determined the search locations. The locations were high probability areas where the suspect had unlimited access. This search effort involved four SAR organizations, a K-9 IC from one of the SAR organizations, and multiple search teams.

When working with other search organizations, a handler doesn't always know the level of training and education of the other organization's dogs and handlers. In this case I did know that the dog teams used were qualified for lost- and missing-person searches and had some cadaver training. But I didn't know to what degree. The handlers were well trained and certified in many areas of search and rescue. Highly trained, experienced canine search teams are very capable of finding a deceased person or body part in the active stages of decomposition. However, a cadaver team must be trained in many other necessary aspects of this specialty search. The complexity of this case involved searching for many things, including trace evidence as well as human remains. Due to the large and numerous speculative areas that needed to be searched, all available maintained mission-ready dogs were used.

The priority area designated was more than 100 acres. It was an expanse of woods, pastures (with and without cattle), and an old hay barn at the end of an uninhabited dirt road. A couple of dog handlers reviewed and sectored the areas to be searched. But before the K-9 IC fielded any dogs, the authorities changed the priority area. The new location was an additional approximately 50 acres and included a dilapidated, partially empty house, which belonged to the suspect's brother. It was just a couple of miles from the previous priority area.

The new area was re-sectored and assigned. Teams worked river bottoms, fields, pastures, and barns. Three cadaver dog teams were assigned to search the old house and the trash-littered yard surrounding it. My dog, Mercy, and I were one of the teams assigned to the house and yard. We began working a perimeter outside the house. Since some old houses have unusual places for rooms or storage areas, we checked the general configuration of the house. We also checked the foundation and looked for places not visible from the inside that led into or under the house.

While my dog and I were searching outside, the K-9 IC and a couple of the investigators gathered around a small stove to keep warm in the front room of the house. The rest of the law enforcement and search personnel waited outside. When Mercy and I entered the room, the heat from the stove enhanced the foul odors in the house. There was also a slight odor of bleach. Mercy alerted in one area of the old bedroom. One cadaver team said her dog had alerted in the kitchen, and the other cadaver team stated that her dog had alerted in a small room off of the bedroom. However, the investigators did not obtain blood or any other evidence from the three dogs' alerts. The yard searches were negative as well.

The authorities told us that a few of the other dog teams had hits in their sectors. A couple of the dog teams directed the investigators to a bloody area and a blood-covered hammer in the barn. The blood, however, turned out to be animal blood. A variety of syringes were found strewn about the barns but it was determined that the syringes were used for livestock. When the other teams finished their sectors, everyone drove back to the previous search location.

When we arrived at that previous location, the K-9 IC assigned me a sector with a wooded hillside with many long ravines. Most of these crevasses had little plant life on the sides, but quite a bit of dead brush at the bottoms. I was assigned two flankers from one of the other search organizations to assist me. They did a good job of mapping the sector and charting a couple of areas where Mercy showed interest. Mercy later re-checked those areas but had no secondary interest, so we eliminated them. We worked crosswind where it was feasible, but changed strategy at the ravines. We worked the rims of the crevasses first because we knew that if there was any scent in the crevasse, it would rise as the day warmed. When Mercy did not hit on anything, we inched our way down to check if anything was concealed in the dead branches and brush below. The flankers stayed on top doing a visual search of the sides, advising me if they saw anything out of the ordinary.

The authorities stated that a couple of the other dog teams hit on a few spots, but after further investigation those areas were eliminated. Our long day ended with nothing major to report.

The following week the Young County Sheriff's Department used a few volunteer search teams, but there is no record of who they were or what was done. During the rest of the month of February, Mercy and I and another certified cadaver team from one of the other SAR organizations (hereafter referred to as Cadaver Team One or Cadaver Dog One) were unavailable. While we were unavailable, several search efforts were made including another massive search using multiple search teams.

In March, Sheriff Pettus contacted the same K-9 IC we had worked with on our initial search of this case. The sheriff requested a scaled-down search. Cadaver Team One, and

Mercy and I were asked to respond. The main area we needed to search was a large amount of secluded acreage adjacent to The suspect's house that was on the hill above us. The suspect paced her yard the entire time we were searching. From her vantage point she could see a large portion of our search areas. Due to the brutality of this murder and the questionable stability of the suspect, the authorities weren't sure of what she might do. Several deputies, equipped with binoculars and telescopes, kept a watchful eye on the suspect while we searched. One of the deputies told us to "hit the ground" and not worry about our dogs if we heard gunfire. Because of the terrain and the amount of acreage, we segmented our search area using natural boundaries such as tree lines, dry creek beds, fences, etc. We searched the segmented areas using hasty grid techniques. The dogs showed slight interest in a few areas but gave no alerts. After flagging and rechecking those areas we eliminated them from consideration.

After we completed our areas, we searched small portions of two different lakes. Cadaver Team One worked the shorelines while Mercy and I worked by boat. We did not find anything.

The sheriff also requested that we follow him to the impound barn where they had The suspect's two-horse trailer. Sheriff Pettus told us that some of the trailer floorboards were covered with a substance that appeared to be washed down blood and tissue. He said they removed those boards in one half of the trailer, and had sent them to the crime laboratory. Our dogs did a detailed search. That is, they worked on-lead and we directed them as to what objects they should check in the barn. Both dogs alerted on parts of the trailer.

Mercy also jumped up on the table where the returned, wrapped boards were placed and gave a strong alert. We later learned that the lab had identified the sub-stance as human blood.

Vi rewarding Mercy after she alerted on the horse trailer. Mercy had alerted where the floorboards had been. There was residual scent on the frame.

At the conclusion of that search day, Sheriff Pettus said he preferred to work with only a couple of dog teams and asked for my phone number so he could contact me directly for future searches.

Four days later, as I was just about to leave my house early in the morning to attend a seminar for my place of employment, I received a call from Sheriff Pettus. The sheriff informed me that Palo Pinto County had issued an arrest warrant for the suspect and also a search warrant for her residence. He said the two agencies had arrested the suspect the night before and he needed me to respond immediately for the search of her house and property. I had to make the decision whether to attend a seminar my company had paid for or to go on a search that I was already involved in. Being the regional manager for the company's southwest office, the decision to even attend the seminar had been mine. It was not something required by the company. I weighed the matter and then made my decision: I'd cut back financially in other areas, reimburse the company for the money they had paid for the one-day seminar, and go on the search. I told Sheriff Pettus that I would contact Cadaver Team One to assist. Fortunately, she was also able to leave work. When we arrived at the residence, we were surprised at the number of law enforcement officers already present. Several crime scene investigators were on the scene scraping various small areas of the floor. They had already removed and placed a couple of cabinet doors from the master bedroom outside to be taken to the laboratory. They had also piled clothes from the closets on the bed.

Sheriff Pettus knew that it was best for the dogs to work first with as little distractions and outside contamination as possible. He told this to his investigators and said he had advised the other department, but apparently there had been some miscommunication. Since the master bedroom of the small house was congested with personnel, we asked them to wait outside while the dogs searched.

Sheriff Pettus and Chief Deputy Barnett told us that the condition of the house appeared to be about the same as when the suspect allowed the Department of Public Safety's crime scene team to search it. That was just after the victim had been reported missing. The crime scene team found that the suspect had taken up all the carpeting in the house and burned it. She had also bleached the floors. The bleached floors gave the crime scene team a false positive reaction when they used luminol for blood detection. Luminol testing is a chemiluminescent presumptive test for the presence of blood. This test can be used to scan large areas. When luminol is sprayed on surfaces in a dark room, blood stains become luminous. However, the bleach that The suspect used to wash the floors caused all the floors to glow. The suspect had also ripped out the closet in her older son's bedroom and had burned it in the field next to her house.

When we entered the house, we saw a dirty mattress on the living room floor that appeared to be the boy's bed. Trash, clothing, clutter, and other filth littered the furniture and wooden floors. Old food and dirty dishes lay decaying in the kitchen.

The master bedroom was the main focus of our attention, so that is where we started. I ran Mercy first while Cadaver Team One waited outside. Mercy worked the furniture-crowded room and checked the clothes-laden waterbed. She showed interest at the foot of the bed, by the closet openings, and worked her way to the small center hallway and then on to the boy's room. The teenage boy's bedroom was devoid of the closet and any furniture. Just a couple of wooden boards lay on the floor among animal feces. The back door that led from the bedroom to the outside had no steps. It was a three-foot drop to the ground. Mercy continued to work in trail fashion to the back door. At that point she became very intense and indicated that she had found something. When I got down to examine the area, I saw a brown drop on the woodwork and a very small, slight brownish smudge on the weather stripping.

The investigator who was with me immediately removed the weather stripping and scraped the paint off the woodwork to send to the laboratory. Mercy and I continued to search the rest of the house. The bedroom that the suspect's seven- and nine-year-old sons shared was as vile as the other rooms. Mercy had no more alerts nor did she show interest in any other areas. When we were finished searching the house, we went outside to allow Cadaver Team One to search the house again. Cadaver Dog One's handler said his actions intensified in the area of the master bedroom and he showed great interest by the closet openings. Cadaver Team One ended their search of the interior when the investigators re-entered the house.

We continued to search the grounds of the suspect's house and both dogs showed interest in several areas. One area in particular was right by the only outside water faucet. The interest by the faucet led the investigators to believe that that was the place the trailer was hosed out. We divided the areas closest to the house into different sectors and each dog worked a separate sector. When we completed our sector, we would switch areas to see if the other dog would confirm any alerts or possibly find something new. We did not discuss any areas of interest or alerts in the sector we just searched. This eliminated any chance of us inadvertently cueing our dogs in that same location, giving a false confirmation. However, if the dog's alert produced a visible piece of evidence, we would call the investigators to that location immediately. In the fields or wooded areas around the house we worked the dogs simultaneously in a grid pattern.

The suspect's sheep pen appeared to be a good place to hide evidence, but a large guard dog that had puppies with her protected it. After awhile, The suspect's teenage son arrived at the house. We felt a mixture of suspicion and sympathy. We requested that he remove the dog and secure her in a way that she could not get loose. I felt that the sheep would stay away from a strange dog so I didn't worry about interference from them. I was wrong. The sheep not only kept surrounding Mercy but nudged her. One actually jumped on her several times. Needless to say, this did not do much for our concentration. We passed by the sleeping puppies and attempted to search the rest of the pen area. Mercy had no interest or alerts in the pen.

Searching the sheep pen with the sheep present was less than desirable, but there was no place to turn the sheep out and we had to work in spite of the sheep because of time constraints. The search warrant was good only for that day. Once we left the property the sheriff's department would need a new warrant to return and there was no guarantee that a new warrant would be issued.

After we completed our search of the suspect's property, the sheriff asked us to search another area and three cisterns located a few miles away. Our last search location for the day was a section of the Brazos River. Mercy and I worked out of a boat operated by the game warden. Cadaver Team One searched from the shoreline. At nearly the midpoint beneath a bridge, Mercy showed a lot of interest. We continued our grid pattern and then approached that area again from the other direction. This time Mercy gave a hard alert. At the same time Cadaver Dog One's handler said he was showing interest from the shore in the same area. We requested that the dive team search that location. However, the dive team was not available and would not be for almost one month.

One week later the sheriff's department received another tip from a confidential source: "Check culverts, creeks, and bridges from the suspect's residence all the way to counties to the south." The authorities believed, as they had all along, that the victim's body parts, weapons, clothing, etc., had been scattered in several areas. At one point we were faced with searching vast areas in possibly seven counties.

Shortly after receiving the tip, Chief Deputy Gary Barnett, another deputy, Mercy, and I were the only ones who went out to search. Cadaver Team One was not available. Our

Sheriff Carey Pettus, Vi, and Mercy at the Brazos River location where the dogs alerted.
All of us still believe that there is something here and in the creek that went unfound.

bridge and culvert searches began with Chief Deputy Barnett designating a specific road from all those where The suspect was seen. That road, or portion thereof, was our search area for the day. We had to ensure that we located and checked all the culverts, creeks, and bridges. We did this by setting the vehicle's trip meter to zero at the start of each new road. We then noted the mileage of the locations checked, along with the results for those areas. For the small areas, we just pulled off and parked on the shoulder of the road since the search wouldn't take much time. While searching, we checked any black trash bags that we found or any probable areas where we felt that a horse trailer could be pulled off of the road safely. At times we felt overwhelmed by the number of culverts and probable areas. Many culverts were only one-tenth of a mile apart. Mercy had no alerts or interest in any of the areas we searched during the first hour.

When we came to a bridge above a wide creek, we parked further off the road for safety reasons. This large, brushy area was going to take much longer to search than the smaller culverts. We worked our way down the steep embankment and began searching east into the wind. I did this to allow Mercy the best opportunity to hit any scent in the area ahead of us on our side of the creek. Due to the creek and the rough terrain we could not work crosswind.

We worked our way east for several hundred yards and noticed some animal bones along the way, but Mercy showed no interest in the area and had no alerts. We came to a section of the creek that was shallow enough to cross, so worked the other side of the creek. This time the wind was at our backs. We searched the rugged banks all the way back to the bridge. We found nothing. We took a short break after making our way up a large concrete retaining wall on the far side of the creek. Our next step was to search the creek area on the west side. We started to cross over the bridge, which was about twenty feet above the water. Mercy began dipping her nose by the drainage holes on the west side of the bridge. On our search back toward the bridge, the scent was ahead of us and being carried further west by the wind. This time we searched directly under the bridge and to the west. We searched the small portions of the shoreline that were accessible and searched high under the girders of the bridge. Mercy kept alerting toward the water away from the steep embankment and dense thorn-covered vines. We decided to do an intense visual check from the bridge to see if we could spot anything. Despite the circumstances and though it had been more than two months since the family reported the victim missing, we were still hopeful. Most all of the objects we were searching for could have been carried away, washed away, blown elsewhere, buried by animals, or devoured by the turtles or fish.

While doing a visual search, we spotted a weathered black trash bag caught in a treetop several yards from the side of the bridge. The bag was in the area where Mercy had alerted. We found a second bag in a tree close to the creek on the other side of the bridge. Both bags were not retrievable but were visibly empty. So we searched the area carefully but did not find anything on the shore to account for the contents of those bags.

There was nothing more we could do at this location. The dive team was still not available. We felt frustrated about not being able to get the resources we needed. We not only wanted to complete our search of this area but we knew human remains would not last very long with the many large turtles and fish in the creek. However, we still had a lot of evidence to look for and many more areas to search. So we moved to another route where the suspect had been seen and we worked several more hours that day.

Finally we got some good news. The results came back regarding the brown spots Mercy had found in the suspect's house. The spots were human blood and the DNA matched the victim's.

The next day the sheriff's department again requested Mercy and me. This time we were out with the chief investigator from Palo Pinto County. We started a different route and ended up at the bridge where Mercy had alerted the day before. At first I was undecided about working Mercy in the same area so soon. I did not want her to think that I expected her to alert again at the same spot. But since we had searched 22 other bridges, creeks, and culverts after working this bridge I felt that it would be okay. The wind was from the north-northwest and I wanted to see if and where she would alert. Her reaction was basically the same as the day before. The location of her alert was slightly different from that of the previous day but this was due to the shift in the wind. When she worked under the bridge she returned to the same spot and gave another alert. After we finished there, we continued on to more creeks, culverts, and bridges.

Several days later we searched again. This time Cadaver Team One was able to respond. The POAs was now subjective and were designated by the sheriff who used the process of elimination. Sheriff Pettus asked Cadaver Team One and Mercy and me to search an old cemetery in the northern section of the county. While searching the cemetery, the sheriff radioed us from his location about nine miles away. They had found a human head. We relocated to a high bridge where Sheriff Pettus waited. We saw Chief Deputy Barnett examining a black trash bag about 45 feet down and 200 feet east of the bridge. The bag was slightly submerged in the shallow waters of a creek that fed into the Brazos River.

Sheriff Pettus told us that he and his deputies had driven over that bridge several times. He said that he had a feeling about that route and as he passed over the bridge that day, the trash bag caught his eye. The sheriff sent Chief Deputy Barnett who was riding with him, down to investigate. As we waited for the crime scene investigators, the dogs hit the scent and got very agitated. Mercy, who does not do a bark alert, kept looking at me and barking. She was insistent on going down to the source of the scent. I praised her but did not reward her. The crime scene investigators arrived within minutes. With our dogs by our sides, we waited as patiently as we could on the ridge above as the crime scene team photographed and examined the head. When the investigators brought the bag up to our location, visual evaluation of the badly decomposed head indicated that it belonged to the victim.

Cadaver Team One, several deputies, and Mercy and I climbed down the hillside. We were all hoping that we would find more in the surrounding area. First we let our dogs work downward into the location where the head had been. This would give them more motivation and let them know that we needed more than that area searched.

Above: Looking down from the bridge at the area where the head was found. The Brazos River is at the top of the picture.

Below: The other side of the bridge, which we also had to search. Because this creek circled around, we had to search the whole thing.

The rough banks and sheer drop-offs by the creek were difficult to cover. The dogs worked down the silt-bottomed creek bed as far as they could. Next they climbed the high banks, with each dog working a different side of the creek. At a point above the creek, where the water fed into the Brazos River, Mercy gave a subtle alert. Cadaver Team One was working the opposite bank and called out that her dog was alerting in the same area. The game warden was contacted and asked to bring a boat so that we could search that part of the Brazos River. When the boat arrived, it had to be lowered about thirty feet by ropes over a barbed-wire fence, through brush and around trees to get to the water.

While Mercy and I worked from the boat, Cadaver Team One continued to search the narrow shoreline. Mercy gave some hard alerts. She leaned over the narrow edge of the boat and pawed at the water. At first we thought she had made

another find. Further checking led us to believe that both dogs had hit on residual scent that was flowing from the location where the head was found about thirty yards up the creek. To be sure about this we needed the dive team to check the area.

Two weeks later the dive team arrived. We went to the first water location where the dogs had an alert. However, before the dive team went into the muddy water we wanted to confirm the location of the dogs' prior alerts. The flowing water could have moved the object a long way downstream. It had been one month since the busy dive team was requested. Again we worked the dogs by boat and at the shoreline. Again the dogs alerted. The location was within a few yards of their first alerts. The dive team searched but did not find anything in the area except a deep hole with many fish.

The next morning we resumed the search in the area where the head had been found. We were fortunate that Cadaver Team One was able to come again. Later that day another very good team, Cadaver Team Two would be available as well (both teams belong to the same SAR organization.) As the dive team searched the Brazos River, Cadaver Team One and Mercy and I worked other areas of the rugged banks simultaneously. We also had to search the creek area upstream on the opposite side of the bridge, since we were not sure if the head had been washed downstream to where it was found. We searched wherever the steep terrain and thick vegetation allowed us access. It was possible that body parts had been dragged some distance away by predators. Cadaver Team One said her dog did not give any alerts. Mercy had no alerts either and the dive team found nothing. Although nothing further was found we felt we had at least eliminated another area.

Later that day Cadaver Team Two met us at a designated location. The game warden led our convoy of cadaver teams and the dive team to the bridge where Mercy had alerted. I assigned Cadaver Team Two to work her dog first while I flanked for her. As is our practice, I did not say, nor did Cadaver Team Two want to know, what Mercy's actions had been in that area. The handler was surprised when I asked her to start her dog on the bridge rather than under it by the creek. Cadaver Dog Two confirmed Mercy's alert by his intense interest in the same spot on the bridge and his determination to get under it. When we hiked down under the bridge, the dog continued to alert in the same spot Mercy had. The dog became so excited that he leaped off the nearly vertical bank and into the water. In order to get him out of the water, his handler laid on her stomach part way over the edge of the bank. While I secured her, she hung her dog's lead down into the water. She had taught her dog to grab his lead in his mouth and hold on. When he did, we pulled him out of the water and back onto the bank. After shaking himself off, he remained so insistent about the location to the point that he tried to stop his handler from leaving the area. Cadaver Team One worked next and said her dog also gave an alert in the same area. I did not work Mercy at that location that day.

We advised the dive team of the exact location where all three dogs had alerted but we requested that they search the surrounding areas as well. The only way they could get their dive equipment down to the water was to lower it, by ropes, over the rail of the bridge. We waited with great anticipation as the dive team searched the murky creek. The water searches were done strictly by feel since it was impossible for the divers to see anything in the murky water. We were confident that the divers would find something since the dogs had such strong alerts. The dive team said they found rocks, one beer can, and masses of twisted roots that protruded from the eroded banks under the water, but nothing else.

We were incredulous that the divers found only one beer can and no other trash. We wondered what had been in those trash bags since there was nothing on shore to account for their contents. Although we were disappointed, we still believed our dogs. However, we ended our search for that day.

In preparing to plan our next search routes, I felt that we needed one large, highly detailed map that included all the different counties that were within our search boundaries. No such map existed. So using smaller maps I reduced and enlarged, cut and pasted a 4'x5' map showing all of the roads in five counties. I made two such maps, one for the sheriff and one for myself. I color coded where the massive searches had taken place, where Mercy, Cadaver Dog One and Two worked, and where the dogs' areas of interest were located. In addition, I highlighted and labeled the suspect's house, where the torso was found, and where the head was found. This gave us a much clearer depiction of the routes The suspect could have taken from her house to get to the location where she had discarded the torso. This also gave us a complete view of many other probable areas based on where the suspect had been seen at the time of the victim's disappearance.

Sheriff Pettus and Chief Deputy Barnett designated additional roads and areas to be searched. Then, new information from a variety of sources, came in that expanded our search boundaries. In spite of the highly speculative locations, the remote possibilities and the extensive amount of time already spent on this search, I was compelled to continue each time I was asked. The victim's family needed us to finish the search. The Young County and Palo County Sheriff's Departments were exhaustive in their investigations but did not have a vast amount of resources. Also, the local citizens were frightened because things like this just didn't happen in their community. In addition, the sheriff's departments received telephone calls every day from the media, asking if there were any new developments in the case. Fortunately, all through this search Mercy and I were able to avoid the media and remain nameless. That is exactly how we wanted it to be. The only people who had to know who we were and what we were doing were the law enforcement agencies.

During the next few weeks the temperature and humidity rose. We would start early in the morning but due to the heat we had to work shorter periods and give our dogs more frequent and longer breaks. This shortened our search time each day. Several times as we drove back to the sheriff's department, we would note the location of probable areas we passed. Our next search effort would usually resume with those areas. Occasionally Sheriff Pettus or Chief Deputy Barnett would determine that there was a different area of higher probability than the ones that we'd noted. In those cases the noted areas were added to a list labeled "Areas to be Searched." I kept this list updated with the date the area was finally searched, who searched it, and the status of that location.

On May 30, 1996, a deputy driving down a road several miles outside our determined search boundaries found a part of a human leg in a small dried creek. The remains of a black trash bag were near by. The portion of the leg was from the knee down and included the foot. The leg was both badly decomposed and mummified. It belonged to the victim.

The location of that discovery meant that we had to add yet another county to our total search area. Information from this newly added county entailed checking on "smells" that residents had noticed months earlier but had not reported. Not until the leg was found did the residents report this information. They now thought the smells might have been the odor of human remains. We searched those areas with deputies from that jurisdiction

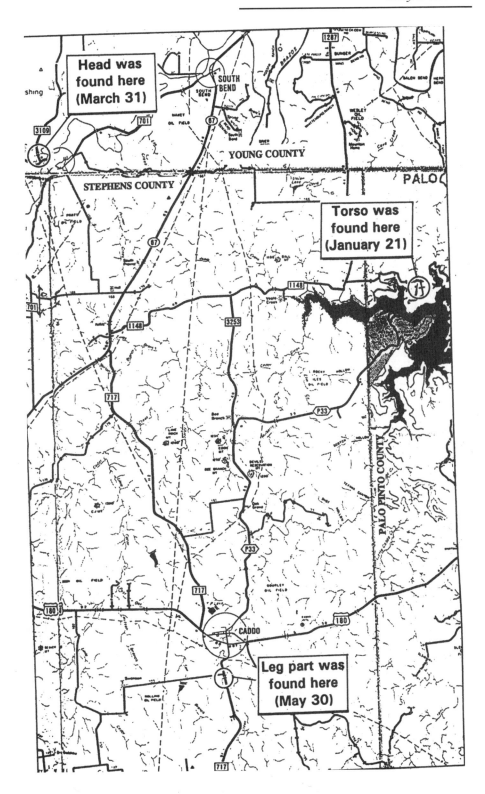

Head was found here (March 31)

Torso was found here (January 21)

Leg part was found here (May 30)

besides other places the suspect had frequented. We also searched more creeks and culverts in our expanded search area.

The suspect, who was indicted on capital murder charges, remained in the Palo Pinto Jail as the search stretched further south. The POA changed again but nothing more was found based on the new information. The dogs showed no interest and gave no alerts in the new area. Once, sometimes twice, during a search day when we did not find anything we ran motivational problems for the dogs. We wanted to keep them encouraged and at the same time ensure that they were still working well and hadn't "shut down." Speculative areas, especially when there are so many, are frustrating for both dog and handler.

We curtailed searching during the hottest parts of July and August. At the end of August, a plea bargain allowed the suspect to plead guilty to the lesser offense of felony murder. The judge sentenced her to life in prison and she must serve a minimum of 30 years before she will be eligible for parole. A condition of her plea bargain was that she would show the authorities where she disposed of the rest of the victim.

A short time later Sheriff Pettus drove the confessed killer down different routes through many isolated areas. They were routes she thought she had taken when discarding the victim's remains. Stops were made at creeks and culverts along the way but she claimed that she really couldn't remember where she had scattered the parts of the victim. She said that she had been drinking, took some pills and then drove around for 12 hours with the dismembered body in the horse trailer. She described how she would stop along a road, go back to the trailer and toss a piece out. She stated that the body parts were all bagged separately with the legs cut into two pieces. That meant that there were still five bags somewhere. When the sheriff asked her about one creek in particular, she looked over the side of the bridge at the rocks below, then calmly told the sheriff that she would never have thrown any part down there because she "didn't want to bruise him." After she had discarded all the parts, she just drove around with the torso in the horse trailer. This accounts for all the places and roads that she was seen driving on. She did not dispose of the torso until the next morning. She said that she forgot it was there.

Things calmed down and the case was closed. However, Sheriff Pettus felt that he wanted the victim's family to have more to bury than what they had. Searching continued but was sporadic. Everyone was trying to catch up on other long-overdue projects that had taken a back seat to this case.

Suspension

November 13, 1996, ten months after the victim's murder, the final effort was made to find any remaining parts of the body. Everyone needed to put an end to this case. The sheriff requested only Mercy and I to search a couple of creek areas that in the months past, had been subjected to drought and floods; strong winds, erosion, and evidence of high animal activity. Nothing was found.

Results of the Mission

Fortunately we did not have to go to trial but we knew that there would be a conviction based on all of the evidence obtained. During this search we were also able to eliminate many areas of concern to residents. This calmed the nerves of several landowners who felt that portions of the victim's body could be on their property.

The authorities later told me that the victim's body had been removed exactly how Mercy had worked and alerted in the house. The victim, who died in bed, had been given an extreme dose of morphine pills by the murderer, to supposedly relieve his headache. Once he was dead, the murderer tied a rope around his chest, ran it through the house, out of the front door and tied it to a pickup truck. By driving forward she dragged the corpse off the bed and into the center hallway. At that point, the murderer untied the rope and drove the pickup truck to the back of the house. She changed the position of the rope by feeding it from the hallway through the older boy's bedroom and out the back door. Next, she pulled the rope into the horse trailer, which she had already backed up to the stair-less doorway. Once in the trailer, she put the rope through one of the small feed doors at the trailer's front end and again tied it to the pickup truck. By once more driving forward, the murderer was able to pull the victim's body through the rest of the house and into the horse trailer where she dismembered it. It appeared that a trail of leaking body fluids created a problem in the house so she destroyed the carpet. The authorities believe this murder was committed for a $150,000 life insurance policy. The murderer, however, will not give a reason other than she "wanted him gone."

What are Your Feelings About the Mission?

Although I am pleased with the way Mercy worked, I feel a sadness that more of the victim's remains were not found for the benefit of his family. Because of the magnitude and complexity of this case, it was featured on HBO's "Autopsy IV" in 1998. Although this was a long and difficult search, it was a positive experience working with the cadaver dog teams from the other group. We worked well together and shared knowledge, experience, ideas, and strategies.

Additional Comments

My employer, who lives and has offices in the Pacific Northwest, was completely aware of the amount of time I spent searching. He knew that I would take care of my obligations at the office and I would never do anything to destroy that trust. So, I worked long, hard hours, often into the night and on weekends to make up for any time I took off. I also used up all of my vacation time. But, we all set priorities in life, how we're going to spend our time and money. I have set mine. With each search I try to bring some good into a terrible situation and, in some small way, to be a reflection of the Lord's love.

Search Tips

Trust your dog but be honest about your dog's capabilities. Do not lead the authorities to believe that you have a "wonder dog" if you really don't. There are many different K-9 specialty areas in search and rescue. Don't think because a dog can do one type of search that he can automatically do them all. Each type of search work requires specific and comprehensive training for both you and your dog. If a dog knows the smell of human decomposition, it does not mean it is a cadaver dog. It takes consistent training, studying and evaluation for both the dog and the handler to make a credible team. Information supplied by the dog teams may play an important role in the successful conclusion of a case. The potential that you will have to testify in court increases dramatically in cadaver work. If a dog team has to testify, the handler will have to provide documentation of all dog training and maintenance records to prove the team was working within their capabilities. Some people think that because the subject is deceased, it is not going to hurt to field unqualified dogs or dogs that have not been maintained. In reality homicide investigations can cost a phenomenal amount of time and money, not to mention the prolonged anguish for the families involved and the emotional strain on the authorities. Remember the quality should go in before the name goes on.

You are going to search many more areas where nothing is located than ones where you make a find. Do not be so eager to make a find that you cry "alert" because you think your dog should have done something or because you heard that another dog alerted in the area. You must be willing to say if your dog had no alerts or areas of interest in your sector. In cadaver work a false alert can be worse than no alert. Alerting on human waste can be construed as a false alert. This is not a true "false" alert but it is also not what you were searching for.

Know the honest qualifications of the person instructing you on how to train your dog. Research several sources on what you have been told and use common sense. Also go to as many hands-on, quality training seminars, outside your team, as possible so you don't get tunnel vision.

Try to learn at least one thing each training session and search mission. Do not go out there and run a problem then complete your training log or search report and consider that the end. Go over your log immediately while everything is fresh in your mind. Look at wind direction, terrain, obstacles, etc., and the areas of interest your dog had. Sometimes you may never figure out why your dog did something, but you can also learn a lot about your dog and yourself so you can constantly improve as a team.

Let your dog work. Don't try to second-guess where you think the dog should go. If we could see scent, we wouldn't need our dogs. But remember, there is no such thing as a perfect dog and most certainly no such thing as a perfect handler.

Biography

Vi Hummel Carr has been involved in SAR for more than seven years and is affiliated with two different sheriffs' departments. As a K-9 unit, she and Mercy were operational in Airscent and Trailing before deciding to specialize in Cadaver Search. Vi and Mercy have received training from top nationally and internationally known experts in SAR. They received their national certifications in both Basic and Advanced Cadaver Search through K-9 Specialty Search Associates and have been credited with many finds on some difficult cases. Vi holds certifications in many other areas of SAR. She is also trained in Advanced Peer Support Counseling through the International Critical Incident Stress Management Foundation. Vi is the founder of Southwest Specialty Search and Rescue and is a long-time member of NASAR. She is a life member of the Homicide Investigators of Texas, a member of Dogs Against Drugs/Dogs Against Crime. Vi and Mercy were the first canine cadaver team—nationwide—to be appointed to the Federal Disaster Mortuary Operational Response Team (DMORT) and also the first canine cadaver team appointed to the Texas State DMORT Team.

THE SEARCHER

Carey Pettus, Young County Sheriff

Who are You?
Carey Pettus, Young County Sheriff

The Callout
I was home Saturday night when I received a phone call from my deputies. They explained that the subject was missing and there was blood on the front porch of his residence. (The blood later turned out to be pig's blood). They also said that during their interview, Hank's live-in girlfriend was casual about his disappearance and was somewhat uncooperative. The next morning I met with Chief Deputy Barnett and instructed him to call a Texas Ranger for assistance. Barnett and the ranger went back to the girlfriend's residence, interviewed her and inspected the premises again. Hank's description was also put out on the law enforcement Teletype as a missing person.

Sunday afternoon I was playing golf when my department notified me of the discovery of a male torso in a bordering county, which might be our missing person. I immediately left the golf course. The evidence at the scene indicated that someone had killed and dismembered the man elsewhere.

The next day I compared crime scene photos of the torso with a portrait of the missing subject and formed my own opinion that this was our missing person. It took six weeks to verify his identity by DNA testing.

The Search Sector
The investigation began by interviewing family, friends, and associates. We coupled the investigation with reports of a suspicious vehicle around the river bottoms near where the victim and his girlfriend lived. This led us to believe that the body parts might have been disposed of in the river bottoms or alternately on property owned by the girlfriend's brother, which was within several miles of her residence. Based on this information, the girlfriend was now our primary suspect.

The search began by using search dogs to clear nearby river bottoms and the property owned by the suspect's brother. This search started as a process of elimination and was equivalent to looking for the needle in the haystack.

We assigned the dog teams to search several miles of the Brazos River bottoms. We also assigned them to search about fifty acres belonging to the suspect's brother. The fifty acres included an old house and cattle pens. The brother also raised hogs and had hog heads in an old freezer in the house. The remains of dead livestock were located several hundred yards from the house. These areas were searched with many hits by several of the dogs in use. However, no human remains were found. After leaving these places we still were not sure how reliable the dogs were. We were only sure that we had not found anything. If the hits were valid, we could only theorize that someone had walked through the areas with blood on their feet.

Problems Encountered

After becoming reasonably sure that the torso belonged to Hank—although at the time we had to wait for DNA evidence to be certain—and that his girlfriend had killed him in or around their residence, we devised a search plan. We decided that the best search technique was to search along the most probable route she would have taken to dump the torso. There were several routes to consider. We started with the most direct route by walking the bar ditches and using dogs at all creek crossings. Bar ditches are long, grassy drainage ditches that run parallel to the roads and intersect with culverts. The dogs were used primarily on weekends when the handlers were available.

Weeks later we received information from a confidential source. This source indicated that we should concentrate our search efforts in a southerly direction toward another city and check all culverts and bridges. We began this task using the dogs and jail "trusties." During this period a local man who claimed to be psychic began telling us of feelings he had regarding this case. He had feelings about how the murder was done and where to look for body parts. Some information was of such a nature that we felt that we could not ignore him. We added locations to the search that he felt were worthwhile.

I had worked with some Police K-9s but this was my first experience using volunteer search dog teams. I assumed that all the dog teams that responded were capable of conducting a search of this nature and that the dogs were more scent discriminating. As we began using the dog teams on a regular basis, we came to trust some teams more than others. Many times the dogs would hit on an area where there was no reasonable explanation for the hit. At other times the dogs would hit on suspect areas, which led to expanded foot searches. We came to a point where we relied on only two teams. This was because we had confidence in their dogs, the handlers' knowledge, and their professionalism. These two teams were dependable and would stay on searches for as long as needed. Even though their dogs had a couple of false hits or at times stopped working after several hours, the dog handlers retained our confidence by the interpretations they made of their dog's actions. We eventually assigned law officers and dog teams together to search specific areas.

At this point in time the search areas were determined several ways: on assumptions of the possible routes taken by the suspect, available physical evidence and instinct. The psychic influenced some of our decisions. The psychic presented information that indicated that missing body parts would be associated with water. This information corresponded to information that we had previously received from confidential sources so we began seriously considering what the psychic had told us.

Vi Carr's dog had a strong hit on a creek crossing in another county. Conditions around this creek and the depth of the water made it impossible to accurately determine if in fact part of the body was in this water. Applying Mercy's alert and the psychic's information to the probable route that the suspect had taken led me to the area where the victim's head was found in a creek bed.

We called the two dog teams to this creek when the head was found. They spent several hours searching the woods around the creek. We dragged this area and later Department of Public Safety divers searched the area again with no results. After this search, we felt reasonably certain that if any other body parts had been disposed of there, they would most likely have washed into the tributary of the Brazos River. The discovery of the head led us to concentrate our efforts further south. We conducted numerous searches again of all creek crossings but nothing was found.

On May 30, 1996, a Young County deputy found the lower portion of a human leg in a creek crossing. Deputies from a different county had previously searched this crossing, which was outside our initial boundaries.

Ultimately, the suspect pled guilty to murder in August of 1996. She agreed to show me areas where she might have thrown the missing body parts. One of the dog teams searched these areas but no other remains were found. The search was terminated based on the wishes of the victim's family.

What are Your Feelings About the Mission?

Cadaver search dogs are valuable assets. However, there must be a working relationship between the dog handlers and the investigators. Investigators must remain persistent in their investigative knowledge, but they must also have confidence in the qualifications and capabilities of the dog team and know what limitations there are. They must be able to trust the handlers' interpretations of their dog's actions without dismissing other theories. In this case, Mercy found blood in the victim's house under a door sill that two crime scene search teams had previously missed. This evidence was crucial to the successful conclusion of this case.

I believe the number of dogs should be limited in any search effort and at least two dogs run separately on any suspect areas. A dog's false hits can lead to wasted searches and wasted manpower. Keep in mind that dogs cannot talk to humans; if they could, there'd be less false alerts. And sometimes dogs can be confused by the smells they register but can't tell their human counterpart that they're confused, only that they've registered something. This means that the handler must know their dog as well as possible to help avoid false hits. If the use of dogs is kept in perspective and recognized as an investigative tool, they can be a very valuable resource.

Dog handlers should prepare written reports documenting areas they have searched. Grid searches should be used and included in the written reports. Any evidence found by the dogs should be collected and documented in reserve as any other evidence.

Search Tips

From a case manager's perspective about the use of dogs:

The case manager should pair the dog handler with an investigator.

The team should be assigned to a given area, which is to be searched systematically.

The dog handler should prepare a complete written report.

The dog handler should be briefed about the circumstances of the case.

The dog handler must keep all case information confidential.

The dog handler should make it clear what the dog's capabilities are and are not.

If the dog is having a bad day or does not want to work, the handler should so inform the investigator and terminate any further search efforts that day.

Maintain an open relationship with the handler. The handler should not hesitate to communicate with the investigator regarding his or her instincts, hunches, or anything else that might have to do with the case.

Before the search begins, the handler should discuss false hits with the case manager.

The dog handler should always remember that not only is the dog looking for something, the case manager is also using the dog as an elimination tool to help narrow searches. Keeping this in mind will make the handler feel useful and a part of the team and also avoid feeling discouraged if they don't find anything.

Biography

Sheriff Carey Pettus holds a Bachelor of Science degree in criminal justice. He has 26 years of police experience and has earned a Master Peace Officer's Certification. Sheriff Pettus has an extensive background in investigation. He served in police departments in two major cities in Texas before returning to Young County. Sheriff Pettus has worked as a police patrolman, a detective, a criminal investigation division supervisor, and a division commander. He has also served in administrative, technical, and field operations. Sheriff Pettus has been the sheriff of Young County for eight years.

Plane Crash

Deputy Sheriff Roger Kendle
Alameda County Sheriff's Search and Rescue
Office of Emergency Services
Mission Location: Wauhab Ridge, California
Mission Date: December 22, 1995

Mission Type

The actual search time was very short, just over three hours. Several factors contributed to this:

- The general area of the search was narrowed significantly because of the activation of an Emergency Locator Transmitter (ELT) upon impact of the aircraft.
- The use of satellite location of the ELT gave the general vicinity of the crash site.
- The use of Direction Finding equipment by our ground teams and the Civil Air Patrol team narrowed the area even more. Triangulating the signal provided an accurate location.
- Though the previous night's weather had been severe, it broke for several hours, just long enough for air resources to find the crash site.
- However, most important, the area where the crash had occurred was familiar to many members of our team. We had trained in the area and had responded to other crashes that had occurred in the same general geographic area. Additionally, we had previously worked with the local Watershed Rangers and called upon them immediately to help us get to the crash site.

The Victims

Both victims were in their mid to late 20s, in excellent health and physical condition. Both were not only experienced pilots who were very familiar with the area, but close friends. The lead pilot had a reputation for being an excellent trainer and evaluator who would give a fair but accurate evaluation of flying techniques. Both had landed at various Bay Area airports literally hundreds of times. The aircraft they were flying was a twin engine Piper Chieftain. It was owned and operated by a company that hauled freight from smaller air terminals to the major carriers at the Oakland International Airport.

The training flight departed from the Oakland International Airport about 2300, Friday, December 22, 1995, and was to last several hours. It included several practice landings at the Oakland International Airport. During the flight, weather conditions worsened and Oakland Air Traffic Controllers diverted them to another smaller airport about 15 miles south of the Oakland International Airport.

Point Last Seen

Why did the incident take place?

Sometime during the flight, the aircraft was vectored to an area some 25–30 miles south of the Hayward Municipal Airport. Once there they were to begin a controlled approach to the airport. Due to the increasingly bad weather conditions and the large number of aircraft in the area, the flight was not contacted again. Sometime shortly after 0130, the aircraft disappeared from the radar screen.

The area where the plane disappeared is very rural, mountainous terrain. Cattle sparsely populate the area ranches and access is limited to unpaved dirt roads. Weather conditions were very heavy rain and wind during the night, some partial clearing in the early morning hours, then increasing fog and rain during the day. The location of the crash was nearly 15 miles from the nearest paved road. Several days of heavy rain had made them extremely muddy and in some areas virtually impassable. Roads closer to the crash site were very narrow with drop-offs on both sides.

Scenes from the wreckage, December 23, 1995.

Copyright 1997, Maptech, Inc.

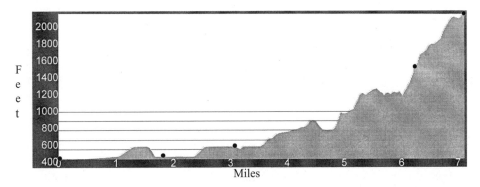

Total distance: 7 miles, 547 feet   *Climbing: 2,196 feet*   *Latitude: 090° 00' 00.0" N*
Ground distance: 7 miles, 793 feet   *Descending: -475 feet*   *Longitude: 180° 00' 00.0"W*
Elevation change: 1,721 feet   *Min/Max: 441/2,167*

Any Other Special Information

Sometime after 0700, the weather conditions allowed two helicopters, one from the Coast Guard, the other from East Bay Regional Parks Police to lift off and help with the search. Both aircraft informed us that they were receiving strong ELT signals in the area southeast of Mount Rose. However, weather conditions were deteriorating and they would have to end their search patterns if it got worse. About 0900 they informed us that the crash site had been found and the Coast Guard had lowered a rescuer who confirmed two fatalities in the aircraft. We diverted to the area and directed the closest ground team to the location by the East Bay Regional Parks Police helicopter.

Search Personnel and Equipment

Due to the remoteness of the crash site, a command post was set up nearly 15 miles away at the nearest access point. This is where we staged and deployed all incoming resources including all search teams in the field. All incoming resources that needed access to the area were checked in at the command post and escorted to the crash site. The recovery operation was going to be a long term operation. Local news media coverage of the crash had stirred considerable public interest.

Several local newspapers and an affiliate of CBS were on scene at base. Although California law allows the media to have access to any disaster scene, the private property owner does not have to allow them on the property. In this case, the property owners did not want to allow the media to have access to the disaster site. It became our job to mediate between the media and property owners. The area was so remote that by the time we had contacted the property owners and gained permission for the media to go to the crash site, both bodies had been recovered and removed.

Search Strategy

The search itself was relatively easy. Teams from the local Civil Air Patrol Unit had begun the search early. Once we found the general location of the crash site, we activated both the Alameda County and Santa Clara County SAR Teams because of the intersecting jurisdictions. Although the use of helicopters shortened the search time significantly, I feel that, with the use of direction finding equipment, we had the crash site narrowed to an area we would've easily searched. The major operation was the recovery of the victims after finding the crash site.

Assigned Resources

Resources deployed to the incident were more than adequate to perform the operation safely and professionally. Logistically, our team is well prepared to operate under a variety of conditions. We maintain personnel and equipment at a level that makes most responses easy.

Suspension and Results of Mission

We suspended the mission about 1830 after we recovered, packaged, and transported both bodies to the command post. The overall results of the mission were favorable. The team performed as expected and accomplished the task without incident.

Additional Comments

After reviewing the incident, several things came to mind that I discussed in the preceding information. However, one area that we did not cover was that of critical incident stress debriefing. Our team has required that they will follow up all incidents of this nature with a stress debriefing. What added emotional stress to this incident was that it occurred just two days before Christmas, and the fact that both victims were burned beyond recognition. In addition, some two weeks after the incident, the family contacted and asked me to help them obtain permission to visit the crash site for a memorial service. This turned out to be one of the most moving experiences of my life. See the attached article by Bill Weber.

Search Tips

Training too much is impossible. Our team of sixty personnel put in more than 15,000 hours of volunteer time annually. Approximately 60% of those hours are training, preparing for every conceivable incident with which we could be involved.

Be sure to perform frequent equipment checks. Although our procedure calls for each vehicle to be thoroughly checked after each call, our team members recheck them at least twice monthly.

Desensitize your team members to death and dying. Visit the local coroners' offices with new team members. Nothing can prepare searchers for some scenes that they'll come across. However, previous desensitization will lessen the effects.

Establish an ongoing critical incident stress debriefing team. It will prove invaluable when dealing with some incidents in which searchers may become involved.

Be prepared to deal with the news media at any event that draws even minor public attention. Make sure that all team members are aware of your team's policy for media contact. Ensure that all team management personnel are current on your team's policies and are aware of the legal rights of the media.

Biography

I am a 23-year veteran of the Alameda County Sheriff's Office, in the eastern-most portion of the San Francisco Bay Area. I have been the sheriff's office search and rescue coordinator since February of 1989. I have completed the Managing the Search Function Class certification through the California State Office of Emergency Services. Additionally, I am a qualified public information officer and have attended several 40-hour classes offered by the California State Training Institute. I am currently assigned to the sheriff's office of emergency services and the search and rescue unit. I also coordinate the sheriff's two diver rescue teams.

The Memorial on Wauhab Ridge

By

William H. Weber

It was two days before Christmas, about 0130, when the plane with two aboard disappeared from the radar screen. We were not the first units to be activated, but at 0630 our pagers went off as the search moved north into our county and became our department's responsibility. It had rained heavily overnight. Once the weather broke, helicopters from the Coast Guard and the local park district were able to over fly the area and locate the wreckage with the coordinates provided by the FAA. Because of what they found on scene, the rescue operation slowed its pace to that of a recovery. If you allow for the time it takes the necessary officials to respond and to complete the required investigative work before being able to remove the remains, you can fully understand why we got the trucks back in the barn about 2100. Other than dealing with some mud-related access problems along the dirt roads that we traversed to get to the site, the operation had been uneventful. We had held a critical incident diffusing before breaking down the command post and would hold our critique of the operation at our next meeting. Other than telling war stories to new recruits in the future, I figured that the whole mission was over. That was until I received a phone call from our coordinator ten days later. He asked for my help.

Dealing with the family or friends of the victims on scene can be one of the most difficult duties to be assigned to. Over the years, I've had to deal with frantic parents while trying to interview them when their young child was missing. While divers worked their search patterns, I had been responsible for offering support to an embracing family, their gaze fixed upon the spot they last saw their loved one hours ago, as if they still expected to see them walk out of the water. At a recovery operation, I've felt at a loss for the right words to say when I saw the haunting sense of responsibility in a kayaker's tear-streaked face, knowing the effort he made to reach his partner's pinned kayak in time. If I had my choice, I would prefer that others handled the task. However, the most qualified members get the duty. It's a job that comes with the territory, a job some do better than others. A job I feel most do better than me.

I make my living fixing mechanical equipment, so I seldom encounter this type of responsibility in my day-to-day work environment. Others in the unit deal with it daily as part of their jobs as EMTs or health-related professionals. As part of our ongoing training, I have qualified as a peer counselor as part of our teams critical incident stress debriefing program. But the only real-life experiences that come close to preparing me to offer this type of support was when I had to deal with the death of my father and loved ones. My experience with church-sponsored support groups while going through a divorce has also helped. I wasn't quite sure of what to expect when our coordinator explained his request. However, I was more than willing to help.

Several family members of one of the victims had requested, through channels, if they could visit the crash site so they could see where their brother had died. They wanted to say a final goodbye. The site was on private land, 15 miles off the closest paved road. There was no public access for miles around. The landowners were contacted for permission to cross their land, and a date was set with the family to escort them to the site. Our escort party consisted of three of us: two trained CISD counselors (our coordinator and a fellow volunteer) and myself. Having been the first ground unit to reach the scene, I would act as the primary guide, knowing which fire roads to take to get back to the site.

Our coordinator had not been to the crash site on the day of the call. He had been the initial public information officer at the command post. After that he had to help the coroner's unit, the FAA and NTSB get to the crash site for their investigations. My fellow volunteer had been on-scene with me to help with the retrieval of the victims. He had also acted as the safety officer making sure that all the proper precautions were taken. While driving from our base to the prearranged meeting point with the family, we discussed our concerns about what kind of reactions the family members might have and how we could respond to their needs.

The morning sun was hidden behind the overcast sky, which shrouded the hills that we would be heading into shortly. We hoped the skies might clear to help brighten the day as well as the mood. As we waited for the family, we dealt with our nervous energy with humor and teasing developed from having to deal with these types of situations. As the family started to arrive, we learned that the original group of four had now grown to a party of fourteen. There were family members and their significant others, friends, and a coworker, all drawn to this location because of their love for the victim. After gathering together for introductions and a quick briefing, everyone was loaded into the fewest four-wheel drive vehicles possible, and the hour-long slow drive up to the site began.

The coworker and one of the friends rode with us. As the nervous tensions eased away, stories began to go back and forth. We talked about the call, then they talked about their friend—our turn, then theirs, and on it went. Although we tried to keep our distance, we slowly started becoming members of their group, no longer just the searchers, but people who'd been a part of their friend's life, even if it was only at the end.

We parked about 200 yards from the scene in a clearing with room enough for our caravan to turn around. My partner and I went ahead to make sure that the site was free of hazards. We had to verify that the salvage crew had left the area in a condition that would be acceptable for the family to visit. Our coordinator oriented the family to the surrounding terrain while we were gone, showing our location on maps of the area to them. We gave them the okay over the radio, and met them halfway down the hill to point them in the right direction. It was interesting to watch how they approached the area, each in their own way. Each looking for a little something that would help with their closure, yet stay with them for a lifetime. We tried to stay on the periphery as uninvolved observers, giving them a vague explanation of how the wreckage was situated in response to their questions.

Dan loved to fly. He was a commercial pilot employed by a nationwide carrier that specialized in handling the smaller freight shipments between major hubs and smaller airports throughout the states. His fellow pilot had waited to do his required check ride under Dan's watchful eye. They took off at 0030 because it was the only time their schedules allowed them to get together. It didn't matter that they were friends. He knew Dan would be an honest and fair evaluator. These traits were one of the many reasons that "everyone wanted to fly with Dan." This was one of many stories we were privileged to hear that day, stories that they punctuated with vivid and colorful details, which allowed us to visualize the type of life Dan led, to whom they had come to say good-bye. Everyone had something to offer. Some stories were unique, while others shared a common theme, some generated laughter, and a few brought tears. They obviously felt safe enough to express themselves honestly in this environment. Dan's coworker and fellow pilot was very patient with his explanations. His curious audience learned how the traffic control system for the area works and what might have been going on during the last few minutes of the flight. He identified the remaining bits and pieces of the plane that they had found while scouring the site for some small token of remembrance. He even showed where the part of the plane would have been located relative to where Dan may have been sitting.

For nearly two hours it went on. They gathered in groups or sat alone. They walked around the site or chose a spot to meditate. They took pictures or made notes. They joked and they cried, they reminisced. Among the many things we learned about Dan that day, was that he enjoyed visiting micro-breweries and smoking a good cigar. Had he been with us, I am sure that he would have laughed as hard as we did when his sisters sipped his favorite beer and smoked their first-ever cigars in his honor. They'd brought along several things to leave as a memorial: a statuette of a bronzed angel, votive candles, freshly cut flowers, and laminated pictures of Dan and the family. While they gathered stones to support the angel, to hold it for all time at the base of an adjacent tree, they passed out flowers to everyone there. After placing their flowers at the base of the statue, each member of their group paused and lit a candle. As they stepped away, a circle began to form and their hands joined. Although invited to joint them, I think this is where we intentionally stayed back as observers, to allow them their final moments alone. Our distance though, did not prevent us from hearing the quiet words of a poem shared by his sister, nor did it keep us from joining in the recital of the Lord's Prayer and the singing of "Amazing Grace." Many grand cathedrals have not witnessed a service as eloquent or so filled with love.

It was time to go. As some took final pictures, others headed up the hill in quiet solitude, alone with their thoughts. From where we had parked, the view of the countryside between us and civilization spread before us, becoming the perfect backdrop for a group photo. The sun had come out and warmed us, like a sign of someone above smiling down on us. The mood was upbeat and jovial and the family was very appreciative of our efforts. There were hugs and handshakes all around.

The drive down the hill found the conversation drifting back to generalities rather than specifics. The closer we got to where they parked their cars, the more distance crept into the conversation. At the bottom of the hill, we said our goodbyes. They offered homemade preserves as a token of their appreciation and thanked us profusely with handshakes and hugs once again.

As the three of us headed back to the "barn," a spontaneous release of emotion erupted in our vehicle. Each of us sharing our feelings and reactions to what we'd just experienced, but held inside because we were outsiders and supposedly detached observers. Each one of us had been moved by the love shown for Dan. How the family and friends had approached and dealt with the situation. We'd been a witness to a special moment that families share when they gather for the last goodbye, and yet we felt as if we were part of the process. My fellow volunteer and I were both grateful that our coordinator had asked us to come along. It is an experience that has been unique to my 24 years in the unit, a mission I'll always remember as special because of such a touching ending to it.

Since that memorial, the sheriff's office has received several thank-you notes from the family, some included tins of cookies and photos from our excursion. Surprisingly, we have received several phone calls from family friends who, having been told of our efforts, also wanted to thank us. I brought the subject up at a recent meeting of our local search and rescue council to see if any other teams may have had a similar type of experience to share. None did, which made the event even more special.

We had prepared for the worst and anticipated in many things that could have happened other than what did. It is funny how we usually look at our responses as helping a person lost, injured, or deceased. Here, our response was to help the living. Our success was seen in their faces, though we had done nothing special other than simply being there. In some ways, though, I think they gave us something. We found a type of closure we hadn't known before, and may not again.

This experience of sharing, of being invited to be a participant, of being included as part of this special group of people, will stay within me for a time that is too great to measure.

Dan must have been someone very special, certainly, he was part of a very special family and circle of friends, and now I, too, have fond memories to share.

Biography

Bill Weber is a 25-year veteran of the Alameda County Search and Rescue Team. He presently serves as the unit's training captain as well as being a peer counselor for the unit's critical incident stress debriefing team. In addition to teaching at a community college, Bill is certified by NASAR as an instructor for the Managing the Search Function course and by Rescue 3 International as an instructor of the Swift Water Rescue Technician I program. Bill has taught classes throughout California and was on the founding board of the NorCal SAR School.

Fire Storm

Deputy Sheriff Roger Kendle
Alameda County Sheriff's Search and Rescue
Office of Emergency Services
Mission Location: Alameda County, California
Mission Dates: October 20, 1991

Mission Type

The search that resulted from this fire would be one of the longest and most intense in recent California history.

On October 20, 1991, a firestorm in the hills struck Alameda County California above Oakland and Berkeley. Twenty-five lives were lost; the fire damaged or destroyed more than 3,000 homes, and it burned more than 1,800 acres. Both cities and the county declared local emergencies. The governor proclaimed a state of emergency, followed by a presidential declaration of a major disaster. Overall damage estimates would exceed $1.5 billion.

It all started on Saturday, October 19, 1991, when a small, insignificant brush fire broke out in Oakland Hills. The Department of Forestry extinguished the fire in about two hours and damage was limited to about five to six acres. Many area residents recalled a similar blaze in 1970 that grew into a fire that eventually destroyed thirty homes and caused more than $2 million in damage. The major difference between the two fires was that on this day, winds were calm and the Department of Forestry air-attack planes doused the flames quickly. Fire crews returned in the early morning hours of October 20, to patrol the burn area and to put out any smoldering hot spots. About 1045, as a very hot, dry wind began to build from the east, a small fire flared up and began to smoke near Buckingham Road. Soon the small fire grew to a large column of fire, then quickly gained strength and became a wall of flames. The original fire was located at the base of a very steep canyon. This allowed the fire to grow rapidly, burning up hill. A "chimney effect" resulted and as the flames crested the top of the ridge, some estimates put the temperature at over 1,000°F and traveled at speeds in excess of 600 mph. As the fire grew in intensity, the firefighters on the scene were rapidly overwhelmed.

The fire spread at an alarming rate on very narrow winding streets. The neighborhoods were nestled among pines and eucalyptus trees. The underbrush was tinder dry after five years of drought. Many trees were further weakened because of an unusual hard freeze the preceding January. As the wind-driven fire continued, trees, homes, and automobiles in its path literally exploded into flames. Residents ran for their lives as they evacuated their homes. They were not able to pack clothes, gather beloved pets or save lifelong mementos. Many rushed along streets on foot or in automobiles with the flames snapping at their backs. Some never made it out of the area and perished in the fire.

The fire continued its hellish rampage, fueled by years of dried underbrush, and turned into a monster firestorm. It fed upon itself, burning fuel, sucking in the hot dry air and causing a bellowing smoke cloud that towered 10,000 feet into the air. As the wind whipped, firebrands fell to the ground, some landed blocks away from the fire. As a result, other major fires broke out.

At the center of the storm, they estimated that heat reached 2,000° Fahrenheit, boiling asphalt, searing concrete, and melting metal. At the height of the storm they estimated that one house was being ignited every three seconds. Winds increased to 50 mph. Yet the winds did not affect the direction the fire was spreading. It was creating a wind of its own. A major eight-lane highway was only a minor nuisance and the fire continued onward to another major firebreak, the Warren Freeway. This too, only caused the firestorm to pause momentarily until it gained enough momentum to jump that freeway. As it continued roaring south and west of the original starting point, firefighters made their last desperate stand against the onrushing inferno. Suddenly, winds shifted to the east and began to build, blowing the fire back into itself. Finally the much-needed break had come and as the winds died and nighttime fell the firestorm subsided. The monster had been beaten.

The Victims

By the time the firestorm had subsided and the fire departments declared the fire controlled, we knew that many people had perished in the holocaust. The total number of missing people ranged from as few as thirty to as many as seventy, their ages ranged from teenagers to the elderly. What we did know was that not everyone made it out of the burn area alive. We were going to have to conduct an extensive search to ensure that all of the remains were found and removed.

Points Last Seen

This posed an enormous problem. No one was certain where any of the victims were. In addition, there were literally hundreds and hundreds of calls from concerned relatives, friends, and loved ones concerning the residents of the burn areas. The Oakland Police Department had the overwhelming task of receiving, documenting, and acting on all of theses calls.

Terrain Features

The terrain varied from steep hills and canyons to flat surface streets. The firestorm had destroyed all of the homes, including one large 250-unit apartment complex. The burn area looked like a bombed out city. All that remained of some neighborhoods was the scorched rubble. Rubble that represented the treasures of the families who lived there.

Weather

Weather conditions changed from extremely hot, 90°F or more with humidity as low as 12%, to about 40°F with rain and windy conditions by the conclusion of the search.

The area to be searched posed a myriad of dangers to not only the human searchers, but also to the search dogs. The dangers consisted of things such as partially destroyed dwellings, more than 1,500 miles of downed power lines, hundreds of power poles, smoldering rubble, and untold numbers of public utility trucks. Besides all of the physical dangers, searchers suffered from mental anguish after spending hours sifting through the remnants of family dwellings.

Any Other Special Information

The firestorm search operation had a much different environment and conditions than the "normal" search operation. The edges of the fire clearly defined the boundaries of the search. The fire had created such intense heat that everything was reduced to a white ash. This made it nearly impossible to distinguish burned wallboard from cremated remains. Often instead of a body, clues were all we had to determine if someone had died there. Clues might be some small fragments of bone, eyeglasses, watches, rings, teeth, perhaps a belt buckle, arranged in such a pattern that might suggest a possible find. Each time a team discovered anything that we could remotely connect to a body, they reported it to the command post. Police officers from the Oakland Police homicide unit along with coroner investigators where sent to the place where the clues were found. The intensity of the search took its toll on searchers. Many got tired quickly. The dog teams also became exhausted quickly and we replaced them at regular intervals.

Search Personnel and Equipment

The one resource we lacked that would have helped tremendously, especially planning the mission, would have been better and more accurate maps of the area. As it turned out we were forced to use maps that were several years old. This caused some problems in the newer neighborhoods since part or all of them were not on the map.

As for the resources that we did receive, from Tuesday, October 22, 1991, to Saturday, October 25, 1991, 762 people from 16 different agencies from Northern California expended a total of 7,374 search hours. Included in that total were 828 hours logged by 84 different dog handlers with 57 different dogs.

The command post resembled a small city. It consisted of:

California State Office of Emergency Services command motor home
California State Office of Emergency Services command trailer
California State Microwave Telephone command trailer and system
Sonoma County Search and Rescue command trailer
Contra Costa County Search and Rescue command motor home
Alameda County Sheriff's Search and Rescue lightning trailers
Alameda County Search and Rescue Lighting and Electrical Generator Unit
Thirty-five portable toilets
Three 20'x20' tenets and generators for lighting and power
Two 2.5-ton personnel carriers

Also at the command center was a fully operational helicopter base that accommodated many helicopters, which arrived and departed daily. The other resources that we used included several C-130 flyovers by aircraft from the NASA-Ames Research Center. They provided infrared photographs of the burn area. Additionally, California Air National Guard from March Air Force Base provided two F-4 Phantom reconnaissance aircraft for updated black and white photographs of the area. Both proved instrumental in identifying the search area and pinpointing hot spots.

Logistically it was a full-time job for several people to ensure a steady source of food and drink for the entire rescue operation, which included the command staff and the field search teams. Emphasis was placed on obtaining, high quality, well-prepared food for searchers, as well as a good supply of snacks and water to take into the field. Many groups and people donated food. Donations came from large corporations, such as Safeway stores, and from individual families. There was a constant stream of food to the command post area. So much food was donated that we occasionally took the food from the command center and redistributed it to shelters in the area. The command center purchased other supplies, such as flagging tape, surveyor's marking paint, gloves, etc., as the need arose.

Search Strategy

Search teams consisted of ground searchers and dog handlers. A team was made up of four ground searchers, two dogs and their handlers, and at least one spotter for the dog handlers. The command structure of the operation consisted of all branches of the incident command system. Additionally, an overall management team was made up of paid staff representatives from the Alameda County Sheriff's Office, the State Office of Emergency Services, the Oakland Police Department, and the Oakland Fire Department. Their primary function was to make policy decisions based on the information from the search management teams. All teams operated under a unified command structure.

We divided the entire burn area into three major sections. These sections were based on what was determined to be a reasonable area to cover in one day's operation. Each of these sections was then broken down into smaller sections that we would assign to each search team. We identified each day's objectives the preceding day and the planning staff would work through the night to prepare the following days assignments. Because of the dangerous working conditions and no real need of urgency, we suspended operation each evening at 1700.

As part of an ongoing effort to prevent any major accidents, safety teams consisting of a fire engine company patrolled a predetermined area. They helped search teams in determining safety hazards and decided if a structure was safe to search.

We gave a general briefing at the beginning of each day to inform searchers of any dangerous situations that had developed through the night, what safety precautions they should take for themselves and their dogs, and any other pertinent information. Before each team was deployed, they were briefed on their specific assignment. All teams were briefed on what markings they should use in the field to identify a particular residence, location, or vehicle that they searched. Orange surveyor's spray paint was used to draw an "X" on the driveway, sidewalk, or vehicle. Then each open area of the "X" was marked with the date. In the area between the upper legs of the "X," they also added their team number on the right and on the left, the number of victims found. When the teams returned, they gave us a report on what they found in a debriefing session.

At noon each day, we updated and informed agency liaisons what resources we needed for the next day's operational period. The plan's unit would work through the night preparing the next day's search assignments. As each section was searched and the teams debriefed, the plan's section would determine if an area had been covered to an acceptable POD.

We scaled the final day's efforts down significantly. All resources except 20–25 searchers and six to eight dogs were dismissed. The focus of the final day was a more thorough search of the Parkwood apartment complex and rechecks of specific addresses where the Oakland Police Department still had persons listed as missing. In each case no further suspected "finds" were found. By the end of the day the demobilization process had begun.

Suspension

Upon completion of the final day's operation, we put the demobilization plan into effect. We released all mutual aid resources except the State Office of Emergency Services Communication Unit and the Alameda County Generator Unit that continued to power the Oakland Fire Department Command Post through the night. By the following morning we released all state and local resources and we dissolved the command post.

The actual search operation lasted a little more than three and a half days, the command post was in operation for nearly five days including overnight operations where the plans section made team assignments for the following day.

Results of Mission

The result of the mission was an extremely successful operation that resulted in the complete clearing of all of the Oakland Police Department missing person reports. The Alameda County Coroners Office removed and positively identified all of the confirmed deaths from the various locations. Of the 29 persons who perished in the inferno, 13 were found because of the efforts of the searchers assigned to what can easily be considered as one of the most gratifying applications of volunteer search and rescue.

What are Your Feelings About the Mission?

Of all the missions I have had an opportunity to participate in, this was by far the most important one of my career. The fact that so may agencies pulled together in a short period, planned a search of this magnitude, and then accomplished every goal that was set in the time allowed was just short of miraculous. There was a very logical explanation for this, which will be covered in the next section.

From the first response to the firestorm on Sunday, October 20, until the closing of the operation on Saturday, October 26, I spent 14–16 hours a day involved in the operation. Often the only time I went home was for a quick shower and a few hours of sleep. Many of the search managers did the same. Most of my time was spent in the actual burn area of the firestorm. The constant emotional overload and long hours started to take their toll on many of us, including me.

Often during the day, I was required to drive or escort a variety of people into the burn area. These people included visiting fire and law enforcement personnel, clergy, and local, state, and federal political dignitaries. Each time I took someone into the burn area I was required to explain what had occurred, where more noted tragedies happened, and often where we had searched for and located remains. The area was secured by hundreds of police officers from all over the state. This meant that the state's mutual aid system was tested to the utmost. We used it for fire, law enforcement, medical, search and rescue, and coroner's offices. This mission also required cooperation from all of the utility companies. The electricity and gas had to be turned off, and most of the propane was blown up or burned off.

After so many long hours and return trips into the disaster area, I began to dread the ordeal of taking yet another person back to see all of this mass destruction. The stench in the area was overwhelming, like a million house fires. It was depressing to see all of the razed homes where families used to live and raise their children. It was heartbreaking see the homes destroyed where memories were made and traditions held. Since she was a child, my wife had visited her aunt who lived in the area that was burned. When my wife saw it after the fire, she broke into tears. She said that it looked like the burned out areas of World War II in Europe. Imagine looking down a street where there had been rows of townhouses and seeing only a row of water heaters, the only things to survive the terrible heat. The fire was so intense that it melted the engines of cars. You would see a small puddle of silvery material and realize that it was the engine of a car. It was so hot that the concrete driveways crumbled. Yet strangely enough, in some areas, there would be one or two houses that did not burn. All around them was total ash, yet there they stood without so much as a scorch mark. It was eerie.

The total destruction of the area made it difficult to locate bodies, although there was very little smoke in the area because there was nothing left to burn. The remains of people were not much different than the other remains. All was reduced to ash and all we could look for was some hint that a body was there; a watch, shoe eyelets, a belt buckle, or other items arranged in such a manner that indicated that they were worn by a person.

There were hot spots all through the week. Until Wednesday some areas were so hot that when a dog would sink into the ash he would burn his feet. One of the largest areas that we had to search was the Parkside apartments. This was a complex of about 250 apartments that was totally destroyed. The fire department poured water on it from late evening Sunday until Wednesday night. We were finally allowed to search the area Thursday morning. That was three to four days of water being poured on the area for twenty-four hours a day to cool the area.

What is difficult for people to understand is that almost none of the fire was extinguished in the areas where people perished. The fire simply moved too fast and couldn't be fought. One incident in particular still leaves a lump in my throat. Hiller Highlands, located in a very beautiful point high in the hills, was cut off early in the firestorm. There was only one road in or out. The fire had reached such intensity that there was no means to get anyone out that might be still in there. At the height of the fire, the Oakland Police 911 center received a call from a thirteen-year-old girl who was trapped in Hiller Highlands. No one could explain how the phone still worked. The 911 tape of the supervisor comforting this little girl, knowing that no one was going to be able to get to her and that she was going to perish in the fire is unbelievable. He was so kind and calming, I don't know that I could have done it. He talked to her until the phone connection was cut. Late the next morning we recovered her remains. An Oakland police officer tried to save the wife and mother of one of our deputies, all three were killed.

All of this depressed me and it started to show after the third day. Early in the mission, the search leaders had decided to have debriefing personnel on hand to talk with the searchers. I had never participated in any type of critical incident stress debriefing (CISD) before this operation. The debriefing helped me so much that after the firestorm, several volunteers and I attended a week-long CISD instruction course and became the lay persons for our debriefing team.

Since then our team has been involved in a number of stressful operations that involve traumatic death. In each case, when needed, a debriefing always takes place. We have been involved with such national cases as the Polly Klaas search, and in each incident we have provided CISD to our own personnel as well as members of other teams involved in the searches. We have very strong volunteer leadership that has recognized the importance of CISD and supports all of the efforts made in that direction.

It is interesting to note that as far as we can determine, this was the largest operation where dogs were used to search for totally incinerated human remains. When the use of dogs was first discussed, no one knew what results we would have or could expect. During the following days, it proved to be an invaluable asset to help search the number of dwellings we had to clear.

However, I cannot say with certainty that any human remains were found exclusively by dogs, primarily for two reasons. First, we teamed all dog handlers with a ground search team. When they thought they had found remains, the team would notify the command post. No mention was made whether the find was made by the ground searchers or by the dog and handler. Therefore it is impossible to determine who made the find. At the time, I don't think anyone considered it important, although for future searches, it would have been helpful to know just how effective the dogs were. Second, the process that took place after the suspected remains were located did not allow for positive identification in the field. Often, all that was recovered were small pieces of bone fragments or personal effects that would suggest the remains of a person. If these items looked like they were the remains of a person, the coroner's office would remove and transport them to their office for closer examination and positive identification. This process of identification took anywhere from days to months.

The clean up from the firestorm started right away, as early as Monday morning. There was a long line of blue Pacific Gas and Electric trucks entering the area. They started right away to restore power to the area. The phone company was there right alongside putting in phone lines. The clean up continued for months and some houses are yet to be replaced, seven years later.

Additional Comments

The main reason the Oakland Hills firestorm search was such a success is a direct result of the cooperative efforts of a dedicated group of individual SAR teams that make up the Bay Area Search and Rescue Counsel. This organization came about as the result of a search that took place in Contra Costa County. The search for a missing hiker lasted for seven consecutive days and resulted in the victim's body being located on the seventh day at the bottom of a steep canyon. Typically a search in the Bay area is of short duration, less than 24 hours. This search made everyone realize the need for more regional training, cooperation, and coordination. The council is made up of search and rescue teams from six counties, a regional park district, several dog teams, and a mountain rescue unit. The mission is to promote the exchange of ideas and information and the development of common communications, training, and search management.

The council was established in the fall of 1990 and over the next year took shape and a large-scale two-day training weekend was held on September 27 and 28, 1991. The idea was to get the teams together, interact at all levels, allow the management teams to work with one another and to offer basic classes that reinforced the fundamental skills and set basic competency levels. The weekend was a complete success, attendance was nearly double what everyone had projected, and evaluation sheets commented on the soundness of the training. When the weekend came to a close, no one realized that the Oakland Hills firestorm was less than three weeks away. The council was about to be tested, literally, by fire.

Because the firestorm search and recovery mission was so professional and successful, the State Office of Emergency Services has used the mission, the command post layout, and the overall management of the search as part of their search management training.

The idea that so many teams could conduct a search for a sustained period, mixing management personnel, and continuing the search through many operational periods with no transition problems, is unheard of in many places. Here in the Bay area, it has become the norm.

Search Tips

Be prepared to deal with overwhelming public and political pressure to open the disaster area to the media and public. It almost becomes a controlling factor in conducting the search. Make sure that the management staff is aware of the pressure and does not allow it to become a controlling factor.

Keep in mind how important it is to work with surrounding search and rescue teams. A well-planned and organized operation will allow the flexibility to deal with unexpected problems that crop up during the search.

During a large-scale disaster or search where multiple traumatic deaths have occurred, such as the firestorm, the need for on-site CISD is paramount. Had this not been available during the firestorm search, the difficult search would have been even more stressful than it was. Another part of this is a place removed from the site where individuals can go, relax and unwind. Make sure the area is far enough from the Search Base as to allow for some privacy.

Make sure you are prepared for the large influx of government and public officials that will visit your Command Post. If possible, make special arrangements to have ranking departmental officers or a public information officer (press liaison) available to escort the officials. Additionally, choose your escorts carefully; make sure they are briefed and aware of the operation, the goals and objectives for this operational period. Make sure they can answer the questions from the officials.

Most important, be aware of the victims, not just the ones that perished in the disaster, but the ones that remain behind. Understand that they have emotions, needs, that they have suffered tremendous personal loss, and they need special attention to deal with such a traumatic event. If possible, provide an outreach program to help them deal with the grieving process.

Biography

For Roger Kendle's biography, refer to page 119.

The Bombproof Alert, or It Ain't Necessarily So
By
Marcia Koenig

When searching for a victim that is out of sight, such as under rubble, water, or in darkness, the handler wants an indication from the dog that is unmistakable, or "bombproof." However, occasionally you'll be on a search where even the best-trained dog will not do the bombproof alert. This is where close observation of your dog's body language can help you solve the problem.

The dog's **natural alert** is what it does instinctively when it encounters scent. This includes increasing activity level, changes in breathing to deep sniffing, changes in body posture (ears, tail, etc.) and making direct eye contact with the handler. Each dog displays its own unique combination when it encounters scent. By doing many search problems and carefully observing the dog, the handler learns what their dog's natural alerts are.

The dog's **trained alert** is what the handler has shaped. It may be a stronger indication of something the dog does naturally, such as a down or dig. Or it could be something entirely different such as pull at a toy tied on the handler's waist or giving a bark. Whatever trained alert is selected, the handler shapes it so that it is strong, readable, and the dog does it under all conditions—the bombproof alert. However, there are exceptions when the dog will not do the trained alert. This is the time the handler needs to read their dog's body language and make a decision based on what the dog has done in training.

Examples

A hillside gave way in a Seattle park. A transient had a camp in the area and was reported missing several days later. Ten days later the slide had stabilized enough to allow two dogs and handlers to search the area. Neither handler watched the other work so that they did not influence each other.

My dog, Coyote, worked the pile three different times. She never went to her full, trained alert—a down at the strongest point—but she did keep moving around, sniffing at everything. The area of greatest interest was at the root ball of a tree uprooted in the slide. Coyote kept sticking her nose into a hole at the root base. At times she looked like she wanted to do a down, but she never did.

Andy's dog, Marianne, the old pro at ten, also worked the slide three times. Her trained alert was to grab the toy at Andy's waist then go to the area and do a sit at the point of greatest scent. The root ball was her area of most interest, too. We probed the root ball and brought the dogs back. Still there were no trained alerts for either dog.

Neither of us was willing to say with any certainty that there was a person under the mud. All we could say was that the dogs were interested in something in the area. We couldn't say if it were a person or clothing and other camping supplies from the man's campsite.

Andy assisted in directing digging operations the next day. As the shovel removed the mud, it revealed clothing and food from the campsite. Farther down they found a sleeping bag with the man inside. He was encased in mud five feet down. No wonder the dogs didn't go to full alerts! There was extremely little scent escaping.

Usually dogs will do an animated alert on a drowning victim. Nevertheless, unusual conditions will change this trained indication. Four fishermen died when their boat capsized on the Columbia River. They recovered two on the bank, but two were still missing a week later.

The Columbia River has a very strong west-flowing current, but the Columbia River Gorge has a very strong east-blowing wind. This makes for very difficult scenting conditions.

A local handler's dog had done a weak alert and the handler wanted confirmation from more experienced dogs. Three of us responded to this mission. Eileen Porter's dog, Megan, alerted weakly. Andy's dog, Marianne, tapped her toy but didn't grab it. My dog, Orca, whined softly, as if to herself. Her usual trained alert was whining leading to barking. The only reason I heard the whine was that I was focusing on her and her body language and not even looking at the water.

When the police used sonar, it revealed two body-sized blips 50 feet down. The police were unable to retrieve the bodies with grappling hooks. Months later one of the bodies surfaced one-quarter mile downstream from where the dog had made their faint alerts.

Lessons Learned

Train for the bombproof alert, but if scent conditions are unusual, don't expect to get it. Pay close attention to the dog's natural alert. I'm always comparing what the dog is doing on a search to what I've seen her do in training. I do training problems in negative areas so I know what negative looks like. When you get these tough searches all you can do is mentally compare with what you've seen your dog do before.

Other Tips

If you're not sure if the dog has something or not, don't ask it if it has anything. You may talk the dog into an alert. Let the dog make up its own mind.

Leave the area of greatest interest, search other areas or take a break, then bring the dog back in. Try to approach from another direction. Observe what your dog does without cueing from you; sometimes the dog will have no further interest in the area.

Have another dog work the area. Don't watch the other team, but compare notes when you're done.

Biography

Marcia Koenig has been involved in dog search work since 1972. Marcia lives in Washington State. She is a member of K-9 Specialty Search Associates, King County Search Dogs, Northwest Disaster Search Dogs, and the Puget Sound Federal Emergency Management Association team. For six years, Marcia was the chairperson for the National Association for Search and Rescue (NASAR) search dog committee. She has represented NASAR at the International Rescue Dog Symposia in Norway (1987), Germany (1991), Sweden (1993), and the United States (1995).

Marcia responded to the Wichita Falls, Texas, tornado in 1979 and to several plane crashes including the KAL crash on Guam in 1997. She participates in all types of searches from wilderness missing persons, disaster, water body recovery, and buried homicide victims.

Marcia's experience as a teacher has helped her develop search dog training classes. Currently she teaches search dog classes throughout the United States and Canada with retired Connecticut State Trooper Andy Rebman. She writes search dog articles, has produced the videotape "Training Dogs for Water Searches" and is currently working on other search dog training videos.

Marcia Koenig and Coyote. KAL airplane crash search, Guam, August 1997.

Missing Child
Wilderness Airscenting

Dave Meek
The Kansas Search & Rescue Dog Association
Mission Location: Topeka, Kansas
Mission Date: October 16, 1994

Traditionally, Kansas law enforcement agencies have had to depend on good-hearted but untrained volunteers to provide search and rescue throughout the state. When this failed, they often sought out-of-state resources, as was the case when they called in Missouri Search & Rescue to assist after the Andover tornado. Our organization became operational in 1994, with the goal of providing both training and response for the entire state of Kansas.

Mission Type
The following search lasted more than 12 hours long. It was one of our first searches and demonstrates some aspects that we did well and others that we have since improved on.

The Victim
An 11-year-old male in good health and physical condition who liked to go hunting with his older brother and going to the scout camp. The boy had on jeans and an unknown type of shirt, boots but no coat. He was also carrying a .22 rifle and ammunition, and had two small puppies with him.

Point Last Seen
The boy, "John," was last seen at 1600 hours at his uncle's house where he was staying on October 16, 1994. He didn't know the area well, and was expected back within one hour. John had wanted to go hunting with his brother at the scout camp but his brother was busy and didn't want to go. So John set out alone and took the .22 caliber rifle with him. He wasn't supposed to take the rifle without his older brother being present. The scout camp was about one mile southwest of the uncle's house. When John was not home by dark (1900 hours), the family members called the sheriff for assistance.

We were received the callout at 0025 hours on October 17, 1994. We had a problem reaching some of our members by phone. Since we were still a new group and this was one of our first callouts, several members did not yet have phones close to their bed. Only three members (two of which were dog handlers) responded. Our response time was approximately one hour due to the long drive involved to the outlying area.

The weather was unusual for mid-fall. The temperature was around 65°F and the winds were from the southeast at 10–15 mph. Fog, low ceilings, and occasional drizzle reduced the visibility to a half-mile. It is normally much colder at night. The area in which John had traveled was a mixture of open grassland, timber, cedar tree forest, and areas of heavy underbrush. The terrain was rolling hills leading to limestone bluffs that lined the river valley. Other hazards in the area included old water wells, which weren't plugged.

Any Other Special Information

It was odd that the family members present, all older children, did not appear very concerned about their missing sibling. However, we never learned why they had this attitude.

Search Personnel and Equipment

If I were in control of this search, and could have had everything that I wanted, I would've wanted one helicopter (FLIR equipped), five to ten mounted posse members to search the open areas, 20 foot-searchers to cover the house and scout camp for clues, ten vehicles equipped with emergency lights and a PA system, two tracking dogs, and ten airscenting dogs.

Upon our arrival the first night, we had one ambulance and one Air Ambulance helicopter that had to return to base due to poor weather visibility. The following morning we had one TV helicopter, two law enforcement bloodhounds, one fire truck, three law enforcement vehicles, and about 20 untrained volunteers.

Search Strategy

After we completed the lost-person questionnaire we began to decide our POAs. The sheriff asked us to take over the SAR operation and offered all the resources on the scene. We immediately set up a passive/containment perimeter using the roads within a three-mile radius of the PLS. We instructed the sheriff to oversee this part of the operation. He was to have vehicles equipped with emergency lights and sirens to drive these roads at 15-minute intervals to attempt to draw the victim to a roadway. We requested a helicopter, but were told that the Air Ambulance was forced to return to base due to the low ceilings. However, if the weather improved, they would request a helicopter.

We set up the command post at the PLS. Vehicles were lining the road around the CP for a half a mile in each direction. As we started to search, the only clue we had was that the missing boy had told his brother that he was going to the scout camp. We started our search by looking for footprints to decide a direction of travel. Since our team does not have mantrackers, we require all handlers to be NASAR tested SAR technicians, level III or above. I was the first to find footprints, which were located beneath the ambulance. These footprints were consistent with the missing boy's shoe size as measured from a pair of his shoes that were at the PLS. Furthermore, the sheriff had briefed us that the ambulance was one of the first units to arrive on the scene earlier that evening. After the ambulance carefully backed off the prints, we were able to determine a direction of travel. With the footprints confirming travel toward the scout camp, we now had a good POA. The sheriff assured me that he and his people had thoroughly searched the scout camp. I asked him to return and search it again. When they finished, they radioed that nothing had been found and returned to the CP.

This was one of our mistakes that night. We had assumed that the sheriff's deputies who searched the site had SAR training. We found out later that this was a false assumption on our part. You should always have trained searchers go through areas that contain high POAs.

We were then told that the bloodhounds had not successfully found a trail. Without maps available at the scene, it was difficult to understand exactly where the bloodhounds had worked. Furthermore, we were never able to debrief with the bloodhound teams since we entered the field prior to their return to the CP.

At this point, we decided the best action was to deploy our two airscenting dogs in the highest POA, which was heading south toward the scout camp. They were to search up to, but not beyond, the scout camp. A local individual was sent with them as a guide since no topographic maps of the area were available and the road maps would be of little use. This was another of our mistakes that night. You should always try to obtain topographic maps of the area.

Thunder, an air scenting dog, alerted at the top of a bluff. His alert gave us cause to suspect that the boy was on the bluff. But a search of the bluff revealed nothing so we took Thunder back up to the site of his alert. This time he showed no interest in the area of his original alert on the bluff but alerted in a different area on the top of the bluff. This confirmed that the victim was moving. After making our way down the bluff, we found a footprint at the base, near a dirt road. The footprint was the correct size but the pattern was unreadable due to the high moisture content of the mud in which it was made. We searched for more footprints on the road without success. At this time our guide told us that we had gone past the scout camp. We decided to work back toward the scout camp and away from the road. As we continued, Thunder turned and headed south up the hill and toward the road. We decided to stop and take a break prior to following Thunder's indication. (I had fallen from a horse a few days prior and had bruised the instep of my right foot, which made the search quite painful.) As we were sitting on a log, I mentioned to our guide that the TV helicopter south of us was hovering. We turned up our police radio in time to hear that the helicopter had found the boy and they were sending ground units to him. He appeared to be all right and was standing next to a road. We estimated that he was less than 200 yards south from our position. The vehicle that picked him up confirmed that he was uninjured and then headed back to the CP. We radioed a request to have transport meet us at the scout camp.

We found out later that the boy was not very familiar with the area around his uncle's farm. When he left for the scout camp, it was still light and he could see landmarks. As the sun set, a fog and mist moved into the area limiting visibility to less than a half mile at times. The poor visibility and increasing darkness, combined with an abundance of cedar trees, caused the boy to become disoriented and start walking in circles. The boy told the sheriff that he had been at the scout camp three different times during the night. It was a fortunate situation for the boy that the temperature remained above 60°F all night. Had the temperature dropped he could have suffered from hypothermia and possibly died. When he was found, the local ambulance crew checked both him and his two puppies. All were in good condition and did not need to go to the hospital.

Assign Resources

Since the boy was found near a road, the passive-search resources were effective. The helicopter said that they would not have seen him if he had not been by the road opening. When the TV helicopter arrived, the sheriff asked them to help with the search—since the Air Ambulance helicopter was still unavailable—and they agreed.

The tracking dogs were a good resource to try first but since they were not successful, we deployed the airscenting dogs. This was a mistake, because he told us later that he'd taken the rifle since he was afraid of stray dogs in the area. This could have led to a tragic ending with an injured or dead SAR dog, since airscenting dogs run free, sometimes out of sight of their owners. (A word to the wise: always put an orange identification vest on your dog.) The area had several abandoned water wells, areas of rocky bluffs and cliffs, so because of the dangerous terrain, we decided not to use the untrained foot-searchers.

Suspension

Luckily, the mission ended when we found John. Although we found him, the active phase of the search would have been suspended soon because we were running out of trained resources.

Results of the Mission

This mission resulted in the return of the boy to his family at 1030 hours on October 17, 1994. No searchers received injuries and all resources were returned to service by 1100 hours.

What are Your Feelings About the Mission?

Any search that results in the victim being safely found is a good search. The performance of our team was professional but needed improvement. I made some fundamental mistakes. One, you can't run a search from the field. You are either a searcher or an overhead team member, you can't do both. I should have stayed with the IC to assist him in coordinating the SAR resources and efforts. Instead, I went into the field with my K-9 leaving an IC—who had no SAR training himself—without a SAR liaison from our team.) Two, never send untrained searchers to cover an area with a high POA. The boy told us he had been at the scout camp three different times during the night. In this situation I should have placed an officer at the scout camp and possibly built a fire there as an attraction device. Finally, before beginning the mission, always ask if the victim is afraid of animals, especially dogs. I thought the rifle was just for rabbits. Better information gathering could have revealed this potentially dangerous situation.

Additional Comments

This was only our second callout as a team. Our response times are now better and our numbers are much higher, but we continue to learn from each search.

Search Tips

Make sure that all team members have a phone or alert device with them at all times. The best trained searcher is of no value if they can't be reached.

Go passive early! Passive SAR techniques are often overlooked or under-prioritized. There is no sin in bringing the victim to you and it is also a great way to utilize untrained personnel.

Dogs are an excellent resource for searching in the dark. Attempts to foot-search at night could destroy many clues. Dogs work well at night due to the increased stability of the air and the other micro-meteorological factors that favor nighttime searching. We know that air moves downhill at night and the humidity usually rises, which creates favorable conditions for scent to both move and to last for longer periods. Knowing this, we can perform hasty searches in the low areas using airscenting dogs, which increases the POD of the K-9 teams.

One SAR dog is equivalent to 50 foot-searchers. Learn about search dogs and their abilities so that you can utilize them in a timely (and early!) manner.

Use SAR incident command protocol. Your team will benefit greatly from following this system. You should at least have a SAR IC and an Ops Officer assigned for every SAR response. NASAR offers a correspondence course on SAR Incident Command, so if you are not familiar with this system, learn it now.

Attempt to get all possible resources early. Teams often wait to request additional resources, but this limits your hasty-search abilities. Remember that search and rescue is an emergency!

Biography

Dave Meek is the founder and current director of the Kansas SAR Dog Association. He holds both a bachelor's degree in Education and a bachelor's of science degree in Nursing. Dave works as an RN in the Critical Care Unit of Stormont-Vail Regional Medical Center. He is also a SAR Technician I, SAR Technician Coordinator, Emergency Medical Technician-Intermediate, and Dive Rescue Specialist I. He was a presenter at the International Search Dog Symposium and at NASAR's Response '96. In 1991 he attended training with the BATSAR (Bay Area Training council for SAR) and at SAR City in California. He currently has his operational dog, Thunder, a German Shepherd, and a second dog, Jeremiah, a Border Collie Mix, in training. Finally, he serves as SAR coordinator for the Shawnee County Emergency Management Agency, which includes the capital city of Topeka.

Dave Meek and Thunder.

The Oklahoma City Bombing:
What Have We Learned?

Marilyn Neudeck-Dicken, Ph.D.
Certified Diplomat American Board of Psychotherapists
Diplomat American Board of Medial Psychotherapy
Diplomat American Academy of Pain Management

The Oklahoma City Bombing of the Murrah Federal Building, April 19, 1995, occurred at 0902 on a typical Wednesday morning. The detonation of 4,800 pounds of ammonium nitrate and fuel oil in America's heartland state was atypical. This event will change the course of search and rescue forever. We entered the beginning of a new era; an era of terrorism, manmade destruction and hate! We all experienced the feelings of *fear*, intense fear; *horror* that someone in this nation could be this destructive; *loss of security* and *trust*, because we believed that we were safe and untouchable; *disbelief* that someone in this nation harbored enough hate to kill our own, our children; and last, *violation* because everyone in this nation was stripped of our innocence. We were naked in the eyes of the world. And, even more tragic, we were not prepared for this catastrophic terrorist act.

Background Information

After the blast it was determined that three buildings contained trapped injured and deceased victims: the Alfred P. Murrah Federal Building, the Water Resources Building, and the Athenian Building. Within 20 minutes, police K-9 teams used for patrol, explosive detection, and search/patrol were on the scene. Within six hours after the bombing, the first responding volunteer dog teams were on site attempting to locate live victims in the mass rubble pile. Their command post area was set up in the parking garage underneath the Murrah Federal Building (Neudeck-Dicken 1996, 1997; Duhaime 1998). By 2230 hours on April 19, 1995, less than 14 hours after the bombing, they had extracted the last live victim from the federal building. By the time the FEMA/US&R Response System took over management at 2400, the operation had changed from finding live victims to body location and recovery.

A total of 74 dogs responding to the bombing were responsible for 491 dog workdays at the site (Duhaime 1998). The 16-day rescue/recovery effort ended May 4, 1995 after logging 168 deaths and 450 dog alerts on cadaver remains. The last remaining three bodies were found May 29, by two Oklahoma City Police Department patrol/search dogs. A job well done, but is the story over?

Handlers and dogs were exposed to a vast magnitude of trauma. The air was thick with fumes and debris for days. Dogs experienced exposure to chemical toxins, asbestos, body fluids, eye irritants, and cuts, to name a few. Could the high incidence of cancer and blindness of the dogs who were in the first responding dog teams be a result of these exposures? A study on the dogs present at the Oklahoma City Bombing by Roberta Duhaime, D.V.M., from the United States Department of Agriculture, Veterinary Services, may offer answers to the many questions still asked (Duhaime 1998). However, long-term ramifications of the bombing not only affected the dogs, but also the handlers as well.

Psychological Impacts of the Oklahoma City Bombing

A longitudinal study of 50 dog handlers present at the Oklahoma City bombing demonstrated that the majority of these volunteers were and are still intensely affected by this traumatic event (Neudeck-Dicken, 1996, 1997, Filter Press 1997). Ten months after the bombing, 68% of the dog handlers studied were experiencing symptoms of an acute stress reaction resulting in intense psychological distress (Neudeck-Dicken, 1996).

Prior studies by Mitchell (1985, 1987) have indicated that more than 85% of emergency personnel experience acute stress reactions after a disaster. The Oklahoma City bombing demonstrated that 96% of the participants experienced acute stress reactions. In Mitchell's above studies the majority of emergency personnel experienced temporary stress reactions and recovered within a few weeks. Though Mitchell's research was collected on emergency personnel by profession, only 42% of the dog handlers studied at Oklahoma City were emergency personnel by trade. As a result, the picture was very different. A total of 68% demonstrated acute stress reactions for more than two years and their distress profoundly effected their work, their families, their health, and their happiness.

After examining the signs and symptoms reported after the Oklahoma City bombing, it became apparent that there were three distinctive populations of stress reactions developing after this tragic event. The first were the responses of the *first arriving Oklahoma dog teams*, second was the FEMA/US&R teams that are *non-emergency personnel* by occupation, and last by the FEMA/US&R Teams that are *emergency personnel* by occupation. The intensity of stress reactions was distinctively different for these three groups of participants. However, there were common threads to their complaints. They all felt overwhelmed and victimized by the media, especially the first responding teams. Also, all three of these groups felt their families, spouses, children, and co-workers misunderstood them after their return home. The most frequently reported symptoms of these three groups were intense grief, anger, and guilt.

Since the greatest emotional reaction to the Oklahoma City bombing has been reported by the first responding Oklahoma dog teams, a possible explanation of this intense reaction could come from the following:

1. The command post/staging area for these individuals was the garage of the bombed federal building. The deafening sound of the elevator alarms, the smell of death, and the view of automobiles owned by the deceased all added to their anxiety.
2. The media harassed them, even during their rest periods.
3. They had direct and continual contact with family members of the victims.
4. This was their home and their home state.
5. They were desperately searching for live victims but too few were found.
6. Of the ten first responders in the study, none of the seven that dropped out of search and rescue were present at the closing ceremony nor were they present when the search was called off. As a result, there was no closure to their grief.
7. They reported fraudulent activity with the media by former teammates and indi-

viduals.

8. They were not prepared emotionally for what they experienced.
9. They had never received, been trained in or requested critical incident stress debriefing (CISD) prior, during, or immediately after the incident.
10. This incident was manmade, and contrived by an American, not a foreigner.
11. Small innocent children, friends, and family members were victims.
12. To date, finality to the incident has been delayed due to ongoing trials, legal issues, and ongoing media coverage in their state. Unfortunately these participants experienced profound psychological affects and their jobs, families, health, and happiness were still impaired two years after the bombing incident (Neudeck-Dicken 1997).

The dog handlers that were non-emergency personnel by profession found the daily pleading of family members of victims behind the barricades, along with the daily the notes, flowers, cards, pictures, and toys left on the bunks of the search and rescue personnel not only overwhelming, but emotionally devastating. This population was *not* trained to deal with the families and loved ones of victims on an ongoing basis as emergency personnel experience daily. This group reported that they and their teams passed up CISD during the stint of their stay "in order to distance from the emotionality so that they could perform the job they came to do." Unfortunately CISD was not offered for any of the handlers that were non-emergency personnel by occupation after they returned home. This could be the reason why 25% of this population of handlers dropped out of SAR immediately after returning home (Neudeck-Dicken 1996).

Only the emergency personnel by occupation reported that they overcame the effects of this incident. Only 4% of this group still reported acute stress symptoms ten months after the incident. Close to 70% of the emergency personnel by occupation received CISD before or after they returned home. This may explain the reported recovery rate of this population in the study. However, this population also had a tremendous need to "look good" after their return home. Their jobs demanded that they be intact and at the peak of functioning. In short, they could not afford to express the severity of their stress reaction in fear of losing their jobs. Unfortunately, cumulative stress reactions and delayed stress reactions did develop in this population at a later date.

Since CISD is not psychotherapy but an attempt to lessen the impact of a traumatic event, its focus to the SAR personnel at the bombing was to restore normal functioning as soon as possible. Specialized psychotherapy was still needed by many to lessen the impact of this traumatic stress. One, however, must keep in mind that the critical incident is not the only factor in a stress reaction. We cumulate stress over time, so the critical incident may be the catalyst to a severe stress reaction. In this case multiple factors come into play. The result is often a complete emotional and physical breakdown.

Just over two years after the bombing, 24% of the 50 handlers admit to a cumulative stress response (Neudeck-Dicken 1997). In the middle of a catastrophic stress reaction, it is difficult to sort out the sources or cause because cumulative stress is often ignored, denied, and minimized. This 24% have experienced major life changes over the course of three years. The result has been chronic illness, marital problems and divorce, and a high incidence of burnout and unresolved issues concerning their jobs, their loved ones, and their future.

Guilt that their dog didn't perform well enough, guilt that perhaps they didn't read their dog's alert, and guilt that people weren't found fast enough all played into the stress reaction. Other factors involved were: *avoidance* (of friends, placed and events), *rationalizations* ("I could have done better if…"), *displacement* (angry at a less threatening target like a friend or loved one instead of the unacceptable), and other defense mechanisms used to protect their psyche. As a result, the real issues were not dealt with and the stress only persists to date.

Another population in this study that needs to be addressed is the husband-and-wife team. Psychological distress from the bombing seeped into the core of the marriage itself. Couples looked to each other for psychological support, but the problem was that both were hurting. The result was the breakdown of the marriage as they knew it prior to the incident. Each of these individuals felt abandoned by their best friend. Since a successful marriage fulfills the personality needs of both members, the extent of psychological distress left these individuals unable to fulfill any relationship needs. As one would withdraw, the other would desperately try to obtain the sustenance needed to maintain. Communication between partners then broke down, leaving these couples frustrated, angry, and misunderstood. This led to power struggles, a lack of adaptability, and a redefinition of the marital contract already established by these couples. Statistically these couples had a 50/50 chance of either divorcing or leaving search and rescue altogether. I call this the 50/50 marital impact of Oklahoma City.

The SAR personality intensifies our predisposition for stress syndromes. Search and rescue personnel are known to be perfectionists, driven by an unrealistic standard of achievement (Mitchell and Bray, 1990; Neudeck-Dicken, Filter Press 1997). The unknown, the uncontrollable, and the unpredictable terrorize us, and we have a desperate need to be in control. Our personality demands that our standards of performance be high. Our perfectionist nature often places our goals out of reach. The results can be devastating when we face the unresolved search, the search that ends in tragedy, or an "American made" act of terrorism as handlers faced in Oklahoma.

Future Needs for Dog Handlers

Examining the stress reactions of the dog handlers has demonstrated that we were unprepared in various areas. The following is a list of areas that need to be reviewed by every team.

1. Desensitization in disasters must be an early prerequisite to being mission ready. Many individuals on dog teams have never seen a dead human body or human body parts. Many cadaver dogs have never been trained on whole bodies, only small body parts or pseudo scent. Medical books on disasters, as well as visits to local morgues, medical centers, emergency rooms, and coroner's office, can help desensitize teammates and dogs. Unfortunately being a dog handler became a glorified role after the Oklahoma City bombing due to the media releases. The pictures on the television screen only showed the comradeship, fellowship, and intimacy of frolicking with a search dog during rest periods. What they did not show was the terror, exhaustion, and turmoil of not finding a live victim, only bodies and body parts. Sadly, glory soon turns to reality when the real facts are known about the ramifications of search and rescue work.

2. Preparedness! We may all experience a disaster in our own home state. As first

responders, are we prepared? Disaster preparedness is an ongoing way of thinking and training. All teams need to train and be prepared. The "what if" scenarios are good monthly training projects. Have your teammates come up with as many as they can think of, then examine them as a team.

3. Get training in CISD. Understanding this as a tool to psychological health is half the battle. Assign a CISD coordinator and find a mental health professional (who is trained in CISD, and has been involved in crisis work) to oversee your team. Often clergy and mental health professionals untrained in this highly specialized area can actually be intrusive and harmful. Set up peer support personnel to initiate and assess the need for defusing and debriefings.

4. Have a mental health professional on staff that can assist with educational and psychological referral sources. A trained professional can spot changes in functioning faster than the untrained. Often a small intervention will prevent psychological distress later. However, those in command need to be open to and not threatened by suggestions and recommendations of these professionals.

5. It is the responsibility of *everyone* on the team to demand CISD prior to returning home from the incident site. No one on a team should accept statements like, "If you're going to be in search and rescue, you should be able to handle the ramifications without help." Or "If a person *chooses* to go into cadaver work, they *should* have a pretty good understanding of what it is that they are getting into." I have heard statements like these repeatedly, even from my own commander. Nonetheless, these statements demonstrate ignorance in the area of psychological trauma. If the dog handlers at the Oklahoma City bombing incident had a "pretty good idea of what they were getting into," would the psychological impacts have been as great? Unfortunately the data shows that they were not prepared. CISD is a way of normalizing a situation so that functioning is restored. However, more is needed to avoid burnout.

6. All individuals and teams need to set up preventive stress management programs on an ongoing basis. Stress management is not 'sissy' but a necessary part of mental and physical health. The examination and acceptance of our own limitations are a beginning. However, we need to recognize and understand our own stress reactions so that we are prepared for the worst scenario. Know your signs and symptoms that you have experienced in the past. Recognizing the behaviors associated with stress reactions can swiftly result in interventions.

7. Be aware of cumulative stress reactions. Incidents back-to-back or problems at home can build up over time and lead to burnout. Keep a record of the incidents attended and your feelings directly after the incident. The workbook *Cumulative Stress Management For Search And Rescue* can take you through the steps of preventing and managing cumulative stress in your search and rescue work (Neudeck-Dicken, Filter Press, 1997).

8. In a highly publicized incident, make sure you keep your family informed. Also, make sure your family members attend a CISD before or directly after your return home. This proved to be very valuable to the Los Angeles and Orange County teams upon their return home. We forget the negative impact SAR has on our families. Often relationships become neglected and children feel abandoned due to the long hours of commitment and 24-hour call schedules. Resentment

and anger are justifiable feelings because love dies from abandonment and neglect. Do not ever forget that our family experiences the trauma of an incident too, simply because we are involved in the incident.

9. Survival of family functioning depends upon how much we are willing to work at fulfilling our family's need. After all, we chose to be in SAR and our families may have had little input in this decision. We need to examine from the beginning whether we can juggle family, job, and search and rescue. Do we have the ability to fulfill the needs of all? What is the price?

10. Know your limitations and your dog's limitations. Most of us in SAR are obsessive compulsive by nature (Neudeck-Dicken, Filter Press 1997). However, the fact remains that no one is really Superman even though I know many that think they are.

    Our personalities alone set us up for stress reactions, because we believe we have to be perfect at everything we do. We become guilty, disappointed, and punishing when we cannot live up to our own expectations. Our attitude also travels down the leash to our K-9 partners. This can explain why Roberta Duhaime reported more than a 50% change in appetite and behavior among the dogs present at the bombing (Duhaime 1998). This can also explain why the handlers showing psychological symptoms after returning home reported depression and fatigue in their dogs (Neudeck-Dicken 1997). When we are "up" our canine partner responds with delight. I have trained mine on a "happy voice." A voice of pain or sorrow is mirrored by the sad sighs of my canine.

11. Since couples at the Oklahoma City bombing either left SAR or divorced shortly after their return (the 50/50 marital impact), measures to protect the relationship need to be in place prior to a major incident. The sanctity of the marriage needs to come first and foremost. I truly believe that a couple should not be at the same incident at the same time. We cannot fulfill marital expectations if both are hurting at the same time. Take turns going to incidents; one goes in the field while the other takes care of work and home needs. This way one can remain objective and the other can emote the incident, and both are involved in taking care of the relationship.

Conclusions

The impacts of the Oklahoma City bombing appear to be centered around multiple issues. From arrival to departure, our SAR dog handlers endured the emotionality of a manmade disaster without a way to distance or a way to defuse. There was a fear to use CISD at the emergency site; afraid that the dumping of emotions could make SAR workers unable to perform their jobs. The majority waited to return home to unload their emotions. Unfortunately many never received CISD. Unloading was done on unprepared loved ones and friends.

Our four-legged partners also endured unnecessary trauma. Not only were they subjected to their handler's emotional impact, but also there are issues around exposure to toxic substances and the long-term affects of such. Since only a small percentage of dogs were decontaminated after working, the repercussions may result in premature death of a beloved canine partner. This adds insult to the critical incident itself. Hopefully the long-term studies will give insight into the veterinary needs of our four-legged helpers, thus avoiding the grief of losing a dog.

Another thing we've learned from the Oklahoma City bombing is that we all can be highly trained in our areas of SAR, and, at the same time, lack training in the psychological skills needed to prevent incident burnout. The point here is that commanders are often more interested in obtaining volunteers to fulfill a need but do not look at the consequences of traumatic incidences on individual functioning. There are individuals that have excellent SAR skills, but will fall apart under stressful situations. These issues need to be resolved prior to the first mission.

Cumulative stress prevention and CISD need to be a part of every team curriculum. The examination and acceptance of our individual limitations are a must for everyone in search and rescue. Denial of this is a catastrophe. We not only need to recognize our stress reactions, but we need to be sensitive to others. We also need to examine death and come to terms with our own mortality. In short, we need to examine the negatives of SAR long before we ever take a mission ready test.

The *urgency* to prepare our emergency personnel for future similar disasters, so that psychological effects will be minimal, is paramount. We also need to reexamine our procedures so that SAR personnel and their dogs are protected from environmental harm during and after their searching. Since interventions concerning manmade disasters are different from natural disasters, we need to focus on this new frontier: terrorism and human-constructed disasters. Oklahoma City was unique. It was America's largest manmade horror show. The very thought that we could become a battleground to internal terrorism devastates the normal American concept of goodwill. Let us use what we have learned from this event and develop positive scenarios for the future. Hopefully time and preparation will increase our knowledge and lessen the impact of future disasters.

Biography

Marilyn Neudeck-Dicken, Ph.D., holds a doctorate in Clinical Health Psychology and has practiced in catastrophic stress management since 1982, when she began working as a psychotherapist to the dying and their families at the Center for the Healing Arts in West Los Angeles. Her experience in CISD began with a Cerritos plane crash in 1986 and included the 1995 Oklahoma City bombing. Her theories on psychological wellness in spite of catastrophic stress are revealed in her book, *Cumulative Stress Management for Search and Rescue: A Workbook for All Emergency Personnel*. She has taught, lectured, and consulted on stress management throughout the United States for more than 12 years. She is a mission ready handler for the San Bernardino County Sheriff's dog team and is a member of the California Rescue Dog

Marilyn Neudeck-Dicken and Woofie.

Association. She lives in Wrightwood, California, with her husband, Michael, and her cadaver-specialized canine partner, Woofie, a German Shepherd.

References

Duhaime, R. (1998) "Injuries and Illnesses in Working Dogs Used in Disaster Response After the Bombing in Oklahoma City," *Journal of the Veterinary Medical Association*, 212(8): 1–6.

Mitchell, J.T., and B. Green (1985) "Healing the Helper." *Role Stressors and Supports for Emergency Workers*. Washington, DC: Center for Mental Health Studies of Emergencies, US Department of Health and Human Services.

Mitchell, J.T. (1983) "When Disaster Strikes: The Critical Incident Stress Debriefing Process." *Journal of Emergency Medical Services*, 8(1): 36–39.

Mitchell, J. and G. Bray (1990). Prentice Hall, New York, *Emergency Services Stress*.

Neudeck-Dicken, M. (1995) "A Practical Approach to SAR Stress Management," *RESPONSE*; Vol.14, Number 3, 14–17.

Neudeck-Dicken, M. (1996) "Psychological Impacts of Oklahoma City Bombing: Then, Now, and Future." Proceedings *RESPONSE* '96. National Association of Search and Rescue, May 29–June 1; 176–193.

Neudeck-Dicken, M. (1997) "Psychological Impacts of Oklahoma City Bombing on Dog Handlers: An Update." Proceedings *RESPONSE* '97. National Association of Search and Rescue, May 27–31; 179–196.

Neudeck-Dicken, M. (1997) Filter Press: Palmer Lake, Co. *Cumulative Stress Management for Search and Rescue: A Workbook for All Emergency Personnel*.

Walk Away Children
Wilderness/Residential Scent Specific

Kathy Newman
Minnesota Search & Rescue Dog Association, Inc.
Mission Date: July 16 and 17, 1993

Mission Type

This is a short search, less than a full day, beginning on July 16, 1993.

The Victims

Two children, a boy, age eight, and a girl, age nine, both in good physical condition. "Tyler" and "Kate" liked to go walking to parks and play areas. They were last seen wearing summer clothes. Point Last Seen

The children were last seen in their home around 1830. (See the map for location details.)The surrounding area included homes, yards, farms, fields, woods, and swamps. The weather was mild with no weather changes during the search mission. The temperature was in the 80s with no noticeable wind.

Search Strategy

On July 16, 1993, the two children left their home to walk to a nearby park. Their father had gone to a store that was close to their home for a few minutes. When he returned, Tyler and Kate were gone. After friends and relatives searched and failed to find the children, they called the local law enforcement agency. The police responded at approximately 2352 on July 16. After searching the area on their own, the police decided to call a SAR unit at approximately 0200.

The police department called MinnSarda and requested us to respond to the incident. One dog handler team arrived within 30 minutes. The dog was trained in both airscenting and tracking. The handler collected a scent article for the dog and cast[1] the dog to try and find a track leading from the house. The dog followed the scent through the backyard to a paved road where the dog seemed to lose the track, approximately a half mile. The handler restarted the dog at the house but the dog followed the same path as before. By this time another handler had arrived with an airscenting dog. Both teams were briefed and, starting from the PLS, the dogs airscented.

As more people and dog teams arrived, we set up base near the home of the missing children. We established radio communications for each new team and we sent them into the field. By daylight all of the searchers had searched a very large area, which included the swamp, outbuildings, the yards, and homes in the area. At this point in the search, we

---

[1] To "cast" a dog is to give it scent and command the dog to find the scent. The dog will cast about looking

became concerned that someone may have kidnapped Tyler and Kate. As more people arrived, we made flyers and distributed them in the area. People were going from door to door talking to people in the neighborhood. One person who lived on the route the tracking dog had followed said that she had seen the children walking down the road Friday evening, the night before.

The first dog team that had arrived at the search was about one mile from the PLS and was reviewing search strategies with a support person. It was now about 1000 on July 17. The dog handler noticed a high-power line that ran toward the PLS. The area under the line was cleared of brush. Since this would be an easy route for the children, the handler decided to search this area. As the handler started down the power line path, the dog gave an alert on someone ahead. At the same time the support person

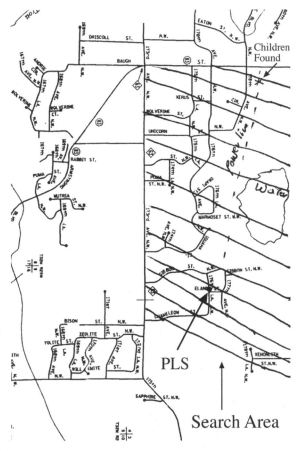

saw some movement. The dog moved further ahead with the handler and support person close behind. They had found them. They were frightened and tried to hide from the search team. However, with a few reassuring words from the team, the children stood up. The team checked the children to be sure that they were not hurt and radioed back to base. Other than being thirsty and having a few bug bites, the kids were fine. A squad car met everyone at the road and drove Tyler and Kate back home to their family.

Apparently the children had walked to the park. When they tried to return home, they got lost. Instead of wandering around they sat in the field waiting for someone to come and find them. Upon investigating the case, it turned out that the trail that the tracking dog had followed was where the kids had walked.

This search was a success because of the team effort made by everyone in the mission. The police called the search team in a timely fashion and everyone worked together.

Search Tips

Be prepared for the types of searches your unit will respond to. Training and maintenance training must go on if you and your dog are in active service.

You've probably heard it a dozen times, but be honest about your skills and your dog's skills.

Keep an open mind about what to do and how to do it. You need to listen to all of the people involved in the search; however, don't be afraid to use your own skills and knowledge when out searching. For example, a family member of the missing person insists that the search team must look near the PLS because the missing person could not walk far due to poor health, yet you've seen people in similar health travel much further than anyone expected. You need to use your own experience and knowledge to make judgments as to where to search.

Having said that, a search is a team effort. Without the support of others many searches would not be successful.

Keep learning. You never know it all.

Keep the search moving. Don't get locked into the idea that the missing person could only be in one area. Encourage the teams to search in new areas.

Biography

Kathy Newman has been training dogs formally and informally since childhood. She has also trained horses. In 1980 she joined the police reserves and started training and working with them. In 1981 she learned about a new SAR unit which was forming in her area and joined it. She is still a member of that unit, MinnSAR Dog Association, Inc. For the past 12 years she has been the director of training for MinnSAR. She has owned and worked four German Shepherds and one Belgian Malinois. In 1985 she had one of the first dogs to have a water find in the unit. In 1990 she trained with Andy Rebman, and her dog qualified as a cadaver dog team.

Kathy has participated in approximately 300 searches, ranging from wilderness, water, cadaver, and evidence. Her present dog is qualified in all of these areas. Kathy has had three homicide finds in her career. Her dog found two ski masks used in an armed robbery that had lain in the woods for three weeks.

Besides SAR work, Kathy trains police service dogs for arson and drug detection, and also trains hearing and assistance dogs. She is a lieutenant in the police reserves and a part-time licensed peace officer.

Possible Suicide
Wilderness Airscent

Deborah S. Palman
 Maine Warden Service
 Maine Search and Rescue Dogs
 Location of Mission: Centerville, Maine
 Dates of Mission: November 6 and November 18, 1996

Mission Type

This search was short and illustrates some "special" search techniques involving airborne scent and some initial poor management, which did not affect the outcome of the search. It is a search with circumstances that are typical of searches involving suicides or other mentally impaired individuals. Particularly those who wish to disappear or are otherwise unable to help themselves when they become stranded or lost. Often relatives do not report missing victims for some time because the victims are loners or the only information their relatives can provide is that the victim left in a vehicle. Without a ground location to search (PLS), the victim becomes a "missing person" of low search priority until their vehicle is found. If the victim's vehicle is left in a populated area, others have usually rescued or found the victim before or shortly after their relatives report them missing. Overworked state, town, or city police agencies typically handle missing persons reports instead of organizations with more aggressive stances toward search and rescue. Searches for these victims usually do not start until their vehicle is found or the relatives contact a SAR oriented organization. The relatives then have to provide the appropriate background information to convince such a SAR organization to begin a search. Unfortunately, this delay often results in the mentally impaired or suicide victim being found deceased. Persons determined to commit suicide will usually be found deceased, but the sooner the search for them starts, the easier they are to find. Overall, suicidal and mentally impaired victims are not found far from their vehicle or the PLS, often within one mile. They generally follow some sort of terrain feature or travel corridor rather than striking off for long distances in thick cover. They travel in easy areas until exposure overcomes them, or until they encounter difficult traveling and they stop or become stuck. If the area is easy to walk through, the victim will travel further. The woods in Northern and Eastern Maine are difficult for able-bodied searchers to walk through. By walking the area on foot to gain knowledge about the travel conditions in the search area, it is possible for an experienced searcher to determine the behavior of the missing person who is physically or mentally impaired. This is difficult to do if the missing person is an outdoor enthusiast who may seek a remote location.

The Victim

Male, approximately 35 years old, in normal physical condition and health, except that he was a drug user (cocaine, etc.). He did some canoeing, camping and fishing in the area, and had outdoor knowledge. He lived alone and often left his home or the area for long periods without telling friends where he was going. He worked in a boat yard.

Our initial information said that he was last seen around mid-September. Later investigation by warden service personnel put this date closer to October 1. His relatives did not report him missing until mid-October. Friends and coworkers felt that he may have committed suicide—he was a drug user and became depressed at times—but they said that he didn't mention this before he left. He did not own any firearms.

The family originally reported him missing to the local sheriff's department. As is typical with the way police agencies handle missing persons, the department put his name and a description in a statewide teletype and added his name to the Maine "wanted and missing" list. No other search or investigation was done at the time. Also, at the time relatives reported him missing, there was no information available to show that a ground search was needed.

In mid-October, a bird hunter or camp owner reported an abandoned vehicle at Great Falls. It was the victim's vehicle. Great Falls is a very remote location and the vehicle was parked as if someone was hunting or fishing in the area. It may have taken awhile for someone to decide that the vehicle was abandoned. The sheriff's office towed the vehicle away and did not try to find the owner except to check areas near the vehicle. Mysteriously, nothing was left in the vehicle that gave any information as to the occupant's intentions, such as a suicide note, ammunition, fishing gear, camping gear, etc.

Point Last Seen

The ground search was initiated in early November when relatives of the victim contacted the Maine Warden Service, the state agency in charge of inland search and rescue. The relatives explained the circumstances involved in finding the missing man's car in mid-October. The warden service classified this search as a "low urgency search" because if the victim had left the vehicle on foot, he had probably committed suicide shortly after leaving the vehicle. November is also a time of peak enforcement activity for the warden service. However, if the warden service had postponed the search until later in the year after the hunting seasons were over, snow might have covered the body and other clues.

Where and when did the incident take place?

When the victim's vehicle was found in mid-October, it was at the end of a branch of a remote woods road, which led to a camp on the Machias River at Great Falls (see map). The vehicle was in plain sight of the river and the camp yard. For the purpose of this search, the warden service assumed that the vehicle was the PLS.

Terrain Features

The main terrain feature in the area of the PLS is the Machias River, which has a moderate current and flat water, except the rapids near Great Falls. A few small hills and ridges border the river, but much of the land next to the river is flat. Paths follow the river's edge, which connect one camp and traveled road to the next. The only roads or ATV trails that were passable where those maintained by camp owners or by people portaging around the falls with canoes. Two camps were within a mile north of the PLS. Although the USGS map shows some structures south of the PLS, these did not exist. The rest of the woods were thick and difficult to walk through since they had been cut over or burned by forest

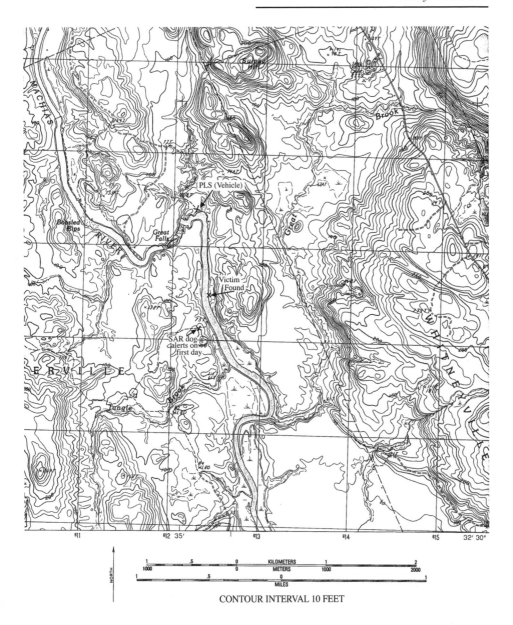

CONTOUR INTERVAL 10 FEET

fires in the past. Except for a few areas where ledges or sandy areas were left bare by the low water levels, most of the eight- to fifteen-foot high banks leading down to the river were steep or covered with thick grass or vegetation. This made walking along the banks of the river difficult.

Weather

The weather from September to November was generally warm for that time of year. Daytime temperatures ranged from 40–60°F during the day with frosts at night. There were a few days below freezing. Rain but no snow fell during October and early November. The leaf fall was complete by the end of October and may have covered some clues. The weather for the first day of the search was low clouds with light winds from the east. Although there was some warming from the sun, it never really broke through the clouds, and temperatures were in the low 50s.

Any Other Special Information

Since this was a "low priority" search with incomplete background information, warden service supervisors decided to run a hasty search. They wanted to cover the high-probability areas that would apply to a victim who had committed suicide. If the victim was not found in that time, warden service responsibility would end unless more definite information developed which showed that the victim was in the woods.

Search Personnel and Equipment

Because of the low priority and the proposed scope of the first day's search, the resources present were probably sufficient. We could have used a good management team or IC. A single commander and planner could have deployed the resources present.

We received the following: five certified SAR dog teams, three trainee handlers from Maine Search and Rescue Dogs, three district wardens, one warden sergeant, one warden lieutenant, a warden pilot and plane with observer, and one deputy sheriff.

I was a district warden and one of the five SAR dog teams. Both the sergeant and lieutenant were newly promoted to their positions and were not past or present members of the Warden Service Search Management Team.

Search Strategy

The initial strategy of the search was based on the assumption that the subject had committed suicide. This would account for the location of his car and the four to five weeks that he'd been missing, and the limited background information available indicated that suicide was a definite possibility. Based on previous SAR statistics, suicides are found close to the PLS (within a half-mile). We deployed four sets of certified dog teams and assistants (wardens or dog handlers in training). We assigned two teams to each side of the river. One team on each side of the river went upstream from the PLS and one went downstream. Another dog team worked in a canoe downstream from the falls. The remaining wardens checked camps and camping places within several miles of the PLS. Grid teams composed of wardens searched areas within a quarter-mile of the PLS, and searched paths on the side of the river where the vehicle was found. The vehicle was parked at the furthest downstream place it could be driven. This made it appear that a downstream location or other location on the river was the driver's objective. Therefore, downstream from where the vehicle was found was considered the highest probability area for the search. We gave the side of the river where the vehicle was found a higher probability because the river could only be crossed by swimming or taking a boat or canoe. However, the victim was known to borrow a canoe from others so we searched the inaccessible side of the river as well. The possible use of a canoe expanded the search area considerably.

We assigned the plane to fly the whole river to look for canoes and campsites and to check boat landings where the victim may have left a canoe. The plane was effective for searching the river, its banks, and open areas. Unfortunately, most of the area was heavily wooded, making it very difficult for the pilot to see to the ground.

The teams that searched areas along the riverbank also searched paths, clearings, or other travel lanes they encountered. We instructed the team searching downstream from the PLS to work deeper into the woods perpendicular to the river. They had to search a small knoll next to the river, which was about a quarter-mile downstream from the PLS. This was done because SAR literature teaches that suicide victims often seek out hills or high places. Contrary to these statistics, this has not been my personal experience in Maine, unless a path led up the hill. The teams started searching about 0800.

The boundaries of the search on the first day were determined more by the "hasty" scope of the search than by the physical features. The overall objective was to search at least one mile on each side of the river from the PLS.

At about 1200 on that first day, most of the teams had returned without finding clues or the victim. One dog team did have some long-distance alerts on a knoll on the opposite side of the river about a mile downstream from the PLS. A "long-distance" alert is an alert where the dog picks up scent in clearings or on hills but is unable to follow it off the hill. This can happen because the scent travels over the tops of the trees from a long distance away, rather than from a nearby source on the ground. In retrospect, it would have been a good idea to investigate these alerts further. However, the dog handler attributed them to the scent from the other teams who were working up wind in the area. The dog handler reported the alerts to base, but the acting IC, who was not familiar with dogs, did not understand what their significance was. The team working in the canoe and the dog teams on the same side of the river as the PLS did not report any alerts. By 1200 the ground searchers and dog teams were tired from working through the thick cover. It had been a hard day, which we ended with a short debriefing. Although the searchers reported what they had found, there was no effective follow-up by management. Therefore the supervisors made no determination about how far the teams had actually searched along the river. As it turned out, the team working downstream from the PLS searched perpendicular to the river and did not get any further than a half-mile from the PLS. The team in the canoe and the team on the other side of the river, which had reported the alerts, did get up to one one-half to two miles below the PLS.

We suspended the search to wait for more information from a warden service investigator who was assigned to the case. Within a week or so the investigator narrowed down the time when the victim went missing from mid-September to the first few days of October. We were able to get a more detailed profile of the victim's clothing, state of mind, and habits. All of the information indicated that he had committed suicide, although no one could determine if he had a firearm or other means of suicide with him.

Two local wardens visited Great Falls again at midday on November 11 to look in the area around the camp again. The weather was sunny and warm with a strong breeze out of the south from directly down river. The wardens walked the riverbank on paths near the PLS. They walked the portage trail on the ridge by the falls, which went over a small knoll on the north side of the bend of the river. This hill blocked the breeze coming from the long straight stretch of water downstream from the PLS. On this hill the wardens reported smelling something rotten. The smell was so strong that they expected to find a body in that area, right there between the path and the river. They searched this area thoroughly, but could not find anything. This was the area I was assigned to cover with my dog on the first day, so I would have been surprised if they located something. Several days later they discussed the smell with me. I recognized it immediately from previous search experiences as the human version of a SAR dog's long-distance scent alert. Obviously the body of the victim was somewhere downstream along the river. From experience I knew that this decomposing scent was detectable by humans for up to a mile or two. With this information I determined that the body was beyond the areas that we had searched. I consulted with the handler of the dog team who searched downstream from the PLS. I verified that they did not go farther than a half-mile from the PLS. If I had remembered the details about the distance alerts and wind direction from the handler on the other side of the river, I could have plotted two lines based on the wind direction and walked right to the victim[1]. However, I had discounted those alerts as alerts on the scent of other searchers.

Based on the new information given to me by the two wardens at Great Falls, I offered to take what volunteer SAR dog teams could respond and try to find the victim downstream from Great Falls. As it turned out, I was only able to find one other dog team, two handlers in training, and my deputy warden to assist. The warden service plane would arrive later.

On November 18, the two dog teams and assistants arrived at the scene about 1030. The weather was mostly cloudy, about 50°F with very light southerly winds. After carefully studying a map, I decided that Great Brook, which was long, flat, and flowed into the Machias River about two miles below the PLS, would be the lower boundary. It was unlikely that the victim would have crossed this brook. My deputy and I decided to search the lower end of our sector working from the brook north to a surveyor's flagging line. We set the flagging line as we walked south along the river. Our sector included the riverbanks and the inland areas. The other team and handlers in training searched the upper area of the riverbank, inland areas, and a knoll, which were south and upwind of Great Falls. Great Falls was where the wardens smelled the rotten smell.

Walking the riverbank and adjoining woods was not easy. There were no roads, paths, or easy travel ways along the river or in the woods. Moderately thick softwood covered the area. Alders covered a moderately steep riverbank, which leveled off about 10 to 15 feet above the river level. Anyone who traveled the river by a small boat or canoe would be unable to see anything on the ground unless it was on the sloped part of the bank. It is also probable that this slope caused the scent of the victim to be lofted up. This would put the scent above the SAR dog we deployed in the canoe on the first day. This dog was an experienced cadaver dog and would've reacted to the victim's scent if it were available.

Below the flag line, about a half-mile below Great Falls, a marshy, grassy area opened up 100 yards from the river. A 75- to 100-yard strip of softwood cover lay between the marsh and the river. Inland from the marsh was an area of thick growth, which a forest fire had burned about twenty years ago. I walked on the inland side of the softwood strip

---

[1] Years ago—before warden service started using SAR dogs—during a search for an elderly man who had been missing for a week during hot weather in August, search managers found that searchers reported smelling something rotten, which seemed to curl down out of the sky in small clearings. The person in charge of the map began plotting these "smells" and found that they were all on a line according to the wind direction. By the end of the week, the search was expanding greatly and the managers expanded it upwind. The wind shifted 90 degrees the morning before the deceased victim was found. One of the "sniff patrols" sent out late that morning reported a smell in a new location. The appropriate wind direction was plotted on the map, and the two lines intersected right where a grid search team found the victim's body that afternoon. The autopsy revealed that he had been deceased for over a week before he was found.

about 50 yards into the marsh. My deputy walked the riverbank. My dog worked the areas between and in front of us. At approximately 1400, one mile below Great Falls, my dog broke her regular searching pattern and ran into the softwoods near the river. Her bell fell silent as she stopped moving. As I started to investigate, my deputy called to me from the dog's location, "I've found him."

My deputy had found a fairly new beer can while walking along the riverbank. When she saw it, she thought that it was likely that the victim would drink a beer before he committed suicide. When she looked up, she saw him lying on level ground about ten feet from the edge of the bank slope. He was lying under a thick softwood canopy among some small trees. He had shot himself with an SKS rifle, which was still fully loaded, less one shot. Because this was a semi automatic weapon it was ready to fire again, and it could have been dangerous to searchers or dogs if a dog had stepped on it. The remains of a small fire were near the body; however, we could not be sure that the victim had built it. A "druggist" fold of paper (commonly used to hold cocaine or other hard drugs) was found between the beer can and the victim's body. There were no other clues in the area that would have led searchers to the body. The only clue was the odor. Later investigation revealed that one of the victim's friends owned the rifle and did not know it was missing

Just when we found the victim, the warden service plane arrived to help with the search. Flying over the victim, the pilot found that the canopy was too thick to see the victim. In addition, the victim was wearing dark colored clothing. The pilot notified the appropriate authorities that the victim had been found. Due to the terrain and distance to the body, state police detectives and sheriff's deputies used a boat and a canoe to get to the victim and process the scene. They removed the body by boat.

Results of the Mission

The outcome probably would have been the same no matter when the search was initiated, since the victim was determined to committed suicide. The search might have concluded on the first day if the management of the search had been better.

What are Your Feelings About the Mission?

On a personal level, I have participated in at least a half-dozen searches for persons that the search team felt would be deceased when found. We felt the victim would be deceased because of suicide, exposure, or because the search was not initiated right away. Some searchers feel that searches that are assumed to be for deceased persons are less exciting or pressing than searches involving victims who could be found alive. Nevertheless, searches for deceased persons provide closure for relatives and for investigative purposes. Finding a dead (long dead in this case) victim is no longer stressful for me. Earlier in my search career, though, I did find this type of mission stressful. I think that my stress was in part due to the fear of finding a body. I did go though a time when I had trouble searching for bodies, but now I have become desensitized to the fear of finding a body.

On a management or searcher level, after reviewing the management of this search on the first day, I realize that I should have been more responsible for its proper management. Two other supervisors at the scene outranked me. I assumed that they would take charge and provide adequate management. However, I was the most senior warden and the one with the most experience and training in SAR management and strategy. My supervisors acknowledged this when they asked me to assign search sectors to the dog teams. The dog teams were our major search resource at the scene. After the assignments, which included an area for my dog and me, I left the rest of the record keeping and follow up to the supervisors. Unfortunately, they did not have the experience or training to do this correctly. At the very least, I should have reviewed exactly how far along the river the dog teams searched.

I also should have taken the long-distance alerts more seriously. As it turned out, this dog was probably alerting on the victim. The victim was found directly upwind from where the alerts were made. The team in the canoe reported no alerts even though they passed within 50 feet of the victim, because the victim was on a level about 10 to 15 feet above the river's surface. This shows that the scent was rising above the level of the water.

Despite the mistakes we made, I felt that the mission was successful. Because the local wardens had returned to the area and smelled the rotten smell, warden service searched the area again. If they had not returned to the area and noticed the smell, we would not have found the victim when we did. He would have been found eventually, since the SAR dog group or a local ground search unit would have resumed the search later as a training exercise. The use of GPS units by searchers and the ability to plot the extent of their searching on a map would have helped. This would have allowed the searcher to know exactly how far the teams had traveled.

Search Tips

Good search management is absolutely vital to ensure that the best and most efficient job is done searching for the victim. Good management and searching is only provided by trained and experienced individuals who have a sincere interest in finding the victim. Because many official agencies do not have these skills or interests, relatives must be persistent in contacting the proper resources to do the job. Sometimes volunteer SAR groups will do a better job than official agencies if those agencies do not have the interest or means to manage or conduct a search. Unless some official agency prohibits them from searching, I see no reason why volunteer SAR groups cannot take the initiative if other agencies do not.

Victims usually follow travel "lanes," natural features, or easier traveling through thick areas until they get lost or stuck in thick cover. They get stuck for many reasons such as mental incapacity, darkness, etc. Search planners can gain insight about where the victim would go or travel if they would, one, have teams walk the areas near the PLS and, two, use reports from experienced woods wise searchers. For example, a conservation officer who is familiar with where and how people travel in wilderness areas can often determine a route of travel. They do this by using any clues left at the scene (like where the car was parked in the Centerville search) or by the terrain itself. Missing people seem to naturally orient to something when they are traveling, such as roads, paths, water, open areas, cover changes, etc. Tracking dogs can determine a direction of travel or check travel routes for scent. Even if the tracking dog does not locate the victim while tracking, the dog team will contribute to the successful outcome of the mission by showing a direction of travel.

Dog teams used at searches should be well trained to a credible and demonstrable level. Agencies that manage searches should be aware of what credible training is and encourage or demand that volunteer ground and dog rescue units meet these criteria.

The scent of live or dead persons can travel and be detected by trained dogs up to a 1.5

miles or more in wooded conditions. This is possible when the scent lofts above the trees and curls down into openings. Human searchers can similarly detect the rotten smell of a long dead person. If the victim cannot be located, the search planners should plot the prevailing wind direction (over the tops of the trees) and weather conditions on a master map.

Dog handlers must report all long-distance alerts given by their dogs. Each must be checked carefully by the handlers and the search command. This clue is no different than if the ground search team heard someone shout back in response to their calls. The search command should know if other searchers are upwind from the dog team and causing the alerts. Dog teams will not always know this, since the search commander doesn't always tell them where they deploy all of the resources.

Bloodhounds working tracks that are more than several hours old often track well in wooded terrain at night. In very still conditions they can have trouble when they encounter the scent pool of the victim who has been lying in one spot for many hours or several days. Sometimes the hound will circle continuously if the cover is thick. The handler can become discouraged and worn out. The handler may assume that the hound has lost the trail. This has happened several times during night searches in Maine. After the handlers thrashed in circles in the dark for a quarter-hour or more, they gave up and walked out, but the victims were found alive (one who was missing for three days in early spring!) in the area where the hound had circled. Apparently the hound's nose is actually too sensitive to localize the source of the scent. This would be similar to a person who walked into a house filled with smoke and was unable to find the exact source of the smoke. Search managers should dispatch an airscent dog team or a ground search team to work the area where the hound was circling. Bloodhound handlers could avoid the problem if they practice tracks where the victim has lain at the end of the trail for hours or days, so that the hound would learn how to work this type of scent pool in training. If the hound circles during the day, it is not as much of a problem, because the handler may see the victim, or the scent can disperse, allowing the hound to find the victim.

Biography

I have been employed as a Maine warden for the Maine Department of Inland Fisheries and Wildlife for 20 years. I have been a police K-9 handler and trainer for 18 years, training and handling three personal dogs who were fully police and airscent SAR trained. I have provided training for other agencies. I have been active in the training and deployment of SAR dogs (primarily airscent) for 15 years, serving as founder and training director for the Maine Search and Rescue Dogs. Currently MESARD consists of approximately a dozen volunteer handlers and their dogs.

I have taken the MASAR Managing the Search Function Course and participate in an average of 20 searches a year as one of the initial responding officers and search manager, and/or as a handler of a SAR dog. My dogs and I have had the honor of finding six victims during searches, three of them alive, one of which was a life-saving find.

Author's Note

On July 29, 1998, Deborah Palman wrote me a letter, which she has given me permission to reprint in this book. Her candid comments express what many of us in SAR have felt or experienced at one time or another.

Last week I had my first live find with Anna, my third search and rescue dog, and about the fourth live find in my 18 year career of wilderness search and rescue work with a dog. I was actually on vacation in Vermont, attending a police K-9 training seminar, when one of the local teams got a call to search for a possibly suicidal woman who had been missing for three days. He asked us for help, and we suspended the seminar to go search. I worked my assigned area for three hours, and, having the only real airscent-trained dog there, was able to cover ground more rapidly than the other teams. It turned out that the woman was near the junction of three of the search areas assigned to the dogs. Being the fastest of the three teams, we got close to her first. My dog hit the scent pool, quite large after three days, and led me to the woman at the base of a cliff. I don't know exactly what happened to her, but she must have jumped or fallen off the cliff as she was in very bad shape with broken bones and severely dehydrated after three days with no water. We were very lucky to find her quickly and find her still alive.

Someone who has not worked with police or SAR dogs cannot understand the type of emotion this type of find brings to a dog handler. It is not just the end product of a day's work with other search resources and the temporary "team" formed for that day, but the end product of raising a dog, training it every day of its life, nursing it through sickness and health, and spending day after day with other SAR dog unit members training for search and rescue work. Training for a year or more, testing for and passing certifications, and searching at many other searches where the victim was somewhere besides your area. Then at a particular search, the dog simply does just what you have trained it to do—locate a person in your assigned area. It is very simple, really, but few others besides dog handlers know what kind of work and emotional commitment have gone into that simple action.

Tragedy in the Heartland:
The Oklahoma City Bombing

By

Dewey H. Perks

The morning of April 19, 1995, dawned bright and beautiful in America's heartland as the citizens of Oklahoma City awoke to start their day. No one realized at the time, but events planned for that morning would forever alter their lives. When the bomb detonated in front of the Alfred P. Murrah building shortly after 0900, not only were 168 Oklahoma residents killed, but hundreds more were injured. As the nation became absorbed with the story and the ensuing dramatic rescue efforts, it could be safely implied that our entire country was affected in a way that would forever change their thinking. This incident, more than any other, brought home to Americans the fact that terrorism could strike anywhere at anytime. Before the emergency ended, thousands of citizens arrived in Oklahoma to aid in the best way they could. This is the story of Virginia Task Force One's role in that effort.

The Federal Emergency Management Agency (FEMA) had been very active during the 24 months prior to the bombing developing a new resource for disaster response. Utilizing a model program developed by the State Department's Agency for International Development, it had begun the process of developing a nationwide response system for Urban Search and Rescue. The process included the solicitation of teams that would be known as task forces. These teams would then receive training and equipment and performing on-site readiness evaluations would validate their preparedness.

The Fairfax County Virginia Fire and Rescue Department was selected by FEMA to be the sponsoring organization of one of the original 26 task forces. As an early player in this arena, the State Department had deployed Virginia Task Force One to Armenia (1988) and the Philippines (1990). Their job during these missions was to assist in the rescue of missing people who were trapped due to deadly earthquakes. Our task force was formed from a core of over 100 members, consisting of five distinct disciplines: management, search, medical, rescue, and technical. If selected for deployment, that group would consist of 56 members (currently 62) who could work and be self-sufficient for 72 hours in a devastated austere environment. In the field, the group could perform the three phases of search, which include physical, canine, and electronic. The team also includes heavy rescue personnel trained in the techniques of breaking, breaching, and lifting reinforced concrete. Advanced medical care, using board-certified physicians, and paramedics are also a part of the team. Technical expertise is also required, which includes hazardous-material defense, rigging, structural analysis, internal communications, administrative support, and equipment cache[1] management. A management group, experienced in incident command procedures, heads these facets of the task force.

In early 1995, FEMA selected discipline-specific experts to form an evaluation cadre to visit the 26 task forces and gauge their operational readiness. This cadre received extensive training so that they could conduct the evaluations and develop a scoring criterion for FEMA's use. By March of that year several task forces had been evaluated, giving FEMA information on the readiness and availability of the teams. This information proved vital for FEMA because now they could identify shortfalls and develop a task force corrective action plan that would make up for these deficiencies in advance and, if necessary, order critical equipment for the task force.

As the magnitude of the destruction became more apparent in the days immediately after the Oklahoma City bombing, FEMA deployed task forces from the nearest jurisdictions and an Incident Support Team (IST), which is an overseer coordination team. It was the job of the IST to integrate federal assets into the local action plan. Along with staff from the national FEMA headquarters, six members from Virginia Task Force One were selected for the IST and they departed immediately via a commercial air carrier.

During this time, task force members from across the nation remained focused on the news reports coming from Oklahoma City. Managers from Virginia Task Force One busied themselves in this initial phase of pending deployment by rechecking the equipment cache, members' availability, and personal gear. As we continued to monitor the situation, we doubted that we would be called out since all news reports showed only the shattered skeleton of the Murrah building. Based on these reports, we believed that the assets already dispatched (other task forces, the IST), coupled with the massive Oklahoma response, would be all that was needed. But our preparations continued, just in case.

FEMA provided daily advisories to the task forces, which kept them up-to-date on the current situation and their anticipated resource requests. As additional task forces and IST members were sent to Oklahoma, it became more obvious that we too would be sent. On April 22 at approximately 2200, we received our activation order. We were to depart on the next day, April 23. All of the work that we had done previously to get ready in case we were called was a great help. Even so, the managers worked through the night to form the task force. As members were selected and the cache was readied, hurried goodbyes were said. Still filled with bravado, loved ones were told to expect us home soon, probably in time for Easter.

The task force assembled at the department's training academy and prepared for the short bus ride to Andrews Air Force Base, its point of departure. Although many of the members selected for the mission had been dispatched to several international and domestic incidents, the majority had never been previously deployed as a FEMA team. However, they had been members of the task force for several years. As the management team continued to gather information and plan its arrival in Oklahoma, the experienced members briefed the others on what they had learned from past missions. They explained what to expect in the next 24 hours.

Andrews Air Force Base is the home for Air Force One, and any presidential movement causes strict security at the base. President Clinton was due to arrive at Andrews Air Force

---

[1] A cache is the term used to refer to the tools, equipment, and supplies that deploy with a task force. For Oklahoma City, this amounted to over 56,000 pounds of equipment.

Base to travel to Tinker Air Force Base in Oklahoma City. Because of this, our base travel was somewhat restricted. As Air Force One rolled out onto the runway, the importance of our mission was amplified. The President himself was going to Oklahoma City to view the work done thus far and to show the citizens of Oklahoma that the thoughts and hopes of the nation were with them. Once we were wheels up, we attempted to rest and prepare for the task at hand. However, anticipation kept most of us awake for the short flight.

Tinker Air Force Base officers and IST members met us once we were in Oklahoma City. They drove us on military buses to the Myriad Convention Center, which became home to many task forces during the incident. It also provided our first exposure to the citizens of Oklahoma. At the time of the bombing, a restaurant association conference was being held at the Myriad. Many attendees stayed on to provide meals for the rescuers. The center was transformed into a beehive of activity. As task forces arrived, other areas within the convention center were established to supply rescuers with creature comforts and amenities. Everywhere we went in the center, we were met by Oklahomans whose only mission it seemed was to make our life there more comfortable. As the days continued these examples of kindness were forever etched into our minds and many lasting friendships were developed.

Soon after our arrival, we established an equipment cache area on the main floor of the center. We were given sleeping space in a meeting area and everyone busied themselves with unpacking. Next we attended a management briefing and the task force was assembled for a team update. Security remained a major factor at the federal building with photo identification required to enter the secured perimeter of the blast site. The group made the short trip to the nearby FBI field office by foot to get our ID cards. Although we were several blocks from ground zero, we began to witness the awesome power of the bomb. Several buildings had cosmetic damage, such as missing glass, trees had been stripped of leaves, and many main streetlights were missing their heads. The streets were eerily quiet and nearly devoid of traffic as the cleanup began.

Once we were given proper identification we returned to the Myriad to gather equipment we would need prior to proceeding to the Murrah building. As we made our way there it became more obvious that the damage we had witnessed on the news was in no way a fair representation of what had occurred. Everywhere we looked, as we got closer to the federal building, we observed a greater and greater degree of destruction. A forward staging area had been established one block from the Murrah building that provided a secure storage area for our equipment and shelter for our members. As we left there and walked the remaining way through the incredible destruction, we became acutely aware of why we had been dispatched. It was then that we realized that we would not be leaving anytime soon.

Approaching the federal building from side three, (each side of the building was numbered for easy reference among rescuers) we observed the rear of the structure that at first glance appeared to be almost intact. Task forces were entering the sub-levels of the structure from an entrance on side four and there was a steady stream of rescuers on the driving ramps of the underground parking area. At the corner of sides one and four a general decontamination area had been established to accommodate everyone who worked in the area. As we turned the corner to face side one, everyone stopped and gaped at the total destruction that we saw. We were not prepared for the sight that met us. Although the news media had shown wide-angle views of the site, most of the coverage had concentrated on the activities at the Murrah building itself and hadn't shown the surrounding buildings. All of us stood as silent onlookers as we surveyed the task ahead of us.

We were directed to the front of the building and were informed that this area would be our operational work site. Around us swirled an ever-present dust cloud while large cranes loomed overhead. Throughout the building, paper debris continued to float to the street while large slabs of concrete (referred to as widow makers) hung by rebar. Our assignment was clear, but seemed insurmountable; we were to remove all debris from the area and rescue any survivors that we found during the operation. With renewed hopes of detecting signs of life, we began our assignment.

A task force consists of an established number of members (56 for this mission) so the group can operate either as a whole or be divided equally to support 24-hour operations. Virginia Task Force One was instructed to operate as a whole for this mission, thus allowing us to work in a full strength (blitz type) mode of operation. Planning called for us to remove all debris from the site using all means available. Since this was a very active crime scene, scores of federal agents were involved. They scanned all of the debris we removed for evidence before it went into a large dumpster. Ever present during these work cycles were the men and women from the Oklahoma City Fire Department and other area departments. They worked hand-in-hand with the task forces and federal agents. A common misconception in disaster operations is that once on the site, FEMA takes over the management of the incident. This is not so and Oklahoma City is a good example of how local officials continuously set operational objectives and provided direct incident management. The task forces fell under the direct supervision of these local officials and worked exclusively for them.

The debris removal plan involved using heavy rescue tools to cut through the intact slabs of concrete. Once the concrete was cut, it was removed by one of many cranes operating at the site. As a new area was exposed, it was thoroughly searched by both canine and electronic means. Countless boreholes were drilled into these slabs where a search camera and fiber optic devices could then be inserted to search for the missing people. The canines had free roam of the debris when a new area was opened in the hope that they would lead us to a find. The explosion had in many instances reduced the building to chunks of concrete, which ranged in size from dust to slabs weighing hundreds of pounds. In many instances the building was reduced to pebble-sized debris that was inspected and then placed in five-gallon buckets for removal. Because of this, long lines of rescuers passed slabs and buckets to remove the debris. Federal agents searched for clues as they observed the collection and removal of each bucket. They had briefed all the rescuers about the types of evidence that could be expected (or hoped) to be found.

As we worked at the site, the incident managers were working on a plan that called for us to prepare to switch to an alternate work schedule. With the constant arrival of additional rescue resources, management decided to place us on the evening (1900 - 0700) shift to ensure that a 24-hour operation could be maintained. Once the decision was made, we rotated from the site very early in the morning to allow us to return to the Myriad for a short rest before we returned to start our new schedule.

Though we were now on a 12-hour shift, it actually equated to a 20-hour workday. To prepare for the day's work, members would get up four hours early to be sure that repairs were made to equipment, eat, tend to personal needs, and to receive medical attention. The cycle would repeat at the end of each shift, with additional emphasis placed on medical attention. The medical team worked very hard during the mission to ensure that no minor malady would develop into a problem that could affect a rescuer's ability to work. The chief complaints of the members centered on the expected aches and pains of skin abrasions and blisters.

The canines were also examined in the same manner; pad laceration from shards of glass were a major concern. Where the glass was located in the debris was determined by the collapse patterns and debris layout following the bombing. While each collapsed building is different, the absolute destruction of this building made these patterns unique. The dust created from the debris can also hinder a canine and cause impactions[2] or eye irritations. Hundreds of pairs of "canine booties" arrived unsolicited in Oklahoma City, but these could not safely be used since they would restrict the canine's mobility on the many uneven surfaces they encountered. As the mission continued, fatigue and stress became more and more apparent in the whole group.

As I mentioned earlier, the kindness extended by the citizens of Oklahoma was overwhelming. Using the Myriad as our home base provided protection from the scores of media that had descended upon the town and the locals guaranteed our security from them. We interacted with the locals at the beginning and ending of each shift, but we were not ready for the manner in which they treated us. Being from Virginia we felt that we were very familiar with the mystique of "the genteel South" and its hospitality. Yet every time we met the locals, they expressed their gratitude and concern that we should be careful. At first we interpreted this as a method to encourage us to work harder, but as the days wore on, we realized that they knew we were truly working as hard as we could. The citizens waited on us hand and foot and we actually had to be careful what we requested since anything we asked for was delivered. Besides having our meals supplied, a small support city evolved within the confines of the Myriad. This included podiatrists, opticians, masseuses, shipment anywhere by United Parcel Service, telephone service by Southwest Bell, and a barbershop. Each day there were new "hosts" in the center. These were people who just wanted to help or others who had family directly affected by the bombing.

The work became personal. We began to think of those who were still missing as members of our extended families. In a disaster the dead and injured usually remain nameless, which helps rescuers stay above that type of attachment. In Oklahoma City, however, we came to know these people and strove to work even harder to help our new friends in the healing process that the recovery of their missing loved one would allow.

Every day we would return to our sleeping quarters at the Myriad to find our cots freshly made. Our cots were also covered with cards from the children of Oklahoma City thanking us for our work for to them. We had somehow become the "Heroes of the Heartland." Their messages of encouragement strengthened our tired bodies and helped us face the stern task still ahead. As we prepared to return to the site one evening, we met a group of teenagers from Deer Creek Middle School who had written their thoughts of the bombing as a class project. Their teacher had made their work into a pamphlet and she had brought half her class to the Myriad to distribute them and to help with the meal preparation. We read the pamphlets and spoke with the teacher, who expressed her disap-

2 An impaction is when dust or dirt collects in the ear or nasal cavities of a dog.

pointment that she'd brought only half her class to the center. We decided that the task force would travel to Deer Creek the next morning to visit the middle school and talk with the entire student body.

After another tiring and frustrating night when no survivors were found in the Murrah, we boarded buses for what we thought would be a quick trip to a neighborhood school. As the skyline of Oklahoma City disappeared, we found out that the school was located about an hour's drive from downtown. We wondered just where we were going and began to question why we were even going. Tired and still very dirty from our shift's labor, we finally arrived at the school. We divided the task force into groups so that we could talk with all of the students in the school. We were amazed at the way the students had rationalized what had occurred, the questions we were asked, and the forgiving manner that they felt toward the suspected perpetrators of the bombing. Their positive attitude strengthened us and we felt refreshed from our visit.

While there, we were told that a staff member from the adjacent high school had lost a family member in the blast. We were asked if we would consider visiting the school so she could thank us for our work. Of course agreed to go and this kind lady met us when we entered the school and greeted each of us in turn as the principal escorted all of us to the school's auditorium. There the entire student body gave us a standing ovation as we filed in. Unable to fathom this expression of thanks, there was not a dry eye in the group. The return trip to the Myriad was atypically quiet as each member pondered what he or she had just witnessed.

As our work continued at the federal building, it seemed that the debris removal would never end. Each evening as we rounded the corner to take up our usual positions, the mound of rubble always seemed to look the same as it did the morning before. As we dug our way into the building, more bodies were recovered. Now over a week into the incident, rescuers were confronted with the unpleasant odor of the natural decomposition of the still missing. A temporary morgue had been established in the parking lot of an adjacent church and as each body was recovered, all eyes watched it make the journey to the church parking lot. While saddened that the person had not been found alive, we took comfort knowing that the family now had the body of their loved one and could begin the process of closure.

The weather remained uncharacteristically mild during the mission, though there were high winds and cold temperatures at times. The winds would sometimes cause all work to stop at the site, as the rescuers were removed for safety precautions. Provisions were made at the site to provide shelter from the elements and an assembly point was established for the rescuers to meet in case of unanticipated structural failure.

The structural stability of what remained of the building played a major role in all of the operational objectives established. Task force and IST structural engineers remained ever vigilant to the constant shifting of the remaining beams and joists as the debris was removed. As we entered the area during our first shift we all noticed a giant slab of concrete that hung over our position. This slab became known as the "Mother of All Slabs," or "Mother" for short. Hundreds of smaller slabs and other office debris were also present. As the building continued to settle, these posed a constant threat of falling. We were often stopped from working as these slabs and overhead debris were cleaned from our work area. More and more shoring was built to support the building as the debris was removed.

The more debris we dug out, the more we began to see the back wall (side three) of the building, which included the boiler room and elevator shafts. Several offices of the federal government, which had been filled with staff and visitors at the time of the blast, were located near this area. Near here, too, was the nursery were so many young children lost their lives. We identified areas of the building by using drawings and then matched up the areas as we dug through the building. We also interviewed maintenance workers, who helped us by identifying the carpet colors that were used on each floor. The papers and files that we found also helped us to determine which office we had uncovered. Several times we found filing cabinets that were no more than a few inches thick, flattened by tons of falling debris.

As we neared the end of our deployment, the Oklahoma City officials decided that the chances of finding any remaining survivors in the Murrah building were nearly impossible. With that decision made, the mission changed from one of a rescue to one of recovery. This decision did not alter the perseverance of any rescuer, however, as they searched every void of the building. The mission did not officially end until all bodies were accounted for and the Murrah building was brought down.

The original charge of the FEMA National Urban Search and Rescue Response System was primarily to assist in the aftermath of earthquakes and hurricanes, with the thought of terrorism a secondary concern. In the face of current events, the thought of terrorism now has new meaning. This is especially true as terms such as "Weapons of Mass Destruction" become interlaced in every community's emergency planning program.

The bombing in Oklahoma City has also made the public safety community more aware of the benefit of critical incident stress management. This process allows workers confronted by a critical incident to defuse using peer debriefers who usually have experienced similar events. At the time of the bombing, recognizing and managing extended incident stress was a new concept with limited public-safety-based knowledge available. The Oklahoma City bombing has since presented mental health experts with numerous examples of this and will be instrumental in the development of stressor recognition for similar events.

The deployment of Virginia Task Force One to the Oklahoma City bombing will forever remain a lasting memory for those members who were involved. During this event, FEMA deployed ten task forces and nearly 100 IST members to aid in the rescue operation. Countless numbers of other federal agencies also sent representatives. Coupled with the outstanding performance of the local rescuers, primarily from Oklahoma City, the mission was completed without a single long-term debilitating physical injury. The 168 citizens killed by the blast and the death of a local rescuer will be remembered by all. But the manner in which the community bonded together to tend to the hundreds who were injured and the rescuers who were sent to find survivors will serve as the yardstick for every future disaster. We who deployed to Oklahoma City will carry with us for the rest of our lives the honor of having been associated with these great Americans.

Biography

Dewey H. Perks is a 26-year veteran of the Fairfax County Fire and Rescue Department and is currently assigned as the station commander of Fire Station 28. Dewey has been actively involved with Virginia Task Force One, dealing with program development and coordination. He serves as a task force leader, plans officer, medical specialist, and is the team's medical coordinator. He has deployed with his task force to Hurricanes Emily and

Fran, the Northridge earthquake, Oklahoma City, and Nairobi, Kenya. He has also been deployed as a FEMA Incident Support Team member for Hurricanes Luis and Marilyn and the Atlanta Olympics. Dewey is a member of FEMA's Phase II Task Force Evaluation cadre, the Command and General Staff Working Group, Medical Review Group, and the Task Force Solicitation Technical Review Panel. Through his OFDA affiliation, he is also a member of the International Search and Rescue Advisory Group, where he has been actively involved in the development of international response guidelines. Dewey is also a consultant for the Special Programs Branch of the National Association for Search and Rescue.

The U.S. Embassy Bombing in Kenya: The American Response to Nairobi

By

Dewey H. Perks

The world was yet again forced to come face to face with terrorism on August 7, 1998, when the United States embassies in Kenya and in Tanzania were bombed. The well-coordinated attack injured thousands and killed hundreds of innocent people. The response to this attack by the Fairfax County, Virginia, Urban Search and Rescue Task Force was the first American international search and rescue mission since 1990.

The Fairfax County Fire and Rescue Department has developed a long-lasting relationship with the U.S. State Department's Office of Foreign Disaster Assistance (OFDA). This humanitarian response arm of the government's Agency for International Development (USAID) has a prolific history of rendering all types of assistance throughout the world in times of need. OFDA is also well known for its early development of modern-day urban SAR response operations. It continues to foster that aspect through its involvement with the International Search and Rescue Advisory Group. When the need is identified, OFDA utilizes specially trained and equipped SAR teams from Miami-Dade County, Florida, and our department to deploy worldwide to assist in disaster operations. Teams from these organizations were deployed to the former Soviet Armenia (1988) and the Philippines (1990) when devastating earthquakes struck those countries.

When the bombing took place in Africa, Virginia Task Force One veterans watched their television in eerie awe as memories of the Oklahoma City deployment flashed through their minds. Again, innocent people had been killed and injured. They were killed and injured only because they happened to be near an American building. Again, an explosive device had left a large swath of destruction. Again, a terrorist had ensured that as much collateral damage as possible was done with no feelings of remorse.

As is the custom when news concerning disasters arrives, the management group of the task force went into operation. They began the advisory phase of operations as it related to this bombing and pending deployment. During this phase, managers ensure that the department's senior staff is notified and that the group's equipment cache is in order. Senior staff then takes the pending deployment under consideration and determines whether the task force may deploy or not. Then we wait for our orders to deploy.

The task force has developed a mobilization manual used by managers to ensure that all aspects of the action are performed safely and efficiently. This manual is composed of numerous checklists, assignment sheets, forms, and organizational charts. These lists and charts give managers a complete guideline to deliver the task force to its point of departure. The managers used this manual to begin the established call-out procedure to staff the team. Next they called the OFDA's Operations Section to inform them of our readiness for a deployment, if deemed necessary.

Shortly after 1000, the OFDA called us and requested that two canine search teams get ready to deploy to Nairobi. As conversations continued, we decided to deploy one canine search team and one task force manager immediately. Sonja Heritage with her canine, Otto, and I were selected to join a State Department Advance team slated to depart from Andrews Air Force Base at 1200 on August 7, 1998. The rest of the task force was activated and would follow.

While the task force began to assemble at the department's training academy, Sonja and I arrived at Andrews AFB and were briefed by State Department representatives. They explained that we would fly to the Naval Air Station at Rota, Spain, for refueling, then continue to Nairobi, Kenya. As we departed, the task force was completing their check-in process and prepared to depart from the same air base. For this mission, 63 members and three search canines were deployed. Additional OFDA overhead staff members were also deployed.

Once we were airborne, I learned that several members of the advance team were familiar with the U.S. embassy and downtown Nairobi. They were able to supply street address, hospital locations, and details about the fire and EMS infrastructure. They were also able to identify the areas that could support helicopter-landing zones for sling-load equipment delivery or emergency medical evacuation.

Before we left Andrews, I had gathered information on endemic health[1] and vector concerns[2] from the website of the Centers for Disease Control. I'd also found out about the climate from the State Department's site. Discovering that Nairobi was situated at nearly 6,000' elevation allayed my concerns about the tiring affect that high temperatures would have on the rescuers. This meant that my main concern would be safety and security. Although safety and security are concerns at a domestic incident, we had to surmount them 8,500 miles from home. For every mission that our team has responded to, Chief-of-Department Glenn A. Gaines stressed one goal to managers: Work smart and keep the team safe. That admonition remained with me until we returned home.

While awaiting transport at Andrews, the task force was faced with two problems: We did not have a secure mode of ground transportation in Kenya and we did not have a definite line of re-supply. Under normal international deployment conditions, the affected country of the requesting organization provides this vital component. This mission was, however, anything but normal due to its terrorist nature. To ensure that adequate transportation was available, task force management decided to include a tractor-trailer and a 16-foot box-style delivery truck into the load plan. OFDA had originally asked the Department of Defense (DOD) to provide a C-5 Galaxy for the mission. That request was quickly upgraded for one additional similar craft to support the trucks, additional food, water, and supplies that the task force would need for its ten-day mission.

Awareness, especially by the National US&R community, of the shrinking size and age

---

[1] Endemic health concerns refer to local health concerns, i.e., disease outbreaks such as influenza, cholera, yellow fever, etc.

[2] Vector concerns refer to native flora/fauna including insects, shrubs, grasses, vermin, snakes, etc.

of DOD assets has led to more domestic responses by ground. Down time awaiting transport has become more common as these platforms are correctly used to support our troops abroad and the many humanitarian missions DOD is assigned. The task force does not idly spend this down time however. As we receive additional information on changes in the disaster, we prepare situation reports. We hold briefings and we conduct training. Training may seem out of place at that time, but a constant review of our response guidelines and the development of operational strategies based on the new information assures that we will have an effective plan of action when we reach the site.

As soon as I arrived in Spain and got off the aircraft, I contacted the task force to provide an update on the information that I had received. I also wanted to check on their departure status. When I called home, our Task Force Plans Officer, Jack Brown, informed me that all plans were on schedule and that the task force should be airborne by 0100 hours August 8. After re-boarding, my plane suddenly developed a mechanical problem, which eventually led to that plane being grounded with a replacement aircraft tasked from Germany.

Meanwhile, the task force had taken off on the first of its two craft with a mid-flight aerial refueling scheduled. During this maneuver, a proper seal couldn't be maintained and the plane was nearly forced to land to take on fuel. However, realizing the urgency of this mission, the aircraft flight commander arranged for a second aerial refueling, which was successful.

Although I had departed nearly 12 hours before the task force, I arrived in Nairobi only 90 minutes before them, because of the breakdown in Spain. Once on the ground, I met with OFDA representative Sydel Maher and discussed the immediate needs that would confront the task force upon its arrival. Ms. Maher decided that the task force would be housed in a downtown hotel to allow better security and food supply. This also put us within three blocks of the bomb site. We drove to meet the task force, which had taken 17 hours to arrive in Africa.

National SAR task forces use an operational system description as its guideline for on-scene disaster operations. Using these guidelines while still at Andrews ensured that the task force had secured the proper equipment to perform site assessments for potential base of operations space and search and reconnaissance. This included structural triage[3] at the bomb site. As this equipment was quickly unloaded, a task force advance group prepared to drive to the embassy area for a first look. They also wanted to meet with the leaders of the Israeli Defense Force Rescue Team who were already working at the site. The British army supplied flatbed trucks to transport to the forward staging area near the hotel all the equipment and supplies that the task force had brought. A manager meeting was held to discuss the objectives of the next four-hour period. This included contacting our department (Fairfax County Fire and Rescue Department) to let them know we had arrived, establishing a base of operations, securing lodging and hot meals for all members, providing secure exercise space for the canines, and establishing points-of-contact with the embassy staff. Jack Brown and I were made team plans officers for the mission. It was our

---

[3] Structural triage is a physical inspection/assessment of damaged structures. This process is used to predict the buildings where the most viable survivors will be located, the level of damage that it has incurred, the level of probability of secondary collapse, means of entrance, and departure.

task to formulate these and all future objectives into an effective plan of action.

During domestic responses, a task force must be self-sufficient for at least 72 hours. This ensures that it is not a burden on the already weakened community. When deploying internationally, this requirement is extended to ten days. Although the team came prepared for this contingency, the State Department continued to require that we quarter in a hotel. The State Department was concerned about a secondary attack, and felt it was safer for us in the hotel.

The advance group soon returned to the hotel and a formal briefing was conducted for all members. During this briefing we were introduced to OFDA support staff, received a cultural awareness briefing, health advisory updates, and a recon report on the findings at the bomb site. The Israelis and a search unit from France were already at work at the collapsed Ufundi Building. A joint operation command post had been established on side four of the embassy and was easily accessible by all teams. An equipment staging area had been identified within a secured perimeter abutting the embassy. All members would assist in establishing this area. A search of the embassy and surrounding buildings was also to be conducted at sunup.

The team was called into formation to begin the short walk to the embassy compound. During this trek, members started to study the explosion patterns as they looked at the damaged buildings. Nearly every building in a three-block area had suffered damage. This included shattered glass, damaged roofs, and marred exteriors. When they were within one block of the embassy, the members who had deployed to Oklahoma City remarked how similar the two incidents were. The same noises, (jack hammers, heavy equipment, and backup alarms) the same sights (rubble, and an ever-present cloud of dust) and the same unforgettable smell of death.

Once on the scene, we had to coordinate with the FBI's Evidence Response Team to clean up the area where we were going to store our equipment. Since we had worked with this group at Oklahoma City, we knew that we could not disturb anything in the area until they had cleared it of evidence. Once they did, we were allowed to clear the area of all debris and get it ready for our equipment. The British army again helped us and we were able to set up quickly. Without them our task would have taken much longer.

The U.S. embassy stood at the corners of Moi Avenue and Halle Selassie Avenue. This is one of Nairobi's busiest intersections. The embassy area resembled an open courtyard with the Cooperative Bank building on the left, the Ufundi House building straight ahead, and the embassy on the right. The streets had been closed since the blast and were filled with trucks, backhoes, and hundreds of spectators.

The terrorists had originally attempted to enter the compound and drive into the below-grade parking area under the embassy. When this was not possible, they drove slightly past the entrance, created a diversion that drew people to the windows in all the surrounding buildings, and then detonated the vehicle. The Cooperative Bank and embassy structures sustained considerable surface-blast-effect damage. They also sustained some smoke damage from the burning vehicle fires. In most instances, the floors of both buildings had remained intact. But the blast wave had emptied shelves and upset desks and filing cabinets. In some places this debris was piled from the floor to the ceiling.

The Ufundi House had received the brunt of the damage from the explosion. Once a five-story building housing offices and a secretarial college, it had been reduced to a large rubble pile. We noticed most of the patterns that you see in a severe collapse, including pancake, lean-to and several voids of varying size[4]. Kenyan rescuers had already ensured that all surface victims had been transported to area hospitals. They continued to provide excellent assistance to the rescue effort.

The Israelis, as mentioned earlier, had arrived first. They worked with ranking Kenyan officials to develop a sound plan of action. The French and American rescue teams were added to this plan. They were given assignments to either assist in or lead the rescue effort based on the task at hand.

As we established our command area within the base of operations, the request for assistance continued to come in. During the mission, more than 150 such requests were received and completed by the team. These requests included supplying staff and equipment to assist with search operations at the Ufundi House and widening the search pattern of collaterally damaged buildings. The team was also tasked with assisting embassy officials to gain access into the many secured vaults located throughout the building. It also became our job to assist with the removal of documents and equipment from the embassy and to provide round-the-clock medical care to the rescue force and members of other federal agencies. The team also supplied staff and equipment to the FBI's Evidence Response Team as they began the arduous chore of determining the cause of the explosion.

At the Ufundi House site, our members utilized search cameras to explore the voids uncovered by cranes. We also demonstrated to the other rescuers how to operate the camera. This way they could use the tool when our members were involved in other aspects of the rescue mission. The same was done with our rebar cutters and other tools. Since the tools and equipment used by formal task forces are not common in the rescue community as a whole, it was necessary to teach the other rescue crews how to use these tools. The maintenance of our extensive and expensive list of equipment is one of the reasons a task force was developed. Typically a local unit does not need these tools and will not have them on hand in an emergency.

Just as in all missions, true camaraderie developed among the members of the rescue force, unhindered by language, driven by the common goal of hoping against hope to locate and find any living victims of the bombing. The same was true with the search canine groups from all teams. As they rotated from the building, they would often meet and discuss common training principles and methods during their infrequent rest breaks.

It is common during operations in reinforced concrete buildings to use rigging to lift large sections of concrete out after it is freed from its web of rebar. This was the main method used in Nairobi, using either acetylene torches or cutters to free the slabs. Before lifting, a core hole is drilled where a search camera is inserted to check for victims. Acoustical devices[5] supplied by the French and American teams were also used during the mission with the hope of detecting sounds of life from the deadening pile. The French had confirmed such sounds and had determined the general area of origin, but the victim unfortunately died before he could be reached.

---

[4] The floors of buildings will collapse in different ways. Pancake: floors fall one on top of another, similar in appearance to a stack of pancakes. Lean-to: the floor collapses but is supported by one wall, which leaves a void along the supporting wall.V-collapse: the center of the floor collapses, forming a V, and the supporting walls create a void at either wall. Cantilever collapse: when one end of the floor is hanging free because of one or more wall failures. Voids can occur near large appliances, AC units, and other load bearing structures.

[5] When acoustical devices are in operation, all work is ceased at the rescue site to make it as quite as possible.

The search mission at the Ufundi House sadly turned, as it did in Oklahoma City, into a recovery operation when it became obvious that no additional survivors would be found in the rubble. During this phase of the operation, our members continued to be amazed at the strong will of the Kenyan rescuers, who constantly took the lead in the grim task of body recovery.

The team's medical unit was very busy during this mission. As with any deployment, its primary focus was to assure the health of team members (including its canines) and to provide immediate life-saving intervention to anyone that was found. While in Nairobi, the unit also found that it was responsible for the medical care of staff assigned with the OFDA, the embassy, the FBI, the U.S. Marines and Seabees, the Diplomatic Security Service (DSS), and the Kenyan rescuers working with us.

While everyone worked to clear of the last debris, an observance was held to bring together the joint rescue force to honor those who were injured, or had paid the ultimate sacrifice. The flags of Kenya, Israel, France, and America were placed at half-staff over the site while a somber wreath laying ceremony took place.

Before demobilizing, OFDA coordinated the transfer of critically needed rescue equipment from our equipment cache to the Kenyan rescue authorities. Our members accompanied them to the presentation and spent most of the day demonstrating and providing hands-on training. Badly needed medical supplies were also donated, through OFDA, to several local hospitals to assist them with the re-supply of the goods expended treating the blast victims.

The team returned to Andrews Air Force Base on August 16, 1998 and was greeted by Chief Gaines and dignitaries from USAID and OFDA. After a brief ceremony on the tarmac, the members soon rejoined their families and officially deactivated at 2130 hours.

The team judged this mission a success, having competed all assigned tasks. It would not have been such a success without the on-scene assistance provided by OFDA staff members Peter Bradford, Sydel Maher, Steve Catlin, and Pete Henderson. Their constant presence and ability to rectify problems or alleviate concerns allowed the team to focus on its mission assignments. The department also played a major role in our success by ensuring that our family and personal needs were tended to during our absence. They also held daily teleconferences with the families to keep them abreast of our progress.

Most SAR teams, as was ours, are formed to fill a recognized void in their local community. Terrorism and its affect were not considered then, but are now on everyone's mind. This was our team's second deployment to a terrorist act and the similarities were amazing. The people of Kenya would often stop and ask us "Why did this happen here?" It was the same question we were asked in Oklahoma. The Kenyans are a strong-willed and resolute people who are already on their way to overcoming this tragedy. Three days after the bombing, for example, people had moved back into their apartments near the embassy and had begun to pick up the pieces of their lives.

When we're deployed, we represent our country, and proudly fly our nation's flag over our base of operations, even though, as Americans, we are aware that flag has become an easy target to terrorism. It is because of America's presence in Africa that the bombing happened in the first place. It hurts to know that America and Americans were the target, but it is especially painful and frustrating that innocent Africans were killed as a result. It is our sincere hope that the suffering of those injured and the sorrow of those who lost loved ones will soon be eased, and that will never be the need for a similar deployment.

In the meantime, we stand ready, as do thousands of rescuers worldwide, to place our lives on the line when duty calls.

Epilogue

The African mission was different in one very important area from Oklahoma City. During the Oklahoma City mission we were constantly in touch with the local residents but in Nairobi we had very limited interaction with the residents. This was due to security concerns, the continuous operations we conducted, and the location of our quarters. We did get to meet several locals at the embassy, the U.S. mission, and the hotels that we stayed in. On the last day in Nairobi, we were able to send out small groups to a local market, and they were able to meet and greet the residents there. We were surprised to discover many American missionaries operating in the Nairobi area and we shared updates on the U.S. news with them.

All of the veteran members remarked on this lack of contact with the local people, and spoke of how important meeting and talking with the locals had been in Oklahoma. The human interaction gives a heightened sense of accomplishment and reality to the mission, and brings it that much closer to home.

Tornado Disaster
Airscent

Sgt. William S. Schlichter
Limerick Police Department
Mission Location: Limerick, Pennsylvania
Mission Date: July 29, 1994

Mission Type

It was a short search. The priority search took place in the Hamlet Development because a tornado passed directly through the development; this location was the most severely damaged. Emergency medical personnel, police, fire departments, and other volunteers from the area searched the development.

The Victims

All the people who resided in the 18 residences that were on Victory Way, in the Hamlet Development. I did not know how many total victims we were looking for. The tornado severely damaged several homes in the development. One home was completely destroyed; nothing was left standing except the foundation of the house.

Points Last Scene

The search for victims began at the entrance to the Hamlet since there was only one way in or out of the Hamlet Development. The search began at approximately 2400 hours on July 28, 1994. At the time of the search it was dark, hot, and very humid. The ground was wet and damp from the rain prior to the tornado, and there was a large amount of debris on the ground, consisting of lumber, nails, and glass from the homes that were damaged. There were also tree limbs, electrical wires, and residential belongings, such as furniture, scattered throughout the development. Several houses were unsafe due to the tornado damage; floors, stairwells, and walls were missing or collapsed.

Any Other Special Information

Residents who were not injured were running throughout the development looking for help or other neighbors. Several residents offered to help the police personnel search for anyone else that could not be found in the development. We didn't allow these people to help. Some were injured and none were trained to handle the situation. Instead, we set up a temporary shelter for the victims at the fire station and took everyone to that location.

Search Personnel and Equipment

A total of 75 personnel from police and fire and rescue assisted in the search. The police set up a grid-type search that covered every area of the grounds. The rescuers used flashlights and spotlights that the fire department provided.

Search Strategy

The Hamlet Development was the priority search area since most of the damage was done to that area. Several officers and fire fighters were deployed in the Hamlet area. They first concentrated on the people who were injured and those who were wandering in the development. After the injured were turned over to medical personnel, the search was then focused on looking for other people in the damaged structures. Rescue personnel also looked for anyone who was injured and may have wandered from the area. Initially, a command post was set up at the intersection of two streets in the development (see photo, below). The fire marshal, rescue chiefs, and fire chiefs manned the command post. The chiefs set up five teams of two to three people each. A team consisted of a firefighter, police officer, and EMS personnel. As each house was checked and cleared, they marked it to identify it as a cleared structure. When all of the houses had been checked, Officer Robert J. Matalavage notified me that they could not account for one family.

While the chiefs were operating from the command post in the development, I ordered a code blue[1] requesting mutual aid from any police department in Montgomery County.

---

[1] Code blue is a call to all police departments in the county for an emergency request for manpower.

The command post was set up around the circle, left middle of photograph. One can clearly see the path of the tornado in this photo, as it cut an S-shaped path among the houses. Note, too, how some of the houses (top of photo) were literally untouched.

"I cannot imagine how wind can remove one half of a house and leave a doll sitting in a doll chair three inches away on the other side of the wall, almost like a chainsaw made of air." Notice how the house at the top left has sustained no damage.

With the magnitude of the destruction and injuries, I knew that I needed additional personnel to handle the emergency. Within one hour a total of 35 police officers arrived at the main mobile command center. We stationed the command center in the central area of the township, at the Limerick Fire Department. We deployed these officers to the outer areas of Limerick Township to check any damage or injuries that might have occurred due to the tornado. Officers who searched the area were deployed in groups of four. Within 45 minutes these officers reported that there were no other injuries to humans other than

More of the tornado's destruction.

severe damage to properties within the township.

Suspension

The initial search was suspended when the residents of all 18 homes were located.

Results of the Mission

Limerick Township has never had an incident of such catastrophic magnitude. Through this incident we learned that all volunteers, police personnel, and emergency personnel worked together professionally. All of the search strategies that we learned in the classroom worked well.

What are Your Feelings About the Mission?

I was very proud of all those who assisted in this disaster. All police personnel worked together, carried out all orders to the fullest extent, and performed above and beyond the call of duty. The volunteers gave 100% and gave endless hours of their time and I salute them.

Biography

Sergeant William S. Schlichter is a veteran police officer with more than twelve years of active service. He has received numerous letters of commendation, certificates of recognition, and certificates of awards. Some of the decorations he has received include: Good Conduct Commendation Bar, Lifesaving Commendation Bar, Exceptional Duty Medal Bar, Legion of Honor Bar, and Drug War Pin. Sergeant Schlichter is also a certified firearms instructor and a pistol expert. Sergeant Schlichter has further demonstrated his management skills while serving on two boards for more than ten years.

THE SEARCHER

DOG HANDLER TEAM

Susan Bulanda
Phoenixville Fire Department K-9 SAR Unit

Who are You?

I am a canine handler.

The Callout

At the time of the callout I was asleep. My husband and I both received the call and responded. We had to take our son with us because we could not get a babysitter at three in the morning. It took us about fifteen minutes to get to the search site.

The Search Sector

My husband, Larry, and I discussed the situation with the team leaders of the rescue crews. They briefed us on what all of the rescue teams had found and where they had recovered people in the debris. Because of the nature of the disaster, Larry and I decided where and how to start. We had to search the whole area, including the surrounding fields.

A family was unaccounted for and another had been killed. It was possible that the family was trapped in a house or carried into a nearby field.

How large was your sector? How long did it take to complete?

The force of the tornado had spread debris over a mile-wide area and about thirty houses to check. Our area of highest urgency was the housing development. Rescue crews had quickly searched the open areas around the development but couldn't get into all of the remains of the houses thoroughly and quickly. The tornado had destroyed fifteen houses and partially destroyed fifteen more. It took us about four hours to search the houses and the surrounding areas.

How did you decide where to start your sector?

Because of the degree of damage to the houses, we started at one end of the development and worked to the other end. We checked each house—or the site where a house had been—as we came upon it.

Problems Encountered

We had to maneuver through all of the rubble for each house. I worked down to the basement of each house. We fully expected to encounter what we did, but the sight of it was still awesome. We did not have any problems working this mission. All of the support was there that we needed.

Were you prepared for the conditions you encountered?

We were fully prepared and trained for the conditions that we encountered. The only thing that I could have used was a pair of leather gloves. However, I was and still am amazed at the amount of damage done in less than a minute of time. I cannot imagine how wind can remove one half of a house and leave a doll sitting in a doll chair three inches away on the other side of the wall, almost like a chainsaw made of air. I have never been so awed as I was on this mission, but it didn't hit me until a week after the mission was completed. While we were working, I just didn't think about it.

The Dog

The tornado was rated F3, which means it had winds between 158 and 206 mph. The tornado had killed one family—a husband, wife, and a ten-month-old infant. Their house was reduced to ground level. In another instance, a five-month-old child suffered a broken leg and other minor injuries and the child's father was also injured. Rescue crews had rescued two other people from the debris who were alive. When the rescue crew did a headcount of all of the families whose houses were destroyed, one family was unaccounted for. As soon as Sgt. Bill Schlichter, the Incident Commander, realized that one family was still missing, he called the Phoenixville K-9 SAR Unit to look for them.

My husband and I, with both of our dogs, responded to the mission. Larry worked Jib, a Border Collie, and I worked Scout, a Beauceron. There were two police canines already on the scene when we arrived. One police officer had tried to climb the rubble piles to look for the missing people and in the process he stepped on a nail, which punctured his foot. The other police officer felt that climbing the rubble piles was too risky and that he and his canine would be seriously injured if they attempted it. As much as he wanted to help, he knew that his dog did not have the training that he needed to do the job safely.

When we arrived, we saw that the tornado had spread the debris in an area that was over a mile in size. The tornado could have lifted and deposited the missing people into the fields around the development. Ground searchers had searched the surrounding areas so we focused our efforts on the debris piles. We decided to use Scout to

Susan Bulanda (holding her dog, Scout) and the others sorting through the debris.

search the rubble piles since he was more experienced in disaster work. Larry used Jib to search the surrounding areas. Larry acted as my field technician along with three members of the rescue crew who were trained in collapsed-structure searches. Together we assessed each debris pile to decide which way was the safest way to go. They acted as spotters for me when necessary. We climbed down each pile to the basement of each house. We looked in every room that was still standing and through every pile. Scout did not find anything. Once, he gave a mild alert in the heart of a debris pile. It turned out that rescue crews had removed the injured victims from that spot. After we cleared all of the buildings, Larry took Jib and searched the fields around the development. Jib did not find anything.

At nine in the morning, Sgt. Bill Schlichter learned that the missing family was on vacation. We were notified and left the scene.

Probability of Detection

I felt that we had a 95% POD because the conditions were favorable and we searched methodically. The way the debris was piled, Scout had access to almost every area. It was unlikely that he would have missed anything. He was working in good form that night so I knew that he was not having an off day.

How Successful were You?

The mission was a total success. Scout and Jib cleared their areas and did not find anyone. As it turned out, there was no one to find.

This mission illustrates how well a search and rescue operation can go when people are properly trained. The mission was a shining example of coordination, professionalism, and harmony between many units. The units involved had safe procedures; Sgt. Schlichter knew what to do and where to deploy his resources in this multiple-task incident. The area hit by the tornado had to be secured. Live wires were on the ground, storage sheds were hanging from telephone poles like impaled victims in a medieval war, and rescue crews had to reach the residents still in the development. Once they could get the residents out of the disaster area, they had to shelter them. The electric company had to turn off the power in the area. Rescue personnel and police officers had to secure the area to keep out curiosity seekers. Ambulance and rescue crews had to transport injured people to area hospitals. The hospitals went to a code orange which is their "outside disaster" plan. That means that the hospital administrators called extra doctors, nurses, and x-ray technicians to the hospital. The community rallied to the aid of the victims by setting up a relief fund. I wish all missions worked as well as this one.

What are Your Feelings About the Mission?

I felt as though Scout and Jib both excelled in the task at hand. In this area of Pennsylvania, we rarely get tornadoes or disasters of this magnitude. Therefore, we have little need to train for this type of disaster. Generally we are faced with junkyards, old barns, and abandoned farmhouses and outbuildings.

The most important thing about this mission was the excellent job that Sgt. Bill Schlichter did to coordinate the search and rescue.effort. The whole incident went without a problem. Everyone knew what they had to do and did it. They accounted for everyone, both the victims and the searchers. With only one exception, not one rescuer was injured or hurt.

Search Tips

Train for as many different situations as are feasible for your area. Although we do not normally get tornadoes in Pennsylvania, we do have to search old barns and rubble piles. Though we do not have avalanches, we do have to look for bodies covered with snow. Keep an open mind as to the conditions that you could face.

Try to keep an open working relationship with your local rescue and police departments.

Honesty in your dog's ability to work is essential. If your dog is not ready to handle a mission, do not try to use him. An untrained or green dog could actually hinder a search effort. Depend upon your head trainer to help you with this decision.

Keep your dog fresh and physically fit. In some areas, the number of searches could decline as areas are developed. Training becomes the essential ingredient to keeping a dog ready. If you do not get many callouts for certain types of search work, your training should make up for the actual missions. This is very important for the search dog that is already qualified. You have to keep them interested.

Know when it is time to retire a dog. The older your dog gets, the better he gets, the harder it is to let go. The dog never wants to quit, but you must keep the dog's safety in mind. Losing or retiring a search dog is one of the hardest things to face. People who don't work in this field have difficulty understanding the bond that develops between a dog and a handler. He is your partner, he is your team member, and he is your friend.

Biography

See Upper Merion mission, page 43.

Lost Hunter
Wilderness Scent Specific

Deb Tirmenstein
Missoula County Search and Rescue: Western Montana Search Dogs

Foreword: Montana Searches

Many western Montana searches are tough, on dogs and on humans. This may be the "last best place" in the U.S.A., but it can be unforgiving. Most of the time people get away with making mistakes, but not always. Those of us who've searched here long enough inevitably end up looking for someone we know. "Typical" search strategies that are acceptable in other areas may have only limited use here. Obviously, driving roads that might normally be used for containment would simply be impossible in large road-less areas. Even trails may be limited.

The thing that most veteran Montana dog handlers dread is the first snow of the general hunting season. It is a forgone conclusion that somewhere in western Montana, some hunter (often someone from out of state) will get lost, caught in the snow storm. How bad the situation is depends on the length and severity of the storm, and on the complacency of the unprepared. Some years, Montana SAR groups receive multiple requests in a single day. Hunter searches are particularly tough. The victims of these searches are often in good shape and can travel miles in a single day. They often travel light with minimal survival gear, avoid roads and trails, and occasionally let a wounded animal take them farther and father into unknown areas. While following a drainage downhill may seem like a prudent move in most of the country, it can be a disastrous mistake in some parts of western Montana.

A hunter (or hiker) in good shape can easily travel ten miles in a 24-hour period. It is unusual for a dog team to be notified and fielded prior to the victim being missing for this length of time. This isn't due to the reluctance to use dogs, but rather, it is usually due to the time needed to assess the situation and summon help. Very often, all that can be clearly determined is the Point Last Seen—a trail head, a vehicle parked along a remote logging road, or a campsite. We commonly face a huge circular search area with a radius of up to ten miles. That equals more than 300 square miles of search area. Given a more aggressive hiker or a longer period since the person went missing, the area can easily approach 1,000 to 2,000 square miles! A typical practice area search scenario allows a dog up to four hours to search a one-quarter section, or 160 acres. Using this time frame, one square mile would require up to 16 hours for a dog to search or would take four dogs one half-day. Think about the number of non-discriminating airscent dogs that would be required to cover the entire search area, and it is mind boggling.

Obviously with searches of this type, we have had to rely more heavily on other methods of working a SAR dog. One method that has worked well for me and several other dog teams in my unit is the use of a fast-working, unusually high-drive, scent-discriminating trailing dog. In a best case scenario, this dog can take you directly to the victim. While this can and does happen, given the distance and terrain, it is rare. Occasionally a clue is found such as a footprint, cigarette butt, gum wrapper, etc., which verifies the dog's track and allows us to modify our search strategy. A common scenario is that the dog gets an accurate direction of travel from the PLS and funnels searchers into the correct area. For example, the dog dives down a drainage and search managers then deploy other resources in that area. In this case a helicopter working up from the bottom could find the victim. It does not matter which resource finds the victim just as long as the victim is found.

What qualities are essentials for this type of dog? It takes focus, endurance, an ability to scent discriminate, and, some would say, excessive drive. For me, Black Labs of working/field trial lines have proven to be very capable in this role. However, I know that many breeds of dog would work just as well. It takes a dog that is tireless, with a boundless desire to please. The dog must be tough enough for the weather and terrain and just dumb enough to want to do this more than anything else in the world.

Location: Chimney Creek area, Garnet Range, Powell County, Montana
Date of Mission One: November 7, 1996

Mission Type

The search was short.

The Victim

A 46-year-old male in very good health, except that he was a smoker. "Rob" wore cotton camouflage pants; jeans jacket and was carrying a hunting rifle. The victim was a hunter from Tennessee who was unfamiliar with Montana weather and terrain, and was not woods wise. He did not have matches or other survival gear and was very ill prepared to spend a night out in the season's first snowfall.

Point Last Seen

The victim left a cabin to hunt at 0700 on November 6, 1996. He failed to return by late afternoon as planned. The victim became lost while hunting elk in unfamiliar territory near Chimney Creek/Chimney Mountain in the Garnet Range in Powell County, West-Central Montana. He did not have a map or adequate survival gear. While he was hunting, the weather deteriorated drastically, the visibility was very poor. The area in West-Central Montana is rugged and mountainous with few roads. The terrain was mostly rolling draws and ridges that were timbered with Douglas Fir and Lodgepole Pine. The understory was varied—pine grass[1] in some locations interspersed with areas of thick brush. There were many rock outcrops and cliffs in the search area and some scattered high, open grassy parks.

---

[1] Pine grass is *calamegrostis vubescens*, a common plant in this area.

The temperature was in the low 30s but with the wind chill, it was much lower. The winds were moderate to strong; direction generally was from the southwest. There was a danger of hypothermia. The first snow of the season had fallen overnight. About three inches of snow had accumulated during the afternoon and evening, which obliterated all signs of Rob's tracks.

It had rained prior to turning to snow, which made the footing unusually treacherous because of a layer of ice beneath the snow.

Search Personnel and Equipment

There were ten to twelve ground searchers and one dog team. Helicopters were unable to fly at the time the search was initiated. The IC did request one additional dog team, but since they had to drive some distance to the site, their estimated time of arrival was about four to five hours.

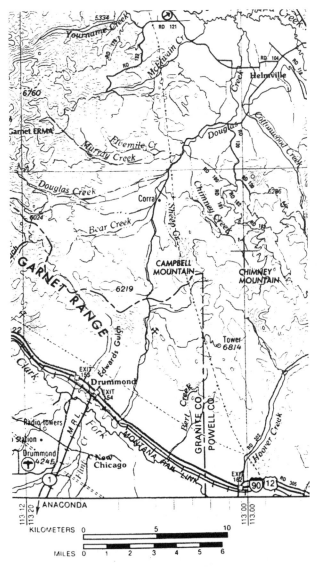

Search Strategy

Two SAR members remained near a cabin, which was the hunter's base camp. This was a precaution in case Rob found his way back to the cabin. They also helped as a radio communications relay for the other fielded search teams. Two other SAR members checked all abandoned cabins within the search areas. We were using the dog to try to determine a direction of travel. If we could find the direction of travel, this would decrease the size of the area we needed to search. We also hoped that the dog could find clues or even follow a track to the victim. Two searchers from Powell County went with the dog team. One of the searchers was an expert in man-tracking. Other searchers focused their efforts on containment by driving along the logging roads. They also contacted residents and hunters who were staying in camps that were in the search area. If the weather conditions improved, we hoped to get help from the helicopter.

Assign Resources

As a dog handler, I was not responsible for assigning resources.

THE DOG HANDLER TEAM

Who are You?

I was the first dog handler who could respond to the incident. The next team was four to five hours away.

The Callout

I was at home 20 miles west of Missoula, Montana. I packed my gear and dog in my truck and met the searchers at the scene at daylight. It took about three hours of driving time to reach the PLS.

The Search Sector

They did not give us any sector. No sectors were established or assigned, since search sectors are not very effective in this part of Montana (see above, "Montana Searches"). They took us to the PLS. The IC hoped that the dog could track the victim from the PLS. If the dog could not do that, the IC hoped that the dog could at least establish a direction of travel despite the snow that had fallen overnight. We asked for a scent article since other searchers and the victim's hunting partners had been through the PLS area, which was a rocky outcrop. Other hunters had been and, we assumed, still were in the search area. We also obtained a physical description of Rob, which included his boot-tread pattern and shoe size. During our interview process we learned the victim's habits and what gear he had taken with him.

How large was your sector? How long did it take to complete?

We did not have a sector. The search area itself would best be described as a circle with a radius of at least five to ten miles.

How did you decide where to start your sector?

Given the *huge* search area and only one dog, we decided to start at the PLS, which was the rock outcrop. I doubted whether my dog could track directly to the victim considering the weather conditions, but I hoped to get a direction of travel. This would narrow the focus of the search efforts tremendously.

Problems Encountered

We faced no unusual problems. I expected to find few, but good resources and a large rugged search area. This is exactly what I got. I doubted if a helicopter could fly in the weather conditions so we did not have one to support our search efforts.

Were you prepared for the conditions you encountered?

Yes. An unprepared searcher in Montana fall/winter searches is a huge liability to the rest of the team.

The Dog

I gave Fergus the scent article at the PLS. Because there was a dangerous layer of ice under the three inches of snow, I worked Fergus off-leash (I usually work her on a leash). Fergus spent some time circling the area on top of a rock outcrop overlooking a valley before she committed to a direction away from the PLS. Fergus appeared to be working well with her nose to the ground as we left the PLS via a logging road. She turned into an old clear-cut or meadow. We continued following Fergus through a series of ridges that overlooked another valley. Fergus worked the wind-blasted ridges slowly and with apparent difficulty. She took her time but in each area seemed satisfied with the route that she was taking and continued to appear to be trailing well. We left the series of ridges and dropped into heavier timber. It was here that we began to notice human footprints that were almost completely drifted over with snow. Communication with the base verified that no searchers had been in this area and the IC believed that these prints were those of the victim. We marked the tracks and continued following Fergus. At this point she picked up speed and soon cut fresher tracks. They were the same footprints, only more recent.. A short time later, Jim Waggoner of Powell County SAR notified us via radio that the search team that was check-

Deb Tirmenstein's Fergus

ing cabins had found Rob. We let Fergus continue tracking with no clues from us, and within fifteen minutes Fergus led us to a smiling victim standing behind a cabin with the other searchers. The dog ignored all searchers and went right to the victim. A big retrieve game followed, which is her reward for a successful find. Rob told us that he had stumbled onto a vacant cabin during the snowstorm. This may have saved his life.

Probability of Detection

Since we did not have a sector, we did not calculate a POD. We worked as a tracking/trailing team and followed a circuitous, mostly linear route to the victim.

How Successful were You?

The outcome of this search surpassed my hopes. Fergus gave us a very accurate direction of travel from a contaminated PLS. We found physical evidence (the footprints) and ultimately our track led to the victim. This was technically not a dog find, because searchers randomly checking abandoned cabins in the area found the victim about ten or fifteen minutes before us. An important bonus was that we were able to dramatically demonstrate to all of those involved the value of a trained search dog as a resource.

What are Your Feelings About the Mission?

This was a special search for me, and a milestone for me in a very personal sense. I was lucky to have a very good first search dog, a male black Lab named Choteau. We worked many searches together and through the years we were more successful than we deserved to be. More than anything, we had learned to communicate—I believed I could interpret his body language and he could read my mind. As time passed and we worked together, the bond grew. Choteau and I were a successful long-running SAR team with many experiences. Is it any wonder that letting go can be so difficult? As this dog aged, I knew I needed to start a new dog. My second dog, Fergus, was another high-drive Labrador who learned quickly and wanted to please, although she often made young dog mistakes. I lacked patience but in response she tried even harder. Her major flaw was simply that she wasn't Choteau. Occasionally, often without realizing it, I referred to my dogs as "the good dog and the bad dog."

On this search, I had to make a painful choice. The terrain was rough, the weather was bad, and the missing hunter had a 24-hour head start. New snow had fallen. It was not a search for an old dog. I put Choteau back in the truck, took young Fergus to the PLS and told her to "go to work." Fergus had participated in many bastard searches, article searches, and had helped other dogs with searches that we knew were cadaver searches. However, this was her first urgent life-and-death search that we faced alone. As I initially watched her leave from the PLS, in some ways I felt more like a critical—very critical—observer than a participant. Intellectually I knew she was well trained, tested, fully certified, and operational, etc., yet on an emotional level, it wasn't the same as being part of a team that had been through it all. Luckily Fergus seemed oblivious to my state of nervousness and continued working from the PLS. As the search progressed, and she dropped into the heavier timber where we noticed indistinct human footprints that were almost completely drifted in with snow. Fergus really had been trailing the victim! It was at this point that I became Fergus's biggest fan and felt like a new dog handler watching dog magic for the very first time.

With search dogs, as in other aspects of life, sometimes we really do get a second chance. This search made me understand that it was time to go on with my new "good" dog.

Missing Hunter
Wilderness Scent Specific

Mission Location: North of Lochsa River in Clearwater County, Idaho
Date of the Mission: September 3, 4, and 5, 1997

Mission Type

The search was long.

The Victim

"Frank" was a 76-year-old male in poor physical condition. He had heart problems and had an angioplasty three months before he went missing. He'd also suffered a stroke some time earlier (the son had reported that after the stroke the victim had become very disoriented). The victim had two artificial knees, and one hip replacement (they did not mention much of this information until later in the search). Frank was a "local" and described as "at home in the woods." According to his son, he was very woods-wise and would never follow injured game without first going back and getting the son. The son said that the victim had never been lost. He firmly believed that he wouldn't deviate from his original plan for the day unless he was either injured or dead. His relatives believed that he would not try to go down brushy draws but would stay in the more open and easily traveled ridges. The victim was a "healthy eater," but one relative stated that he loved chocolates, especially candies such as Tootsie Rolls. Relatives reported that the victim had a "fascination with high mountain lakes."

Frank was wearing pile camouflage pants and shirt, and slick-soled western riding boots. He was carrying a bow and possibly a knife. The victim did not have food or water with him.

The victim was last seen at 0600, Monday, September 1,1997, when he left his hunting camp to scout for elk. The search continued until approximately noon on September 5, 1997.

Other Circumstances or Information

Most searchers and some family members believed that the victim had most likely suffered a heart attack or stroke and died somewhere near the camp. Others suspected a fatal fall.

Point Last Seen

The victim was last seen at his wall tent[2] in the middle of a high mountain meadow. By the time we arrived, the victim had been missing for two and a half days. The camp was

---

[2] A wall tent is a very large canvas tent used by outfitters.

full of mules, horses, caches of food and supplies, a pet dog, packers, and ground searchers.

The victim became lost while bow hunting elk in unfamiliar territory. He did not have a map or adequate survival gear. After he became lost, the weather deteriorated drastically.

The incident took place in the vicinity of Monroe Butte, north of the Lochsa Wild and Scenic River, south of the Clearwater River. This is a mostly trackless area in North-Central Idaho's Clearwater County.

Terrain Features

This area is rugged and mountainous, with few maintained trails or established camps or cabins. The terrain is steep, rocky, and mostly heavily timbered with some small, scattered open meadows. Heavy downfall[3] and dense brush characterize some parts of the search area. The area immediately above the hunting camp was very steep and, in some places, essentially a cliff face. Much of this area was heavily timbered with sub-alpine fir or mountain hemlock. There was an understory of menziesia[4] and beargrass[5], which is very, very slick when wet. Many draws had thick alder understories. Lower areas were mostly forested with Douglas fir and Lodgepole pines, with dense stands of spruce on wetter sites.

Weather

The weather on Monday, September 1, was warm and sunny, possibly the 60s or even 70s during the day. On Tuesday, the second day of the search, temperatures dropped drastically. By Wednesday and Thursday it was cool, in the 30s or lower 40s.

On Monday and Tuesday, I don't recall the wind strength or direction. Wednesday there was a light wind except for a brief period before heavy showers when the winds became strong, gusty, and upslope. During the heavy rains the wind died completely. Thursday and Friday the winds were mostly light during the day.

On Monday there was no precipitation, on Tuesday rain had fallen much of the day. Wednesday was stormy with periods of very heavy rain. Thursday was clearing, and on Friday there was no precipitation.

Special Dangers

Special dangers included steep rocky areas, slippery vegetation, and rough terrain. The area was roadless, requiring long hikes and/or helicopter transportation. The cold, rainy weather made hypothermia a serious possibility.

Any Other Special Information

Supplying the search base became a full-time job for local outfitters and packers.

---

3 Downfall is downed timber and debris that was blown down by storms.

4 *Menziesia ferrnginea* is a common shrub.

5 Beargrass is *exerophyllum tenax*, a common plant in the northern Rockies, and is actually a lily.

Search Personnel and Equipment

There were a few ground searchers on the scene by Tuesday night. By Wednesday there were approximately 15 to 20 ground searchers present and one dog team. Packers ferried gear in and out on horses and mules. Some ground searchers used ATVs or motorcycles. A helicopter flew intermittently on Wednesday, but heavy rain and poor visibility limited its use. Thursday a prison crew joined the ground searchers, but the helicopter was recalled to base. On Friday several of the original searchers left but a helicopter rejoined the search and the IC fielded several new dogs.

Search Strategy

The searchers initially believed that the elderly hunter had suffered a medical emergency somewhere fairly close to the camp. Ground searchers checked likely areas near the victim's hunting camp, grid searching wherever possible. Searchers on motorcycles and ATVs covered all likely trails, checked hunting camps, and attempted containment. The helicopter, when conditions allowed flying, did grid the likely areas near camp. The dog was to pick up a track if possible and to find a direction of travel. If this failed, the dog would be used to search likely areas. Searchers on horseback checked possible trails in the area. Some ground searchers checked areas around a nearby lake and others checked additional trails in the area.

Assign Resources

As a dog handler, I was not responsible for assigning resources. Late Thursday night, however, based on what the dog had done, the IC asked me where I would assign resources for Friday if they were to ask me to do so. I suggested the area behind the ridge (where we lost the track) and in the draw, which was my first choice. I did not feel comfortable making these suggestions and asked "What if we are wrong?" The IC replied, "It's all we have." A helicopter gridding the area found the victim (alive and well) early Friday approximately four miles down the draw where Fergus had alerted.

THE SEARCHER
DOG HANDLER TEAM

Who are You?

Deb Tirmenstein, the first dog handler who could respond to the incident. The dispatch informed me that no other dog teams were available at the time.

The Callout

I was at home at the time of the callout. I packed my gear and my dog, Fergus, a four-year-old Black Labrador, in my truck and drove to a logging road junction north of the Lochsa River. An Air Force helicopter from Malmstrom AFB in Great Falls, Montana, transported me, my dog, and my gear to the base camp at the PLS. What would have taken six and a half hours of driving time to reach the logging road junction was accomplished by the helicopter in about fifteen minutes.

The Search Sector

Who decided your sector?

The IC did not assign or establish any sectors. The overhead team took us to the PLS with the hope that the dog could follow the scent of the missing person. We wanted to establish a direction of travel despite the poor weather conditions and the length of time since the victim had disappeared. The victim's son and other searchers had searched the area around the PLS, which was a wall tent in the middle of a high mountain meadow. We requested and received a description of the victim, which included a description of his boot tread and shoe size. We also gathered as much information as we could about the victim's habits, and the gear he had taken with him. These are important clues. The information that we initially received was quite sketchy. Most of the information was not available to us until very late in the search.

How large was your sector? How long did it take to complete it?

We did not have a sector. The search itself is best described as a circle with a potential radius of up to 30 miles.

How did you decide where to start your sector?

Given a huge area and only one dog, we decided to start at the PLS. I had little confidence that my dog could track directly to the victim given the weather conditions and the length of time the victim was missing. I even doubted whether we could get a direction or travel to narrow the focus of the search efforts. However, they asked me to try and so I did.

Problems Encountered

The primary problems included the accessibility of the search area. Helicopters were very limited due to the poor weather conditions and getting anywhere within the search area was slow going. Additional problems involved the victim's habits, indeterminate information about his physical capabilities, and his exact plans the day he became lost.

For example, searchers believed that victim was frail and unable to travel far. However, on the fourth day we learned that the victim had hiked nearly 30 miles in a single day only one week earlier. On the fourth evening, although we had initially ruled it out, we found out that the victim might have in fact have headed down a draw that the dog had shown extreme interest in on the third day of the search.

An additional, and perhaps an inevitable problem considering the huge size of the search area, was the initial lack of resources. Ideally I would have liked to have enough resources to search both the draw all the way to the bottom and the ridge at the beginning of the search.

Were you prepared for the conditions you encountered?

Yes. The consequences could have been serious if I were not properly prepared.

The Dog

I started the dog off at the wall tent after getting a scent article from the victim's son. At this point, it was raining hard. The victim's son had searched for a full day prior to seeking help. He had tied some ribbon on a tree farther down the trail to mark the last identifiable footprint of his father.

Fergus, who had just spent seven hours crated in a vehicle, raced around the tent and fell head first off a bridge. The other searchers gave me looks of "This is what's supposed to find the missing hunter?" and although they didn't say anything, they were clearly skeptical and quite unimpressed by this hyperactive small Labrador. Fergus quickly settled down and began tracking from camp, ignoring humans, mules, horses, ATVs, and a loose dog. She stuck to the main trail, passed the ribbon, and continued on the main trail for some distance. She was clearly working hard, noting, but not following, where other searchers had left the main trail. The searchers anxiously watched what the dog would do. She didn't veer off onto the route that they believed the victim had followed nor did she show any interest in heading toward a nearby lake, which was considered to be a high probability area. Some distance farther (see map, below), she peeled off the main trail and circled very widely around the butte. She was still working well although, knowing the age of the track, I had trouble believing it. They told me that no searchers or anyone else had been in this area on the previous day.

At the very head of a draw, we caught a huge gust of wind. Fergus' head came flying

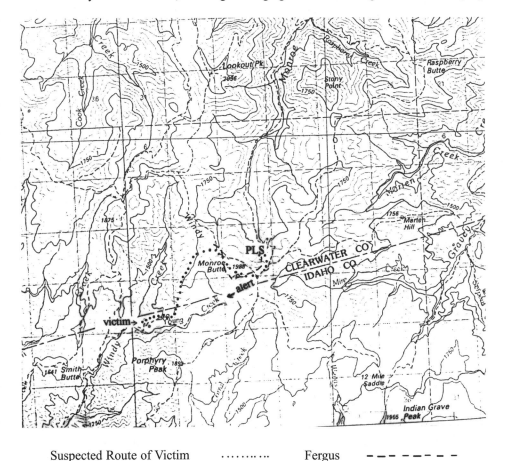

Suspected Route of Victim   ·········   Fergus   – – – – – – –

off the ground and she immediately began to airscent down the draw. Although she can be a dramatic dog at all times, this time her body language was quite extreme even for her. The searchers and I were running as fast as we could to keep up with her. Her interest was so intense that I thought we could literally step on the victim. We searched in the immediate area, but by this time the rain was falling in buckets and the wind was now at our backs. As the wind shifted 180°, Fergus lost interest in this area. Visibility was poor and everyone was soaked. We decided to mark the head of the draw as an area of interest and continued with the track, hoping to find some concrete clues.

Fergus resumed trailing and took us to the top of the ridge. This was the ridge that the victim was supposed to hunt but this wasn't the route they that believed he had taken. The dog showed extreme interest near a fallen log in the manner that she does for human scent. At this point the camp was visible below. While checking this area, we found part of a Tootsie Roll, which was very recent and still had some candy in the wrapper. We continued to the edge of the ridge, but Fergus lost the track. It was raining even harder. We continued down the steep, almost cliff-like area above the camp and ended the search for day three.

The base commander decided that on the fourth day that we, the dog team, would return to do a thorough search of the ridge itself. If there was time after the ridge was cleared, we were to continue searching the route that we thought the victim had followed. They assigned other ground searchers to check the trails—one near the draw where Fergus had a strong hit. The base commander assigned additional teams to search the other side of the main trail. Grid searchers covered portions of the ridge itself. We searched the ridge and the other areas as they assigned us to do but did not find any clues. The dog did not show any interest in the areas we covered, either, although Fergus continued to work very hard. While we were searching, Fergus periodically pawed at the pack that contained the victim's scent article. I allowed her to sniff the scent article, and she kept working as before.

Thursday evening, the third day of the search, we hiked to the base camp, checking the immediate vicinity of this trail as we went along. Late Thursday night, the IC decided to assign the resources for Friday, based mostly on what Fergus had done. A helicopter gridding the draw that we had suggested found the victim on Friday. The victim was alive and well. He was approximately four miles down the draw from where we had searched briefly on Wednesday.

Frank said that he had gone around the butte on top of the ridge (just as Fergus had done). He could see the camp from the ridge. He had shot a buck and followed it, traveling around the back of the ridge and ended up lost in the draw (see above map). After traveling down the draw for some distance Monday through Tuesday, he hurt his leg and did not travel much after that. When he did move, he crawled. We had searched only the top quarter- to half-mile of the draw on Wednesday. It seems improbable that a scent could travel three miles or more on the wind, but all evidence suggests that Fergus picked up the airborne scent from a distance that I did not believe was possible. This experience has prompted me to begin testing to see exactly how far a dog can detect scent on the wind.

Probability of Detection

Since we did not have a sector, I did not calculate a POD. We worked mostly as a tracking/trailing team. We spent most of a day searching the ridge itself and a small area north of the ridge. They did not ask me to give a POD, but I would have estimated our POD on the ridge as 40%. Human grid searchers also covered part of this area and the cumulative POD would have been higher.

How Successful were You?

My dog greatly surpassed what I believed she could do. In this alone we were successful. For those dog handlers who count "finds" like notches on a gun, this search would be a big zero. However, for those of us who understand that many finds are shared, or facilitated by dogs, it means everything! The dog helped a SAR manager direct resources to the appropriate area, and another resource, in this case a helicopter, made the find. The result was a happy one. Through everyone's efforts the 76-year-old hunter was reunited with his overjoyed wife and family. Was it the dog that saved the victim's life? Was it the helicopter pilot or the ground searchers? The answer is clear. It took everyone.

What are Your Feelings About the Mission?

When I initially heard a description of the search area and the scenario, I was certain this would be a wasted effort. I suspected there was very little we could do, given the huge size of the search area, rough terrain, terrible weather, age of the track (around 52 hours old), and the lack of resources. Clearly I was wrong. I underestimated the ability of a trained SAR dog. This search has prompted me to work harder. My goal is to routinely try older tracks and to try experiments with airscenting. I want to learn the distance at which my dog can hit on a specific human scent in various weather conditions.

Search Tips

Train for what is impossible and hope for what is doable.

Learn to speak dog. I'm serious! This is by far the most important tip, but that's another story.

Remember that search dogs are only one resource; strive to work effectively with other resources.

Use your own intelligence and ingenuity to match your style and the type of dog you work to your own terrain and weather conditions. Make sure your dog's drive and style match your area's needs no matter what some "experts" say.

One valid alert is better than ten false alerts. Some dog handlers are fearful of checking an area and finding nothing. So they report many, many "alerts." I've seen handlers report dozens of "alerts" along many miles of river. They can't all be correct. Don't report an alert that did not happen just to say your dog had an alert. Searching an area and not reporting interest or alerts is not synonymous with failure or indicative of an inferior search dog. Sending resources to false alerts can cost precious time. On the contrary, negative results can be vital in helping to narrow the focus of a search area, which can occasionally facilitate a find. Diverting resources to areas of false alerts or interest, on the other hand, can prove deadly.

Always push the limits of what you believe is possible. When we quit experimenting and learning, it is probably time to leave the searching to others.

Biography

Deb Tirmenstein has been working with search dogs for the last 13 years. She is currently working her second dog, a female black Labrador. She has a BA in Biology, a BA in Geology, and a MS in Environmental Studies from the University of Montana. During the summer field session she is employed as a biological science technician with the National Park Service in Yellowstone National Park. During the rest of the year she works as an environmental consultant in Missoula, Montana.

If Only They Were All This Easy

In March 1999, Deb and Fergus were called to Lolo, Montana to search for "Melvin," an older man with Alzheimer's, disappeared. When they arrived at the search, there were people everywhere, everyone was frantic, and it was all very chaotic. Deb asked a deputy to drive them to where Melvin's hat had been found earlier that morning. On the way to the hat, we spotted Melvin just standing by the road. They pulled over and he hopped in the car with us. Fergus believed she had "found" Melvin in the front seat of the police car and proceeded to slobber all over him.

When someone back at search base asked the deputy, "How did you know it was Melvin?" the deputy replied, "The fact that he was wearing three hats was a pretty good clue."

Deb Tirmenstein with Fergus.

Scent Collection at a Crime Scene
By
Chief Bill Tolhurst
Niagara County Sheriff Special Forces Unit

Scent is evidence, and should be properly collected and preserved like all other evidence at a crime scene. To collect scent material or to make scent pads, certain operational procedures must be maintained to avoid compromising the integrity of the scent.

Scent should be the very first piece of evidence collected, since it can be so easily contaminated. The mere presence of other people can contaminate the scent article or the immediate area of the scent article. No one should come in physical contact with the article or the scent. The scent article should be handled with clean rubber gloves (do not use powdered gloves) and should be kept in clean plastic or paper bags, properly sealed, and stored for future use. Do not use garbage bags to collect or store scent articles because some garbage bags are chemically treated to control odors. Only people especially trained in its collection, handling, and preservation should collect scent articles.

Scent pads are made by a special machine called a Scent Transfer Unit[1]. Scent pads can be made from practically anything—guns, knives, etc.—without damaging fingerprints. This scent pad procedure also allows you to collect and preserve trace evidence off these items. These pads can then be used to:

- Trail the subject from the scene of the crime
- They can be used as an investigative tool to check the whereabouts of a subject
- It can also be used to identify a subject in a line-up procedure
- Sometimes, scent pads can establish probable cause.

Scent is also the only piece of evidence that can: Give you a direction away from a crime scene, give you a path to follow to look for other dropped or discarded items, take you to where foot prints or tire prints may be collected, take you to the subject and identify him. It is also possible to work scent at a crime scene long after the crime scene has been destroyed.

---

[1] For more information about the Scent Transfer Unit contact either Bill Tolhurst through the Niagara County Sheriff's Office or Larry Harris at (949) 548-0782.

Searching for a Grave

Before searchers are put afield to look for a grave site, considerable investigation should be done. Often, however, very little information is available, and confirmed or verified information is nearly always nonexistent.

Some of the questions asked should be:

1. Why are we searching this location?
2. How big is the anticipated search area?
3. How long has this body been down? Why do we believe the subject is buried?
4. Do we know: Sex? Age? Weight? Height? Clothing?
5. What do we know about the subject?
6. When and where was the subject last seen?
7. If an informant is involved, law enforcement should take him to the scene, in private, before any search is considered.
8. Is the informant reliable? What is his track record?
9. Law enforcement should make a careful, quiet evaluation of the area before they put searchers out into the field.

After getting as many answers to the above questions as possible, investigators can decide whether a physical search is practical. If a line search is to be made, it will follow the procedure explained in "Line Search", below. There are many more things to be examined. Therefore, it should be a slow search with careful attention paid to details. The things pointing to the grave are more difficult to see and understand. Let's look at some of the things that indicate a grave site, and why they do so.

1. Just the fact that a hole is dug changes the natural environment. Piling dirt on the side of the hole will kill or damage the vegetation.
2. When they put the body in the hole, it will replace much of the dirt, so there will be excess dirt left over. Maybe they mounded the excess dirt over the grave, or maybe they spread it around. Then the grave will sink as the dirt settles and as decomposition takes place, which is why knowing how long the body has been missing is important.
3. If the body is in advanced stages of decomposition, grass and other vegetation should be green and taller over the grave for two main reasons. One, the body furnishes nitrogen (fertilizer) to those plants, and, two, water runs to the path of least resistance, which will be the loose soil of the filled grave. In doing this, it starves the young grass around the grave and, sometimes, the grass will turn brown around the grave and green over the grave.
4. When the body is in advanced stages of decomposition, predators will find it and dig holes over the grave. Careful examination may show you footprints or droppings of the predators.

Larger stones, broken roots, and damaged vegetation may be evident in this area. Often after heavy rains, graves attract swarms of flies and other flying insects. If predators have opened the grave, scavenger birds (crows, hawks, blue jays, etc.) may be in the area in larger numbers than normal. Predators also may have dragged pieces of clothing, shoes, and even bones or other body parts around the area. Each predator has a definite feeding pattern. In our area, the main predators are foxes, coyotes, raccoons, and stray or wandering domestic dogs. A fox will usually take carrion parts into heavy cover, some distance from the find. They will also go to their dens, if it is not too far away. A coyote will usually take theirs to high ground in fairly open areas, where there is enough cover to disguise his appearance, but open enough that he can see and scent the area. Raccoons will usually go near trees where their escape into trees is possible.

All these predators will eat at the scene until they are disturbed. Therefore careful examination of the scene for droppings, foot prints, tooth marks on bones, and hair will help identify the predator. This will give a possible location to look for missing body parts.

Generally, searches for graves are not practical in very cold, snowy, and freezing weather. The only exception may be searching for a grave in open country using an airplane. Aerial observation may be productive as light snow, frost, and even rain accents the soil disturbance where they dug the grave.

A preliminary search with cadaver dogs and knowledgeable handlers should be made before foot searchers are put into the field. The dogs should be kept at the scene to check suspicious areas found by line searchers.

Line Search

Each company is to train at least four line captains. These captains will be the men in charge of their company's searches, and each line captain must have a radio. A line captain will be on each end of the search line, and can talk with the captain at the other end. One captain will be along a road and will be the guide for all of the searchers in his line. When the line is in place (searchers ten paces apart), the deep boss (the line captain at the end of the line opposite from the road) will radio the road captain that they are ready. The road captain will give the order to start, and each searcher passes down the order. The road captain sets the pace.

It is the responsibility of each searcher to keep the line straight and together. If the searchers find the pace too fast, let it be known and have the road captain slow the line. If a searcher sees something, he sings out, "Hold the line," and the whole line passes the word and stops. The line stays in place until the searcher is satisfied that the item was not important. Then the command to go on is given again and passed down the line. If something significant is found, the line still stays in place. It is the responsibility of the line captain to see that this is done. Only one person should approach any important item, and then only close enough to be sure of what you have, but the line stays in place. At that point, each line captain marks his location with tape or a paint marker. The closest captain goes down the line to where the searcher is that made the find.

If it is something that could be related to the search, put markers around the object to mark the spot. Be sure not to touch or go any closer to the object than necessary. Try to keep an uncontaminated 15' radius around the object.

The line captain will then instruct the searchers that are in line with the object to go around the object. Then line up again and continue with the search when the line captain gives the order. The line captain directs the searcher closest to the object to either go to his left or go to his right and stay with that next closest searcher. This will keep at least 30 feet around the object uncontaminated. The line captain should clearly mark and follow the route the finder took toward the object and away from the object.

Now assume that the search is back underway and a body is found. The searcher sings out and alerts the closest line captain. Again, the captain marks his location, then walks down the search line, checks the route the finder used when the find was made, and marks it plainly. The line is still in place. No one walks around. They stay put.

If crime tape or any other article is needed, they can pass them down the line to the scene. This way each man only has to walk thirty feet. There is no need for anyone else to enter the area except at the discretion of the line captain. The line captain then calls the road captain to tell him to notify law enforcement and that he is sending the searchers out. The road captain makes proper notification to law enforcement. The line captain has the line turn toward the road and walk single file out to the road captain. The last searcher going out marks the route with spray paint or tape, all the way to the road.

Now the line boss at the scene puts up a crime tape around the body, at least 30' (or more) to maintain the uncontaminated area. One man is left at the crime scene, knowing where the route to and from the scene has been marked. The plainly marked route to and from the crime scene is the only one that all investigators should use.

From this point on, police personnel should take over the crime scene responsibility. When appropriate, search dogs and handlers will precede the line searchers.

The line search captains should:

1. Instruct all searchers not to drop litter; these items can cause confusion in the crime scene area.
2. Control very carefully, all information that goes over the air.
3. Make sure that all people follow the marked route to and from the scene.
4. Post a guard at the road entrance to the scene, so that only authorized persons are allowed back to the scene.
5. Make sure law enforcement is notified as soon as possible. Radio transmissions should be limited with as little information transmitted as possible.
6. Keep track of all pertinent data: location of items found, time, who found it, etc. until the scene is turned over to law enforcement.
7. See that no information is released to the press.
8. The deep line captain should mark his line every eight or ten paces, when possible, so they can follow this line if the search has to be extended back farther into the area.
9. The mark to show the route of a line captain shall be one stripe, at least half way around a tree. The mark showing where a find has been made will be an "X" on the tree. If no trees are available, spray paint the vegetation or the ground. You can also put a stake in the ground with tape attached to it. Use anything that can be found easily. Each department can use whatever works for them, as long as it is easy to spot.

Bill Tolhurst with Candy, a Labrador Retriever cross (left), and Comanche, a bloodhound (right). Comanche is a trail dog and a crime scene dog. She has been trained in trailing, cadaver search (both land and water), article search, accelerant detection, and is a hearing dog as well! She has found 174 year-old graves in her career.

Drowning

Kay Cooper-Watt
  Central States SAR, Inc.
  Mission Location: Lake Charleston
  Mission Date: May 14, 1996

Mission Type

This was a short search, which illustrates efficient search techniques, and how fluid dynamics works to solve complicated water search problems.

The Victim

Male, age 23, in excellent physical health, with no known habits. "Eric" was last seen wearing cut-off blue jeans. He went missing at 1530 on May 9, 1996. He was a member of the Eastern Illinois University wrestling team.

Point Last Seen

The victim was last seen in the spillway from Lake Charleston into the Embarras River, which is in Coles County, Illinois. Four wrestling team members decided to slide down the spillway during a flood. Two drowned. One body washed out of the spillway the following day. The accident happened, in part, because the victims did not understand the power of water and how dangerous sliding down a spillway can be. Traces of alcohol were found in one victim.

Weather

The weather at the time of the incident was clear. The river was in flood stage with high-water conditions. The river current was seven knots. The air temperature was 75°F, a southwest wind at 15 mph, with no precipitation.

Special Dangers

There were dangerous hydraulics created by flood waters pouring over the spillway, creating a low head dam hazard. (See the list of terms at the beginning of the book for a definition.) The river and spillway were filled with debris, which included large trees.

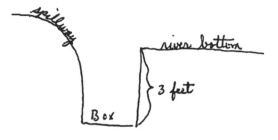

Body trapped in box, held in by debris.

Search Personnel and Equipment

We had all the resources we needed. Our resources included experienced boat handlers, a dive team whose specialty is low head dam rescue and recovery, and a professor of fluid dynamics.

Search Strategy

Recovering the subject's body for the family was essential. We did not want to leave the body in the river to be found later in the summer when the water receded.

The only canine alerts were in one area on the Embarras River, three-eighths of a mile from the PLS, about 30 feet from a flooded tree. We marked the location of the alerts with engineering tape.

After talking with a fluid dynamics professor from the

Oren Lockhart (left, front) explaining the science experiment to Eastern Illinois University's wrestling team members. Lake Charleston, Illinois, May 14, 1996. (Photo by Kay Watt)

University of Illinois at Champaign, we learned that the dog was alerting on scent coming from the spillway. The river's bottom current was carrying the scent. The more the river receded, the farther downstream the alert would be. The professor suggested an experiment to pinpoint the exact location of the body in the spillway.

Following the professor's instructions, we measured the depth of the river, which was twelve feet. We filled six one-gallon plastic jugs with river water and tied 12' lines to the jugs. We marked each jug with an orange buoy. Our objective was to drop a jug on the spillway so that the bottom current would carry it to the very place where the canine had alerted. When the jug passed through the alert area, this would establish the subject's location on the spillway. This was possible because the current and turbulence of the river were holding down the scent and preventing it from coming up for quite a distance. Since water does not always travel the way it appears on the surface, the jugs would show exactly where the scent of the body traveled. So if the jug was tossed into the water where the body went in, it would be swept along the bottom, where the body would sink to, and follow the path that the scent of the body did. This would confirm that the area where the dog's had an alert is the area where the body was located. In essence, the dog confirms the jug and the jug confirms the dog.

Fortunately, Coles County ESDA already had a cable on the face of the spillway for body recovery. Several members of Eastern Illinois' wrestling team helped to ferry the jugs along the cable and drop them. When the jugs popped up in the river, divers in the zodiac observed their flow patterns. They reported these patterns to Oren Lockhart who was in charge of ferrying the jugs along the cable. Finally one jug "hit" the canine alert area, confirming that the body was still within the PLS area. Because there were several varying accounts given by eyewitnesses about where the body was last seen on the spillway, we needed to use the jugs. Due to the turbulence of the water, determining an exact location was difficult. The one jug that hit the alert area gave us an exact location on the spillway. Using the jug enabled us to observe the flow and current patterns, which were unique due to the height of the river and its expansion. The experiment gave us the exact location on the spillway, which proved to be correct.

Using drag hooks to breakup debris in the spillway at the exact location, Coles County came in contact with the body four times before they could dislocate it from the spillway. The body moved downstream where it was recovered within ten feet of the boat.

EIU wrestling team members and Oren Lockhart (nearest to the water's edge) ferrying a jug on the cable across the spillway, Lake Charleston, Illinois. Note the buoy hanging from the cable; the jug is on the cable line. (Photo by Kay Watt)

The dog had the alerts before 1200 but Coles County did not recover the body until 1902. that night. After it was established where the body was on the spillway, Oren had to figure out how to safely recover the body, which he did.

Suspension and Results of Mission

The search ended with the recovery of the body.

What are Your Feelings About the Mission?

Although I felt badly for Eric and his family, this was an exciting mission because we used fluid dynamics to determine the location of a body, and everyone worked together without any problems.

Additional Comments

People would benefit greatly by using science in water searching.

Water Search Tips

If you have a PLS, begin searching outside of it and work toward it. In water searching, you cannot see what is going on under the water. Rarely does the body stay where it entered the water. The water currents will take the body someplace else. The only exception would be a body of very still water with little or no current, such as a pond, lake, or quarry. Even in those cases, there can be current below the surface that will move the body.

Use a slow, tight grid. Again, you are looking in an area that you cannot see. By using a slow, tight grid, you give the dog every chance to catch the scent. Keep in mind that when the scent hits the surface of the water, air currents move it further. So the dog may hit in an area that is nowhere near the body. By studying wind and water currents, the handler must determine where the body is located in relation to the available scent.

Map out all canine alerts and study them for flow pattern and current information.

Think about what possibilities you might have before you suggest a POD area for divers to search.

If you cannot figure out the problem, call someone who can help you. Don't be afraid to experiment with different techniques to solve the case.

Biography

Kay Cooper Watt has been in search and rescue since 1991. Her Golden Retriever, Hawthorne, was the first search dog in central Illinois to be specially trained in water search. Training with the Springfield Underwater Search and Rescue Team (SUSART), Hawthorne found SUSART divers 22 times before his first mission on the Illinois River in 1992. Today, Kay and Hawthorne are members of Central States Search and Rescue, Inc., in Wentzville, Missouri.

THE SEARCHER

DOG HANDLER TEAM

Who are You?

Kay Cooper, a dog handler, whose specialty is water searching.

The Callout

We were driving to another search when the callout came at 0800 on May 10, so we did not hear the callout message until late that afternoon. By that time, another canine team had been contacted. The second callout came around 1900 on May 13. We left at 0600 on May 14. It took us almost two hours to reach the search site.

The Search Sector

Who decided your sector?

The IC determined the area that I was to search. I requested the following information: What the circumstances of the drowning were; the witnesses' reports; the weather/river conditions at the time of the incident and if weather and river conditions had changed since the incident took place. I also needed to know what had been done before we arrived. I asked to be briefed as to what the other canine teams had found. Since they had posted observers on the bridge, I wanted to know if there had been 24-hour coverage and how long they had been there.

How large was your sector? How long did it take to complete?

Our sector started as close to the boil line[1] as we could safely get and ended about two miles down river at a large snag in the middle of the river. The first search lasted from 0843 to 0953. The second search took from 1002 to 1145.

---

[1] In a low dam situation, a boil line is a break in the water where part of it goes downstream while the other part circulates back to the dam. If you cross the boil line and get into the water circulating back to the dam, you will be drawn into the face of the dam and most likely die.

How did you decide where to start your sector?

Since the commander of the dive team wanted to search the area closest to the spillway, that is where we started.

Problems Encountered

While doing the water search I discovered that the pads on my dog's dew-claws were raw and cut. This resulted from the last search we were on, on May 10. Since I had checked him after that search, I was surprised that I had missed the dew pads. We cleaned, medicated, and wrapped the pads.

Were you prepared for the conditions you encountered?

Running close to the boil line was scary. I knew from training with Marian Hardy how dangerous this situation was. I knew Oren Lockhart and had worked with him often, so I was not nervous while he was handling the boat. However, when someone from another agency, whom I did not know, became my boat handler, I did feel nervous.

The Dog

My dog is very sensitive and I knew something was wrong because he had a hurt look in his eyes. He was acting hesitant in the Zodiac, which was unusual since he had worked from that same boat on trainings and missions. I kept asking myself why he was acting this way, since I knew he loved working in that boat. I felt that he was physically uncomfortable. Because of this, we switched boats and worked out of a Jon boat. This made Hawthorne more comfortable and he seemed okay in the Jon boat.

Probability of Detection

We had a 100% POD due to the scientific experiment and canine alerts.

How Successful were You?

I felt that the expansion of the river into a lake was interesting and I would have liked to search

"Find my son" is what this fisherman is asking a SAR dog to do on the Illinois River in the winter of 1993. (Photo by Kay Watt)

the river some more. I thought the scent would be in the shallow water near the alert and work back toward the dam. However, due to the water conditions I could not work the area further.

Search Tips

The following search tips come from Hershel McAlister.

Be prepared prior to leaving for a mission. Be sure you have everything you need to do your job, even if that means staying overnight when you hadn't planned on it. Do not rely on your contacts to take care of you by providing the equipment you need to complete your mission or house and feed yourself and your dog.

Gather as much data as possible from primary sources.

Don't take unnecessary risks. Remember that no lost or missing person—especially one that you know is dead—is worth another human life.

Always keep a positive and upbeat attitude because people see you as a professional.

Be careful of jumping to conclusions that are not based on facts. Assume nothing. You must check and double-check everything. For example, don't assume that a missing elderly person can't walk more than a mile. A determined elderly person can cover many miles.

After a four-hour morning search in November 1993 on the Illinois River near Havana, this dog was pulled out of the search, as airscenting conditions rapidly deteriorated due to a cold rain and a fog, with winds at 20 mph. (Photo by Kay Watt)

Biography

Hershel McAlister, principal founder of Central States Search and Rescue, Inc., County of St. Charles, Missouri, is a member of the Lincoln, Nebraska Task Force and Missouri Task Force. He is a Type II evaluator and instructs on a national level. Hershel McAlister is also Central States' coordinator and principal training officer. His five-year-old chocolate Labrador, Max, is a Level I FEMA search dog.

Drowning

Dee Wild, Director of Training, and Lisa Higgins
Louisiana Search and Rescue Dog Team (LaSAR)
Location of the Mission: Manchac, Louisiana
Date of the Mission: February 8-20, 1998

Mission Type

This search was long, due to several issues that hampered the search effort, such as swift currents, heavy underwater debris, wind, and low water temperature (mid 50s), which meant the bodies (if any) would take longer to float.

The Victim

This drowning involved two subjects. Subject one, "Sam," was a 19-year-old white male in excellent physical condition. He had been known to take drugs in the past. He was considered an outdoorsman and was known to fish and camp out often; his parents considered him a strong swimmer. His clothing and change were thrown about as if they'd been taken off in a hurry on the turnstile where he and his friend had been camping.

Subject two, "Ron," was an 18-year-old white male, who had a history of diabetes and was taking daily insulin. Like Sam, he also had used drugs in the past. Ron was not a strong swimmer but was an occasional fisherman. Ron had taken off his jacket and neatly hung it on a piece of rebar that stuck out from the bridge tenders structure.

Other Circumstances or Information

The deputies found Ron's insulin, along with a soft drink and candy. Based on the remaining insulin found, his family determined that he had taken his last injection Saturday morning, February 7, 1998. His Saturday evening dose was untouched. This gave authorities a time frame of when the incident occurred. According to his family, he was very diligent about taking his insulin injections. (See drawing, opposite, which shows location of items found by deputies upon arriving at the turnstile.)

Point Last Seen

Both victims were last seen Saturday, February 7, 1998, camping out on a cement turnstile, which was used to open the railroad bridge in Pass Manchac. It was approximately 75 yards from the railroad bridge tender structure to the turnstile. This turnstile housed the gears and a section of the railroad bridge that manually turns the track to allow boats to go through the channel. This cement turnstile was part of an old railroad bridge that had long since deteriorated (see photo, opposite).

Both parents knew that the boys had planned on camping and fishing from the turnstile. Sam had a small flat boat that they would use to paddle out to the turnstile. One of the victims had pulled the boat up on the turnstile. There were no eyewitnesses to the actual drowning.

On the left, the new railroad bridge and platform. A blue T-shirt and black sweatshirt were found hanging on the rebar.

On the right, the abandoned bridge and concrete slab that stuck up out of the water, where the items were found.

A - ice chest
B - fishing pole
C - fishing pole
D - keys, ball cap, lip balm, lighter, blue flannel shirt, one quarter, one box of fishing worms, one small smoking pipe, and one small bag of marijuana
E - black backpack
F - tree limbs piled up for a fire

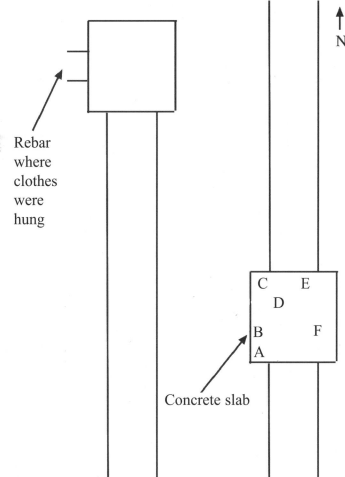

N

Rebar where clothes were hung

Concrete slab

The cement turnstile where the boys camped.

Why did the incident take place?

Neither boy returned home at the designated time

Where did the incident take place?

Pass Manchac connects lakes Maurepas and Pontchartrain. There are three railroad bridges, one new cement railroad bridge, and two old wooden railroad bridges. All of them run north to south across the Pass. The only evidence remaining of the two wooden railroad bridges is their support post sticking out of the water. There is also considerable underwater debris caused by the deterioration of the old wooden bridges. The new cement railroad bridge has a computerized bridge tender. The bridge tender on the new bridge houses the computer system and/or personnel that raises a portion of the railroad bridge for boat traffic to pass through the channel (see photo, below).

Weather

The current was running out of the west; the Beaufort scale is a means of measuring wind speed at sea or over water. Our winds were six on the Beaufort scale, which meant a strong breeze, some large waves, extensive white foam crests, and some spray. The water temperature was 51–54°F, and the air temperature was 60°F.

Any Other Special Information

The current, winds, and underwater debris caused problems during the search effort. Strong currents made navigating the boat difficult. When fighting current like this, the navigator had a very difficult time keeping the heading that we required. He also had a hard time responding to needed changes, since the boat wasn't able to turn as we would have liked. The boat rose and fell so much on the waves that the dogs obviously felt insecure about their footing, which made it tougher for them to do their jobs, divided as they were between keeping their balance and working the area. The winds pushed the boat around and made navigation difficult. It also took the scent from the place where it was breaking surface and threw it around. Underwater debris seems to be the norm rather than

The new bridge tender.

the exception in much of Louisiana's waterways. Dragging procedures were used in an attempt to make recovery; unfortunately, the hooks ended up catching on all of the debris, and we lost over 100 hooks. Diving in this type of water way with zero visibility amidst a collapsed structure, with strong moving currents would seriously endanger the diver.

Tangipahoa Parish Sheriff's Deputies located Sam's flatboat was found along the shore, approximately one mile from the scene. The flatboat still had the oars neatly in place inside the boat. A container of fish bait was sitting on the seat. This indicated to authorities that foul play was not a factor.

The Beaufort Scale for use at Sea

Beaufort Force	Description	Sea State	Knots
0	Calm	Sea like a mirror.	< 1
1	Light Air	Ripples with appearance of scales, no foam crests.	1–3
2	Light Breeze	Wavelets, small but pronounced. Crests with glassy appearance, but do not break.	4–6
3	Gentle Breeze	Large wavelets, crests begin to break. Glassy looking foam, occasional white horses.	7–10
4	Moderate Breeze	Small waves becoming longer, frequent white horses.	11–16
5	Fresh Breeze	Moderate waves of pronounced long form. Many white horses, some spray.	17-21
6	Strong Breeze	Some large waves, extensive white foam crests, some spray.	22–27
7	Near Gale	Sea heaped up, white foam from breaking waves blowing in streaks with the wind.	28–33
8	Gale	Moderately high and long waves. Crests break into spin drift, blowing foam in well marked streaks.	34–40
9	Strong Gale	High waves, dense foam streaks in wind, wave crests tumble and roll over. Spray reduces visibility.	41–47
10	Storm	Very high waves with long overhanging crests. Dense blowing foam, sea surface appears white. Heavy tumbling of sea, shock-like. Poor visibility.	48–55
11	Violent Storm	Exceptionally high waves, sometimes concealing small and medium-sized ships. Sea completely covered with long white patches of foam. Edges of wave crests blown into froth. Poor visibility.	56–63
12	Hurricane	Air filled with foam and spray, sea white with driving spray. Visibility poor.	>64

Search Personnel and Equipment

Search personnel from several agencies came together as one unit to help find and recover the subjects. Agencies represented were Tangipahoa Parish Sheriff's Office, Louisiana Wildlife and Fisheries Agents, St. John Parish Sheriff's Office, Baton Rouge Parish Sheriff's Office divers and St. Tammany Parish Sheriff's Office canines from Louisiana Search and Rescue Dog Team.

We used Wildcraft 18' Patrol boats, Reno 21' flatboats and flatboats with "go-devils." A go-devil is an air-cooled engine, rather than one cooled by by water, has a long drive shaft for balance with a flatboat, which enables it to work well in marshy areas. It only needs a few inches of water to push the boat.

We were fortunate to have several individuals with the sheriff's office who were accustomed to working with dogs on the water. Captain Perkins was very knowledgeable regarding the use of dogs, since we had worked several other incidents with him. Captain Perkins served as our boat operator on day one.

Search Strategy

Captain Perkins, the Tangipahoa Parish Sheriff's Office IC for this scene, held a detailed briefing on the incident based on their department's investigation on Monday, February 9, 1998. Captain Perkins ascertained that the search area was approximately 100x50 yards. They held the briefing at the sheriff's substation office prior to our team going out to the site.

Probability of the Area

The sheriff's office had a theory based upon their investigation as to what might have happened to the two subjects. They believed that as Ron was hanging his clothing on the side of the railroad bridge tender structure, he fell out of the boat and was in trouble. Sam, hearing his friend's cry for help, jumped in from the turnstile where he was fishing and swam out to help him. The agency believed that both subjects would be found close to each other. Investigators noticed the manner in that Sam had thrown his clothing down, as if he was in a hurry.

After the detailed briefing, we proceeded to the scene. An officer with Louisiana Wildlife and Fisheries took us out by boat, without the dogs, to survey the area. He pointed out the turnstile where the boys had been camping and where the clothes were hung at the tender structure. While out with the agent, we noted the current and wind direction to decide our search pattern.

THE SEARCHER
DOG HANDLER TEAM ONE

Who are You?

Dee Wild, trainer/handler with Louisiana Search and Rescue Dog Team (LaSAR), and her K-9 partner, Spice, a Curly Coated Retriever.

The Callout

I received the call at 1040 on Monday, February 9, 1998 from Captain Perkins of the Tangipahoa Parish Sheriff's Office requesting dogs for Wednesday, February 11, 1998, at 0800. I was at work at the time, my boss, David J. Fine, Regents Professor and Chairman of the Department of Health Systems Management at Tulane University believes in the work I am doing with Spice and allowed me to take the day off. Getting the time off is the only special arrangement I have to make in order to respond to callouts. It took me no more than an hour to reach the Tangipahoa Sheriff's Office Substation.

Who decided your sector? How long did it take to complete?

Based on the information provided us during the briefing by Captain Perkins, we knew the area that needed to be covered. Therefore, once Captain Perkins arrived on the scene, Spice and I, along with Lisa Higgins, serving as my backup, made the first sweep of the search area.

How large was your sector?

The search area would be approximately 100x50 yards and would take approximately 20 minutes to cover.

How did you decide where to start your sector?

The current was moving west to east. The wind was blowing out of the west and the new railroad bridge runs north to south. Based on these factors, I decided to have the boat run the length of the new railroad bridge on the east side.

Problems Encountered

Since we had to work out of high-sided boats, we decided to work the dogs across the wind as much as possible. This would help bring the scent to the dog's level since the scent would hit the side of the boat and bounce upward toward the dog. By working the dog on the east side of the new railroad bridge, I understood that if Spice alerted, the subject would be to our west, although the boat was facing south.

Were you prepared for the conditions you encountered?

On the first sweep, I noted Spice's alert between two of the cement pilings and marked the location. Clearly Spice had

Spice showing airscent alert toward the new bridge.

switched from checking the area to working scent. She turned toward the new bridge, leaning down toward the water. She began tasting the air with her tongue. As the boat was leaving the scent area, Spice began working down the side of the boat following the scent. Upon reaching the back of the boat, she reached out and tasted the water near the motor. By tasting the water, Spice used her Jacobson's organ[1]. She kept herself between the scent source and engine fumes, which allowed her to stay in scent and away from the contamination caused by the fumes. Once out of the scent area, she returned to the front of the boat and continued checking the area. We continued working along the railroad bridge until we reached the bridge tender structure, where the dog gave another indication. At the east base of the bridge tender structure, my dog got caught up in a scent pool. This was where Ron's clothes had been hung on the rebar, and it was here that Lisa and I had noticed an eddy. The current created the eddy as it came around the northeastern corner of the structure. The eddy was holding scent. I had to get my dog out of the eddy to find the location of the scent source. After working this section for several minutes, I opted to have the boat operator move into the channel running between the structure and the first cement piling to

This is where the victim's clothing was hanging on the rebar. Spice had an alert here in an eddy which held scent.

the north. Lisa observed Spice's reaction as she entered the channel. Lisa saw Spice's head following the scent around the northern corner entering the channel. The boat ran within inches of the cement apparatus. Halfway along the structure, Spice lost the scent. The boat continued along the cement apparatus before moving across the channel to work between the old and new railroad bridge structures. This put us between the old railroad bridge with the turnstile and the new railroad bridge. We worked between the two bridges toward the turnstile. Spice continued to check the area but did not indicate scent. When we reached the cement turnstile, I noticed that she did not indicate on the turnstile where the victim's personal belongings had been found. As we passed the turnstile, I decided to turn between the two cement pilings where she had indicated earlier. When we reached the east side of the new railroad bridge, Spice again began to alert to the area.

The Dog

Lisa and I asked Captain Perkins to position the boat away from the new bridge and into the lake where we could see the entire area. From there, Lisa and I discussed every-

---

[1] This organ allows the dog to taste scent in the same way retrievers are able to pick up specific objects touched by the handler at the bottom of a waterway.

thing Spice had done during the search pattern. We have often found that the backup (which in this case was Lisa) is in a better position to pick up key information since they tend to observe the search area as well as the dog, while handlers tend to spend most of their time observing their dog. Therefore, we strongly advocate that the handler and back-up talk before the handler makes the call. This way the handler has all the information before approaching the IC.

Probability of Detection

After running Spice, I ascertained that we had two clear alert areas. I felt that Spice indicated heaviest between the two cement pilings on the Northern side of the turnstile with a lesser indication at the channel. The two alerts were approximately 50 yards apart. Based upon this information, the second handler, which was Lisa, could determine how she would work the area with her dog. We explained this to Captain Perkins.

How Successful were You?

After working the area, I was confident that Spice had given me the correct information. I also felt very confident that I had read my dog correctly. Although she had given me a mild alert in one area and a strong alert in the other, I had no problem understanding both of them. I did not try to force or discount her alerts based on the information I had about the incident. Upon completion of her work, I decided that her strongest alert was northeast of the turnstile and her mildest alert was on the north side of the tender structure. Spice communicated to me that she had scent in both locations, it was up to me to make the call and stand behind my dog. It was now time to let Lisa and Molli work the area.

THE SEARCHER
DOG HANDLER TEAM TWO
Same Day

Who Are You?

Lisa Higgins, a trainer/handler with Louisiana Search and Rescue Dog Team (LaSAR), and her canine partner, Molli, a black Labrador Retriever.

The Callout

When the call came in I was exercising my dogs in obedience, agility, and endurance training at the Bogue Chitta Wildlife Management Area. Since we had more than a day to respond, all that was necessary was to check my equipment that evening. The drive would be only about one hour from my home.

The Search Sector

Who decided your sector?

With role reversal, I now became the handler working my canine partner, Molli, and Dee Wild, became my backup. Once again, Captain Perkins was at the helm of the boat.

How large was your sector? How long did it take to complete?

Having watched the first team, I was certain that we had two clear areas where we needed to concentrate. It is the policy of Louisiana Search and Rescue Dog Team (LaSAR) to always verify all water searches with a second dog. We realize that a diver will risk his life for those he can not save, therefore we verify our alerts in order to prevent a diver from going down without just cause.

How did you decide where to start your sector?

Because the conditions had not changed since the first dog had worked, I worked the area the same way. The only thing I did differently was that I chose to spend more time around the bridge tender section. I decided to do this because we did not have a clear area pinpointed there like we did with the other location. Working Molli into this area in a different way allowed us to get her into a position where she could define the scent source more accurately.

The Dog

When we entered the search area, Molli gave a soft alert at the same location as the other dog, by reaching downward to the water. By continuing to the bridge tender section, I was able to pinpoint the scent source in this location. As we approached the bridge tender structure, I did not spend time around the eddy. We already knew that scent was pooling in this location. Since I knew where the first dog lost the scent, I worked into the channel approximately eight to ten feet from the tender's structure. This time I believe that we were able to get right over where the scent source was breaking through the water's surface. Molli indicated this spot by following the scent down the side of the boat then trying to reach down for it. She then began whining and finally barked her alert. We reported this information to the agency. With this information, the agency searched both areas for the missing teenagers. The heavy debris hampered search personnel in their efforts.

What are Your Feelings About the Mission?

Prior to leaving the scene on the first day (Wednesday, February 11, 1998), Lisa and I spoke to the parents of both subjects. We had cleared these meetings with the IC before approaching the parents. Sam's parents did not understand why Spice was picking up scent to the north of the cement turnstile. They believed that their son would have swam toward Ron, not

Molli alerting on scent near the bridge.

away from him. I could not explain to them why the victims were not closer together, I could only trust my dog's alerts. Lisa Higgins told the family that we did not know what actually took place that day, all we could tell them was what our dogs had shown. At that point, all we could do was pray with them for the quick recovery of their sons.

THE SEARCHER
DOG HANDLER TEAM THREE
Return to the Scene

Who are You?

Lisa Higgins, trainer/handler with Louisiana Search and Rescue Dog Team and her canine partner, Frosty, a Golden Retriever.

The Callout

When the call came in on Thursday, February 12, 1998, I was at home. Baton Rouge Parish Sheriff's Office Divers would be on the scene the following morning and the agency would like the dogs to return one more time. I did not need to make any special arrangements to respond and I knew that it would take approximately an hour to reach the search scene.

The Search Sector

Friday, February 13, 1998, recovery divers from Baton Rouge Parish Sheriff's Office needed to know if the bodies had moved since Wednesday, February 11, 1998, when we were there last.

How large was your sector? How long did it take to complete?

The search area would be enlarged if I did not get any of the indications where we had them on Wednesday.

How did you decide where to start your sector?

This time Dee was unable to return to the scene. Therefore, I opted to work my "old partner," Frosty, my eight-year-old Golden Retriever. He is the team's founding dog. Although he is semi-retired, I maintain his training and knew he could handle the job. I made this decision because we do not like to work the same dogs repeatedly over the same site. We are concerned that the dog may work from memory. If the dogs do this, they can give a false alert, which is something we do not want to encourage.

Problems Encountered

Due to the greatly improved conditions, I realized that it would not take long to verify whether or not the bodies had moved. The water was much smoother, no waves to bounce us around, and the wind was almost nonexistent. The temperatures were cool so we could work a longer period of time without tiring the dog.

Were you prepared for the conditions you encountered?

As the conditions were much calmer, I worked the area the same as I did on Wednesday, in a north to south direction with one exception; I worked closer to the bridge. Frosty gave alerts in the same two areas that Molli and Spice indicated.

Even though I was confident that we had the areas for the dive team to work, we also went on and checked areas that we could not get to when the water was rougher. Remember, clearing areas is also positive information as it can reaffirm the indicated areas. However family members can and will ask that you check certain areas if they feel that they have not been given attention. In this case the father of one of the boys asked that I go behind the old bridge. He also asked that I put the dog up on the turnstile that the boys had been seen camping on. I could have explained why I believed that we did not need to check behind the old bridge but elected to do the search as was requested for two reasons: It would clear the areas but would also give the family members the piece of mind that all that could be done had been done. Put yourself in their place. Their job is the toughest one of all. They must sit around watching us, unable to help, feeling helpless. If they are able to let you know of anything that might have been missed, then they feel that they have helped, too.

Checking behind the bridge was not easily done, as we could not get the boat into much of the area due to shallow water. It hurts to think that if the boys had gone in that direction, instead of the direction they did, they could have better helped themselves.

Getting to the turnstile looked easy enough, but we were to learn the hard way that it wasn't. As we were working toward our new area to search, the boat hit underwater debris so hard that it threw Frosty out of the boat. It was no big deal for a Golden Retriever, but we learned there were jagged pylons just far enough under the surface to be invisible but could easily stop the boat and could have impaled the dog. We were lucky this time! I got out of the boat onto the turnstile and pulled Frosty up with me. Like the trooper he is, he went on and checked every nook and crack on the surface as well as the entire outer edge. We located nothing out of the ordinary and Frosty gave no alerts.

The Dog

This time the family members, having watched what we had done, were satisfied that we had covered everything possible.

Probability of Detection

The agency was satisfied with the work of the three dogs—all three were seasoned veterans of water recovery—who had all indicated the same two areas, and was ready to let the divers try to recover. The dive team took three boats out with them and all their gear. There were safety divers assigned to every diver that went down as well as personnel monitoring the progress of the divers from the boat. The divers were unable to do a thorough job because the current in the channel at the depths they were working was so strong that they were having to work hand over hand, holding on to debris to maintain their positions and feeling with the other hand. The water was throwing them back under the boat and the debris was sharp in many places, which could have caused injury to the diver or damage to their equipment. Though the divers did an outstanding job under the conditions, it was decided to have them resurface, as the conditions were just not safe. The agency did not want to risk losing a diver for a life that could not be saved. It was decided that the agencies would run the waterway daily waiting for the bodies to surface since the hooking operations were hampered by the debris and it was not safe for the divers to dive the area due to strong currents and heavy debris.

How Successful were You?

After working the area, I was confident that all three of our dogs had provided the divers, agency, and family with the information they needed. Even though I knew our dogs had done their job, it is still very difficult to leave a scene knowing that the subjects were not recovered. We want to always provide the agency, and especially the families, with results every time. When we do not get instant results, it is sometimes very unsettling. I walked away, confident that Frosty and the other dogs had performed to their best capability, yet sad that the search was not able to conclude with recoveries. This time nature's conditions won out by hampering the divers and the dragging efforts.

Results of the Mission

A commercial fisherman found Sam on the bank, east of the bridge, eleven days after the incident. He had suffered a head injury caused by hitting underwater debris upon entering the water to help Ron. The blow to the head was the actual cause of death. The fire chief of Manchac, Louisiana, found Ron 12 days after the incident. According to Captain Perkins, both subjects were found in a direct line from where the dogs alerted.

What are Your Feelings About the Mission?

Both of us feel that Tangipahoa Parish Sheriff's Office was extremely organized and methodical in their approach to the scene. They did an outstanding job making us a part of the effort by giving us detailed information. Without their thorough investigation and their theory of what happened on the water, we would have checked a much larger area. Their detailed information helped us decide where to search. We in turn gave them the information they needed to confine their search efforts. We accomplished this by doing two things, allowing the dogs to work and reading our dogs properly. It took everyone working together to bring an end to a very tragic situation, we were proud to be a part of that effort.

Search Tips (From Dee and Lisa)

Understand the conditions and limitations that can hamper a search effort. Boats do not stop on a dime, and divers can have zero visibility or unsafe working environments. Without witnesses you may not have a PLS to work from. Don't become upset if they cannot make a recovery immediately. Be part of the solution and not part of the problem.

Do not position yourself over your dog. Instead allow the dog to work the entire boat. If you force the dog to only work the bow of the boat, you have limited your dog's capabilities to pick up scent. By giving the dog space to work you will place yourself in a better position to observe your dog's body language.

Do not talk your dog into a false alert. Stay quiet. You will take your dog's focus off their work and place it onto you if you talk too much.

If you are the second dog out to verify what the first one did, do not force an alert to make sure both dogs' alerts coincide. Remember that the conditions can change from the time the first dog went out to when the second dog searches. A simple wind change can cause the second dog to alert in a different location. By marking each alert on a map, you will find that the alerts will show the highest probability area. The second handler may not want to know where the first dog alerted, in order to keep a clear frame of mind. This is especially true when a seasoned dog goes out first, followed by a less experienced dog.

A word of caution, some dogs alert aggressively by jumping out of the boat and swimming to the area in question. This is not a problem in a safe waterway. However, on waterways that may pose underwater hazards, you will want to keep your dog in the boat. Therefore, you may want to have a secondary alert.

Making the call and standing behind one's dog is not always the easiest thing to do. Often handlers will not acknowledge an alert because they do not get their "canned" alert. This often happens when the handler does not have the conviction to believe in their dog's capabilities. Sometimes they do not believe their dog's signal because the alert is not where they believe the alert should be or the alert does not fit the picture that has been painted. Other handlers will force their dog to alert by leaning over the front of the boat and talking the dog into an alert. These handlers tend to do this in the location where the agency has suggested the subject will be found. This type of handling promotes false alerts since the handler is trying to satisfy the agency and not letting their dog work. In both cases, the dog team has let down the agency and the family of the victim. The handler is not allowing the dog to communicate what it has found or not found. Believe in your training. If you have a solid training program, trust your dog. Your dog will do their job. A training program is like building a house, if your foundation and framework is solid, you can build the rest of the house. Do not skip steps in your training trying to get your dog operational.

Finally, remember why you are doing this. It isn't for the glory, but rather for the victim, the family members, and the agencies that require your services.

Biographies

Dee Wild is the director of training for Louisiana Search and Rescue Dog Team (LaSAR), the first search and rescue dog team in the state of Louisiana. She co-founded the team with Lisa Higgins in late 1989. She put together an extensive training program before the first dog entered into training in March 1990. Since the first callout in May 1991, Dee and her canines have responded to over 70 callouts in Louisiana, Mississippi, Texas, Florida, and Arizona. Her first field-operative canine, Maggie, is now retired. Maggie is a Whippet and was certified in Wilderness and Water. Maggie is credited with locating a missing hunter on the seventh day of the search. Dee's current field-operative canine is a Curly Coated Retriever named Spice. Spice is certified in Wilderness, Water, Body Recovery, and Urban. Dee has over 20 years experience and knowledge in conditioning temperament; interpreting structure and movement, and training dogs in search and rescue, obedience, and conformation. She owned and operated a boarding kennel for three years, offering boarding, grooming, and obedience training. She continues teaching obedience classes to the local community where her clientele base is derived from veterinarian referrals. Dee and her dogs have earned many accomplishments. She was the first to train and handle the first field-operational Whippet in SAR work. Both Maggie and Spice were honored by Citizens Against Crime for the work they are doing in the field of SAR and both dogs earned their AKC Canine Good Citizen certificates. Dee served two terms as the first woman president of Slidell Dog Fanciers Association, and her home bred Whippet, Sunrise, who is not doing SAR work, was the number one novice obedience dog in the United States for her breed. In addition to her many accomplishments, Dee is also a reserve deputy with St. Tammany Parish Sheriff's Office and actively instructs at national SAR seminars, where she teaches canine water recovery and other disciplines with Lisa Higgins.

Lisa Higgins has been active in SAR since 1982 as a mounted reserve officer with the Pearl River Police Department. By 1989, realizing that a trained canine would be more effective than just the higher visibility that a horse provides, Lisa and her daughter, Troi, met with Dee Wild and together co-founded LaSAR Dog Team.

Although Lisa began to train her own dogs in obedience as early as 1979, she did not begin to train in earnest with dogs other than her own until 1990, at which time she served as an assistant to Dee within the team. Serving as the team's senior handler, Lisa has worked well over 150 searches, not only in her own backyard of Louisiana, but Texas, Mississippi, and Vancouver, British Columbia, Canada.

Working two dogs of her own, she has certified her Golden Retriever, Frosty, the team's first dog, in Wilderness, Water, Body Recovery, Building, Disaster and Urban. Her second dog, Molli, a Labrador Retriever, is certified in Wilderness, Water, Body Recovery, Building, and Evidence Recovery.

Lisa has been a reserve officer with St. Tammany Sheriff's Office as a mounted officer, working crowd control during Mardi Gras and with local football games for the high schools since 1991, as well as a SAR dog handler with the special operations division.

Since her early days with Pearl River, Lisa still remains active in the Hug-A-Tree and Survive program, having presented to well over 70,000 children at schools, scouting events, and church functions.

Suicide
Wilderness Scent Specific

Susan Williams
San Diego County Sheriff's Department SAR Bureau
Mission Location: Palm Springs area of Anza Borrego Desert State Park, San Diego County, California
Mission Dates: March 14, 1988 and March 19, 1988

Mission Type

This search is a short search (although it encompasses two response days). It illustrates how trailing dogs can detect scent days after the subject walked through an area. It also illustrates the ability of airscent dogs to detect scent from a distance of one-half to one mile.

The Victim

"Bill" was a white male, age 46, who was depressed and unemployed. He had no known habits, and it was not known what he'd been last wearing, nor any equipment he might have taken with him. State rangers found a suicide note in the vehicle, and a weapon was missing from the Bill's home. The victim went missing on March 1, 1988.

Point Last Seen

The park rangers noticed the victim's car parked in the Palm Springs area of the Anza Borrego State Park on Saturday, March 5, 1988. When they checked the vehicle, they found that the owner had locked and secured the vehicle. This is common since many hikers leave their cars in this area. On Sunday, March 13, 1988, the state park rangers checked the car again. Because it had been so long and it appeared that the owner had not moved or disturbed the car, the rangers contacted the sheriff's department. Their investigation of the owner registration led the deputies to an address in El Cajon. The residents at that address told the deputies that they had not seen the victim since about the first of the month. After the deputies received this information, they entered the car and found a suicide note, dated March 1, 1988.

Where did the incident take place?

The search took place in the Arroyo Tapiado, CA quadrangle. The PLS was at the Palm Springs area, approximately four miles south of Agua Caliente off Highway S-2 near mile marker 43. This is part of the Carrizo Badlands area of Anza Borrego Desert State Park.

Terrain Features

The general terrain features are sandy washes[1] with many steep slopes and narrow

---

[1] A wash is a dry streambed.

ridges, making up a maze of ravines. This area was the site of a stage stop on the Butterfield Overland Stage route. It is a popular day hike area in the spring, when many visitors come to the desert to view the wild flowers. A 1000' ridge line forms a natural barrier in the area and a major wash (Arroyo Hueso) runs generally north and south just east of the PLS. To the west lies a jeep trail that runs north to the View of the Badlands.

Weather

Weather conditions during the period the subject was missing varied, naturally. On the date that he went missing, the temperature ranged from 55–64 and was mostly cloudy with a chance of showers, gusty northwest winds to 30 mph shifting to north by late Wednesday (March 2) and continuing through Thursday. Wind advisory for deserts. Throughout, the temperature ranged from a low of 36°F on March 14 to a high of 86°F on March 18. The weather was typical, varying from overcast skies to sunny, but was mainly clear days with the occasional hazy day (March 5 and 9).

Special Dangers

Rattlesnakes are always a danger in this area. During the day heat can be a concern although at this time of year the highs are not excessive. Cactus is a problem in some areas of the desert but not in this area. The sides of the ravines are almost vertical and the tops of the ridges are very narrow in some places. Care must be taken not to fall.

Any Other Special Information

On March 13, the sheriff's helicopter conducted a two-hour aerial search. The helicopter did not find anything. The sheriff's department decided to call in SAR for a search on March 14. They also asked park visitors to be on the lookout for the subject.

Search Personnel and Equipment

It would have been great to receive more dogs and mantrackers for the initial call on March 14 than we actually did. As for the resources that we did receive, we had dogs and mantrackers. (Two dog handlers with three dogs responded to the initial search.)

Search Strategy and Assignment of Resources

Our unit's initial response on March 14 was to deploy a dog team and mantrackers to try and establish the victim's direction of travel. The area was extremely contaminated with footprints from many hikers going through the area. The park rangers had counted more than 100 people in the area on March 13. All mantracking signs around the car and in the nearby wash had been obscured.

We collected scent articles from the victim's residence. Two of the dogs were area search dogs (airscenting dogs), and one dog was a trailing dog. When we fired[2] the dogs on the scent articles, all of the dogs alerted very actively on the subject's car. The trailing dog handler started the dog from the car to see if the dog would show a direction of travel. The dog went northward up a wash for about a quarter-mile indicating faint and scat-

---

[2] To "fire" the dog means to allow the dog to smell the scent article and then command the dog to search for that particular person's scent.

tered scent, but lost the scent when the wash turned westerly. The airscenting dogs also showed the presence of scent to the northwest of the car.

Because it was getting dark and the terrain features made it unsafe for night searching, we decided to launch a full-scale search at 0800, Saturday, March 19. We used the location of the abandoned car as the PLS. We put an advance team in the area Friday night to keep sightseers clear of the scene. At their request, the dog handlers stayed with the advance team so that they could start with the dogs at first light. This is when desert scenting conditions would be most ideal. Two airscenting teams and two trailing dog teams

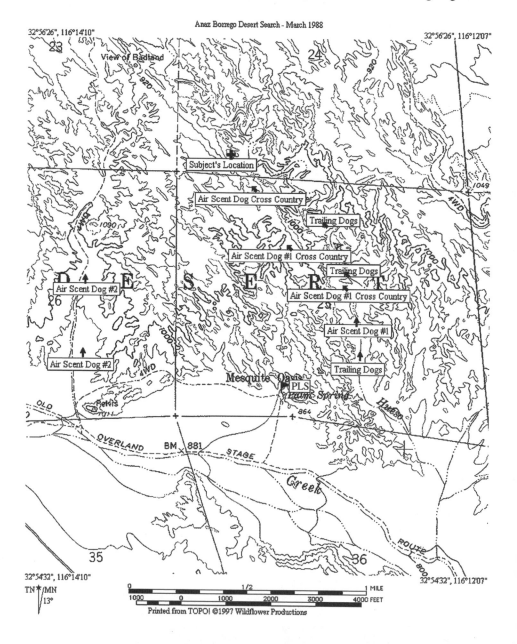

Anaz Borrego Desert Search - March 1988

stayed with the advance team.

A 1000' ridge line forms a natural barrier in the area. Our search strategy on March 19 was to send one airscenting dog team up the wash to search the east side of the ridge. We deployed the other airscenting team up a jeep trail toward the View of the Badlands vista to search the west side of the ridge. The two trailing dog teams followed to search the wash and confirm a direction of travel in case we needed a subsequent foot search.

We deployed the dog teams by 0600. Shortly after that, the airscenting dog that was searching the east side of the ridge gave a very strong alert and "took off cross country like a shot." His handler and SAR team member were scrambling to keep up. The team traveled up and down across ridges for approximately a half-mile to where the body was found in a slot canyon[3]. The dog team found the subject's body in less than an hour after they entered the field. The body was in the general direction the dogs had indicated Monday evening.

Results of Mission

We found the body in a sitting position at the west end of an east-facing slot canyon. The ravine had 40 foot, nearly vertical walls. It was a natural chimney that carried the scent aloft during the day. Because the weather between March 1 and March 19 was relatively constant, with temperatures ranging between a night time low of 36°F and a daytime high of 86°F, the conditions were ideal for an airscenting dog. They allowed the scent from the body to rise during the day, settle and concentrate each night. The trailing dogs were also able to find scent, even after 18 days.

The Palm Spring area probably has higher than normal ground moisture content for a desert region because of its permanent water supply. The area's topographical features, combined with the weather conditions, provided better than expected scenting conditions during this search.

The coroner ruled that the death was a suicide. The victim was shot in the head and the gun was beside the body.

What are Your Feelings About the Mission?

This was an enlightening mission. We had several searches during the spring of 1988 that showed us that scent remained available much longer than we anticipated; however, this search was exceptional for a number of reasons. It showed us how long scent can be available after a victim left a trail. It opened our eyes to the importance of trying the trailing dogs though conventional thought might lead you to believe that the scent would not be found. Earlier in the year we had a search for another suicide victim in which the dogs found scent five days after the victim laid a trail. Before these searches, we felt that 24 to 48 hours was an excessive time to expect scent to be available. We found that when working old scent trails, the scent would not be continuous. However, by letting the dogs keep working they would find the trail in shady, damp areas after losing it in the more open, dry areas. We also found that the dogs will work from desert plant to desert plant under these conditions.

We were also surprised at the distance that the airscenting dog picked up the lofting

---

[3] A slot canyon is a very narrow canyon with nearly vertical sides. In some cases, you could stand in the middle of it and reach out and touch both sides of the canyon.

scent coming from the body. The conditions on March 13 did not result in more than weak alerts in the general direction of the body. However, on March 19 the dog that made the find had strong scent from approximately a half-mile away. Unless you were standing right next to the body, there was no noticeable odor to the human searchers.

Search Tips

Don't assume that scent won't be available for trailing dogs even if several days have passed since the subject may have left a trail.

Attempt to get search dogs into the field early when desert conditions are best for scenting.

Use airscenting dogs to hasty search likely routes of travel and follow up on clues (in this case the weak alerts from March 13).

Use trailing dogs to get a direction of travel.

Using specialty dogs (cadaver dogs) is not necessary when searching for a suspected suicide victim. All of the dogs that we used in this search were wilderness search dogs.

THE SEARCHER
DOG HANDLER TEAM

Who are You?

I am the dog handler who made the find.

The Callout

I was at home when I received the initial callout. It took me more than two hours to reach the search site.

The Search Sector

The dog handlers developed their own search strategy. It was simply luck that I took the wash east of the ridge and the other area search dog handler took the jeep trail west of the ridge.

How large was your sector? How long did it take to complete?

My assignment was not a sector per se. I was assigned to go up the main wash east of the ridge in the direction the dogs had indicated on March 13. My assignment was to see if my dog had any further alerts or found anything.

Problems Encountered

The problems that I had involved negotiating the terrain after my dog found scent and took off cross country. We had to go over several near vertical sandstone walls as we crossed the badlands to get to the subject.

When my dog picked up scent he immediately left the main wash and took off up one the 40' ravine walls to head cross country. He had been working just ahead of us as we went northerly up the wash. He was not ranging any distance at all before he got the scent. When my partner and I followed him and got to the top of the ridge, my dog was already at the bottom of the ravine and starting to climb up to the next ridge. He paused to look back and see that we were coming and then disappeared out of sight over the next ridge as we were working our way down. He repeated his behavior as we negotiated at least three ravines and ridges in this fashion. When we came again to the main wash he waited only long enough to make eye contact again before entering the narrow slot canyon where the subject was found.

Were you prepared for the conditions you encountered?

At the beginning of my assignment I did not expect to have any success at all. I didn't feel my dog was ranging well that day and did not expect him to work well for me. I knew that we were almost three weeks behind our subject and that our potential search area was quite large. I was very surprised when my dog went from a slow walk to a flat out run up the side of a ravine and out of my sight. All I could do was follow him and hope that my partner kept up. We didn't radio back to base camp until we actually made the find because of the difficulty in negotiating the terrain and because my dog would take off and disappear out of our sight. He would do this each time he made eye contact with us, either from the top of a ridge or the bottom of a ravine. Although this was my dog's first cadaver find, he ended up having about as many cadaver finds as live finds throughout his career. He was grandfathered in as cadaver dog when CARDA initiated that specialty.

Search Tips

Following up on dog alerts is important, even if they are weak, as were those on March 13.

Don't assume your dog is not working even if he is not ranging as far as you would like. Most dogs will follow up when they come across a good scent source.

In the right conditions your dog may pick up scent from a very long distance. The PLS, where the dogs were giving weak scent alerts on March 13, was a mile from the subject. My dog got strong scent on March 19 approximately a half-mile from the subject.

Herding dogs such as mine, a Bouvier des Flandres, tend to keep in contact with their handlers. I don't know what would have happened if I were working a dog that didn't keep checking back to see if I were still following him.

A dog does not have to be cadaver certified to make a cadaver find.

Biography

Susan Williams is a reserve lieutenant with the San Diego County Sheriff's Department Search and Rescue Bureau. She is in charge of the SAR canine unit, which is made up of 25 members, 20 of whom are mission ready. She has been a reserve deputy sheriff since 1986. Susan is a member of the California Search Dog Association (CARDA) and has been a mission ready CARDA handler since 1987. She has handled three CARDA mission-ready dogs, two area search dogs, and one trailing dog. Her present dog is certified as a CARDA wilderness area search dog, avalanche dog, cadaver dog, water search dog, and basic urban disaster dog. She has been on more than 300 searches during her career, and has searched throughout California and in Arizona, Massachusetts, Hawaii, and Baja, California. She is a NASAR SAR Tech II evaluator, a heavy rescue instructor, an American Red Cross Emergency Response Instructor, and attended the F.E.M.A. Canine Search Specialist School. Susan presented a talk entitled "Desert Searching with Dogs" at the 1994 NASAR Response Conference.

Appendix

Outline
The Mission

Heading: Name: Address: Phone: Unit Affiliation: Location of the Mission: Date of the
Mission:

1. *Please state* if this search is short, long, or illustrates inefficient search techniques or
circumstances.

2. *The Victim*
    a. Age
    b. Physical condition/health
    c. Habits
    d. Equipment/clothing
    e. Date victim went missing
    f. Other circumstances/information

3. *PLS (Point Last Seen) or Last Known Position (LKP)*
    a. Why did the incident take place (hiker did not return, person fishing fell over-
    board, child wandered away, etc.)
    b. Where did the incident take place (use a topographical map)
    c. When did the incident take place(if you do not want to use a date, state the sea-
    son, such as spring)
    d. Terrain features
    e. Weather at the time the victim went missing, current and expected for the next
    eight hours
        1. temperature
        2. wind strength and direction
        3. precipitation
    f. Special dangers associated with the area, (shaft mines, weather changes, heat,
    cold, swamp, etc..

4. *Any Other Special Information*

5. *Search Personnel and Equipment*
    a. The resources you would have liked to have
    b. The resources you received

6. *Search Strategy* - The following are suggestions and intended to jog your memory.
    You do not need to include all of the example items listed below "a" through "g."
    However, you should include the other categories.

Example:
 a. Did I use the resources I had to keep the search area from getting bigger or to try and find the victim?
 b. Determine the urgency of the search
 c. Determine the boundaries of the search
 d. Segment the search area
 e. Determine the Probability Of the Area
  1. theoretical
  2. statistical
  3. subjective
  4. deductive
 f. Prioritize the segments
 g. Tactics
  1. confinement
  2. segmentation
  3. attraction
  4. detection

7. *Assign Resources*

8. *Suspension*—at what point would you call off the search? Why?

9. *Results of the Mission*

10. *How did/do you FEEL about the mission.* This is a personal response, not a professional one.

11. *Additional Comments*

12. *Five tips* as per instructions above (Mission Instruction #10)

13. *Biography* of yourself as per instructions above (Mission Instruction #12)

The Searcher—Dog Handler Team

Ideally this section should be filled out by someone who used a dog team to search a sector for the above reported search mission. The sector does not have to be one in which a find was made. It should represent some of the problems unique to the search. The person who filled out the Mission part of this report does not have to be the same person who fills out The Searcher part of this report.

Write the report following the outline below. Number each part of your report to correspond with the numbers below. Use the Mission Instructions as they apply.

1. Who are you? The IC, dog/handler, field tech., etc.

2. Where were you when you received the callout? What special arrangements did you have to make to respond to the search? How long did it take you to reach the search site?

3. Who decided the sector you were to search? What information did you need to start your sector?

4. How large was your sector? How long did it take you to complete your sector?

5. How did you decide where to start your sector?

6. What problems did you encounter? Did you expect the problems you encountered?

7. Were you prepared to face the conditions you encountered in your sector?

8. Describe how you and the dog worked. What did you notice and what did you do?

9. What Probability of Detection did you calculate for the sector you searched? Why?

10. How successful were you? Success does not mean that you found the victim. Success is decided by how effectively you searched your area. By the clues you found or by clearing the area.

11. How did/do you **FEEL** about the mission. This is a personal response, not a professional one.

12. Give five tips as per Mission Instruction #10.

13. Give a brief biography as per Mission Instruction #12.

Suggested Reading List

Analysis of Lost Person Behavior
    by William G. Syrotuck

Compass and Map Navigator: The Complete Guide to Staying Found
    by Michael Hodgson

Cumulative Stress Management for Search and Rescue: A Workbook for All Emergency Personnel
    by Marilyn Neudeck-Dicken, Ph.D.

Emergency Services Stress: Guidelines for Preservice the Health and Careers of Emergency Services Personnel
    by Jeffrey T. Mitchell, Ph.D. and Grady Bray, Ph.D.

First Aid for Search and Rescue and Other Working Dogs: A Pocket Medical Guide for the Working Dog
    by Karen Dashfield, DVM

Incident Commander Field Handbook: SAR
    edited by NASAR Staff and Education Committee

Introduction of Land Search Probabilities
    by William Syrotuck

Managing the Lost Person Incident
    editor and senior author: Kenneth Hill

Manhunters! Hounds of the Big T
    by Bill Tolhurst

On the Trail! A Practical Guide to the Working Bloodhound and Other Search and Rescue Dogs
    by Jan Tweedie

Practical Scent Dog Training
    by Lue Button

Ready! The Training of the Search and Rescue Dog
    by Susan Bulanda

Scent and the Scenting Dog
    by William Syrotuck

Search and Rescue Dogs: Training Methods
    by the American Rescue Dog Association

Search Dog Training
  by Sandy Bryson

Search is an Emergency: Field Coordinator's Handbook for Managing Search
  Operations
  by Rick LaValla and Skip Stoffel

Some Grid Search Techniques for Locating Individuals in Wilderness Areas
  by William Syrotuck

Standards for SAR Technician III, II & I and Crewleader III
  by the NASAR SAR Technician Committee

Stress Management, Critical Incident Stress Debriefing: An Operations Manual for the
  Prevention of Traumatic Stress Among Emergency Services and Disaster
  Personnel
  by Jeffrey T. Mitchell, Ph.D. and George S. Everly, Jr., Ph.D., F.A.P.M.

The Police Textbook for Dog Handlers
  by Bill Tolhurst

The Rescue Company
  by Ray Downey

Tracking: A Blueprint for Learning How
  by Jack Kearney
 Note: This is a mantracking book, not a dog training book!

Water Rescue: Basic Skills for Emergency Responders
  by David Smith and Sara J. Smith

 For a complete list of books and videos contact:
  NASAR
  4500 Southgate Place, Suite 100
  Chantilly, VA 20151-1714
  703-222-6277
  bookstore@nasar.org

Or
  Emergency Response Institute
  1819 Mark Street N.E.
  Olympia, WA 98506
  206-491-7785

Abbreviations and Terms

AFB	Air Force Base
ATV	All Terrain Vehicles
CARDA	Canadian Avalanche Rescue Dog Association
CISD	Critical Incident Stress Debriefing
CP	Command Post
DER	Department of Environmental Resources
DOD	Department of Defense
ELT	Emergency Locator Transmitter
FEMA	Federal Emergency Management Agency
FLIR	Forward Looking Infrared
GPS	Global Positioning System/Satellite
IC	Incident Commander
IST	Incident Support Team
LKP	Last Known Position
NASAR	National Association for Search and Rescue
OFDA	Office of Foreign Disaster Assistance (a branch of the State Department's United States Agency for International Development)
Ops	Operations
PLS	Point Last Seen
POA	Probability Of the Area
POD	Probability Of Detection
SAR	Search and Rescue
USAID	United States Agency for International Development
USGS	United States Geological Survey

Terms Used

Airscenting – When a dog looks for any human scent in the area, not a specific scent. It can also mean when a scent specific dog puts his head up into the air to follow a scent cone.

Alerts – When a dog gives a signal that it has caught scent of the victim. It can also mean that he comes back to the handler and gives a signal that he has found the victim. If the dog is taught to do a refind, he will lead the handler back to the victim. If the dog is taught to give a bark alert, he will stay with the victim and bark until the handler arrives. There are many different types of alerts. For a detailed explanation, see the chapter in *Ready! The Training of the Search and Rescue Dog* on alerts.

Attraction Efforts – A variety of things—such as calls, whistles, or other signals—used to try to draw the victim toward you.

Crosswind – As in "working crosswind." When you work crosswind you are working so that you are cutting across the wind instead of going into it or with it. Picture the wind hitting the side of your body as opposed to hitting your back or face.

Hasty Search – The initial rescue effort. In some cases, a hasty team will do a quick search of an area to see if the missing person is nearby. Typically this search will follow obvious paths of travel, such as a path in the woods, or areas near the PLS. If the hasty search does not find the missing person, the full search will start. The hasty search gets people into the field right away.

Jon boat – This is a type of rowboat that has a flat bottom that tapers up on one end.

Low head dam hazard – A small dam where water, such as a river or stream, flows over it. There is a vertical drop where the force of the water causes a hole at the bottom of the dam. The water around the hole tries to fill the hole causing a washing machine effect. This will suck a person in and keep them there without escape. The body will keep circulating around and around.

Mantrackers – People who are trained in the art of tracking, such as the old west "Indian scout."

Zodiac – This is a brand name of an inflatable boat that has a flat bottom and pontoon sides that keep it afloat. This was the first boat of its type and the name has become the catch-all description of the product, in the way that Kleenex refers to all paper tissue.

We've All Been There!

A salesman is trying to call a client. The phone rings and a little boy, in a whisper, says, "Hello?"

Salesman: Is your mommy there?

Little Boy: (whisper) Yes.

Salesman: Can I speak with her?

Little Boy: (whisper) She's busy.

Salesman: Is your daddy there?

Little Boy: (whisper) Yes.

Salesman: Can I speak with him?

Little Boy: (whisper) He's busy, too.

Salesman: Is anyone else there?

Little Boy: (whisper) The fire department.

Salesman: Can I talk to one of them?

Little Boy: (whisper) No, they're busy.

Salesman: Is anyone else there?

Little Boy: (whisper) The police department.

Salesman: Well, can I talk to one of them?

Little Boy: (whisper) Nope, they're busy, too.

Salesman: Let me get this straight, your mother, father, the fire department and the police department are all in your house, and they're all busy. Just what are they doing?

Little Boy: (whisper) They're looking for me!

—Author unknown